ARREST

A Memoir of the American First Lady
of Nice, France and the French Riviera

COUNTESS ILENE MÉDECIN

ARRESTED

A Memoir of the American First Lady of Nice, France and the French Riviera

© 2024, Countess Ilene Médecin

Print ISBN: 978-1-66788-240-6
eBook ISBN: 978-1-66788-241-3

ACKNOWLEDGEMENTS

My husband, Beau, for his incredible editing and loving support

Ruth Sokol for editing and her caring support

Alizabeth James, my loyal producer

The City of Nice, France

Maestro Mathew Savery, for his empathetic understanding and support

DEDICATIONS

**This book was made possible by
the incredible contributions the following people have made in my life.**

My beloved grandparents Sam and Belle

Mom & Dad

My incredible courageous daughter, TK. My reason
d'être and the wind beneath my wings.

My Lilou and Marcel, our loyal Niçois family and caretakers

Jackye mouse, Nic, and Jean-Claude, my true Niçois friends

Corky, my mentor and savior

Ruth and Dennis, my adopted Big Sis and brother-in-law

Laurel and Ken, my wonderful grounders

DDDD, Dennis, my hysterical brother-in-law

Trish, my most fun traveling buddy

Trevor Mound, my dear friend and political confidant

My baby cousin Jills

Selvan, Laxmir and Ram, my Indian family

Beau, my Love who after sixteen years still thrills me

My steppy Tara, who is there to always help me

Bekka, my beautiful Norwegian God-daughter

Mayor Jacques Médecin, who made all my dreams come true

Ganesh, my mystical treasure

CONTENTS

INTRODUCTION

A S I FOUND MYSELF LYING ON THE TOP BUNK IN the cell of the toughest women's prison in all of France, I knew I was in big trouble. I looked down at the three other women in their beds—the French prostitute, the Muslim drug dealer and the young Muslim girl who bit off her mother in-law's finger. I was thinking this would certainly make interesting dinner conversation someday if I ever get out of here.

Many years have now passed since these traumatic events occurred. While the memories remain vivid, I also bear the scars of falling off a wild ride. Fortunately, I was able to recover enough and stand up to lead my life down a very different treasured path.

BOOK ONE

Incarceration

CHAPTER 1

PEOPLE HAVE SAID MY LIFE IS LIKE A FAIRY TALE and it's true. Camelot lifestyle with castle, private jet, bodyguard, diplomatic passport, the whole shebang. But here I was in jail and didn't know why. This was definitely not supposed to be part of my fairy tale.

My arrest and incarceration had come as a great surprise to me. It was Monday, February 22, 1997. One minute I was a free woman happily traveling on my way to see old friends in France, and the next moment I was in confinement. I had been the First Lady of Nice and the French Riviera for more than a decade and now I was in prison.

Remember the old Elvis Presley song *Jailhouse Rock*. I had no explanation. If an elephant had dropped from the sky and landed on my toes, I would not have been more amazed than when the two gendarmes (French National Police) walked up to me in the baggage area in the Nice Airport and crisply announced "Madame Médecin, you are under arrest. Come with us." They grabbed me by my arms—one big policeman on either side and physically hauled me away. I was too bewildered to resist and don't remember walking either. They were pulling me across the floor with my legs dragging like a rag doll, but I was too numb with shock to feel anything.

I wasn't prepared for any of this. Just my name, Médecin, should have protected me from the indignity and obvious mistake. I was the wife of Jacques Médecin, former Mayor of Nice from 1966 to 1991. My husband, "King Jacquou," was the last scion of a century old political dynasty dating back to 1870, beginning with his great-grandfather, Pierre Médecin, followed by his grandfather, Alexandre Médecin, and his father, Jean Médecin. Altogether, they ruled Nice and the Côte d'Azur for over 100 years. How could this be happening?

It couldn't be real. I had been the First Lady of Nice and the French Riviera. It was my title, not something I asked for, but the French media had bestowed this designation in my honor. Jacques and I were friends with Prince Rainier of Monaco and Princess Grace Kelly. It was quite a life we had on the Côte d'Azur. Our sphere included the likes of Claudia Cardinale, Marcello Mastroianni, David Niven and Jeanne Moreau. We were political allies and close friends with Jacques Chirac, the Prime Minister at that time of France, who later became President. I had campaigned for Chirac in the streets of Nice, when he needed our support for the upcoming Presidential election of France. I was by his side shaking hands and doing my best to be a supportive First Lady of Nice. We were on a first-name basis and good friends. His birthday was two days after mine. Every year he would send me my favorite all white bouquet of flowers that filled four vases. That's a generous, free loving, Sagittarius for you.

So, look at me now. I was in jail!

Although rarely addressed with my other title "Countess Médecin," I was, in fact, an actual countess by marriage. The Médecin Family was a dynasty that ruled Nice for over a century, and Jacques carried a title that originated with the eminent House of Medici of Florence.

It didn't take me long to understand there wasn't going to be anything friendly or respectful about this encounter. The gendarmes dragged me to the airport jail and put me in a cell. This was the beginning of a five-day period of grueling detention before I was brought before a magistrate to finally hear the charges. My anxiety level peaked for five days not being informed and not knowing what lay ahead of me.

After three hours in the Nice Airport jail, I kindly asked one of the gendarmes if he would please go to the vending machine to get me a sandwich and some water. My belongings had been confiscated, but somehow I had ten francs in my pocket. I gave it to him and again waited. He finally came back and told me, with a disrespectful smirk, the machine ate my francs. I was not used to being treated poorly and was scared. I couldn't have imagined they would treat me like this—a woman who had been distinguished as the Mayor's wife and had done so much for the city and region. I had devoted my life and energy to the citizens of Nice. Even though the gendarmes were national police, not our municipal ones, they were certainly aware of my name and position. A minimal amount of concern or consideration was non-existent.

After being escorted to my solitary cell with nothing to sleep on but a black tarp on the cold concrete floor, I was still in such shock and couldn't think straight. Eventually, I had to go to the ladies room. I repeatedly banged on the steel door and finally a gendarme came and screamed at me.

"Que veux-tu?" ("What do you want?")

I said I had to use the toilet. He laughed and opened the door and led me to the restroom while he stood outside the stall, like I was going somewhere. I finished and he returned me to the cell. I'm a very private person and strongly objected to being humiliated like this. As time progressed, it got even worse. No one offered me any water or food, and the only chance I had to eat was when I had given some francs to that gendarme. But, as I stated, he stole my money.

Obviously, my circumstances were not conducive to a good nights sleep. I was drowning in the adrenaline of my fear and anxiety as I lay awake all night.

I saw a magistrate at noon the following day who informed me only of my transfer to the Women's Prison in Nice, but still nothing about my charges. He said I would be booked at the prison for a temporary stay. Following that stay, I was told to be prepared for another transfer to Grenoble Court to stand before the magistrate and hear the charges. Apparently, Grenoble Prison would be my final destination.

It sounded like I would be going straight from the court to prison. My adrenaline was surging with my stomach churning to the point of shock, not to mention feeling semiconscious. I was petrified. This was not a good day.

CHAPTER 2

THE NICE WOMEN'S PRISON WAS SO ANTIQUATED it felt like a dungeon from the Dark Ages. The interior was cold, dank gray with depressing darker tones.

My booking included being photographed, fingerprinted and patted down. "Patted down" is not quite the word. I was probed and invaded by a horrid female guard who was getting much too much enjoyment out of her work. She looked up at me as she was on her knees, scrambling around my shaking body. I could see pleasure in her eyes, and just thought, Merde. This was not America. I had no rights. I was arrested and booked into prison, still without being informed of my alleged crime. The continued humiliation was torture day after day. Also, not knowing how long I would be subjected to these conditions was demoralizing.

I clenched my teeth, closed my eyes and tried not to cry, but I was weeping silently inside. Not knowing what was going on behind the scenes and as weak as I was, my only option was to be self-reliant. I mustered the strength not to give them the satisfaction of seeing my tears.

After completing the booking process, a woman guard led me to the bathroom where I was allowed to take a shower. I dried off and was led to a cleaning closet where they gave me two specific products. I had been "appointed" to scrub all the shower stalls and toilets. They were intensely watching every move I made. This was calculated mistreatment. They wanted me to suffer the indignity because of whom I was married to. They went far out of their way to make me even more uncomfortable than was necessary.

It was the third day of my detention and still hadn't been informed why I had been arrested or what I was being charged with. I hadn't seen a prosecutor or any representative of the court. I certainly hadn't seen my lawyer yet, though I knew he had been contacted. Lilou, the head of my household, and Jackye, my best friend, knew to notify him as a result of the incident at the airport. All I had encountered so far were guards, gendarme and jail cells. What the hell had I done? What was going on?

Oddly enough, they didn't issue me a standard uniform, which were dull gray coveralls as the other prisoners wore. I was allowed to remain in the same clothes I had been wearing when I stepped off the plane from London—black slacks, a white crepe blouse with an Hermès silk scarf and a Fendi raincoat. Lovely outfit, but hardly appropriate for prison wear. I wished they had issued me the ugly jail apparel. If I had known how long I would be forced to wear this one outfit, I surely would have demanded they get me a fresh one from my suitcase.

I was ushered down the hall to my cell by two female guards. One of them was the woman who had previously frisked me. The icy floors and walls were gray stone and very old. I was thinking that God only knows just how old for sure, but at least 100 years. The stone floors were worn smooth, probably from the many prisoners unconsciously pacing back and forth throughout the years. How many had been detained before me? Maybe multiple thousands and now I was one of them.

The guard jerked the cell door open and pushed me through. I trembled as the iron bars clanged shut and suddenly realized I was in a cell with three other women. They stared at me. I stared back at them. It certainly was a tiny space for four adult females. There were two bunk beds and a toilet in the corner behind a flimsy curtain with enough floor space for the four of us to stand upright. That was it. It was crowded, smoky, and smelled of human waste. The odors assaulted me. The rancid smell found its way to violently attack my nostrils. I could feel the frigid stone walls closing in on me, squeezing the life out of me like a vise.

The women at once saw my shock and confusion. They were immediately aware that I did not belong in this environment. Do you think it was the way I was dressed? They certainly sensed I had no experience with jail life or being in prison. In short, I was lost and frightened displaying my vulnerability.

It was too much. My world suddenly fragmented breaking into a thousand pieces. I pitched forward and almost passed out and was lucky not to land flat on my face on the chilly stone floor.

CHAPTER 3

I WAS NOT MEANT TO BE DENIED MY FREEDOM AND locked up. I mean, who is, but prison for me was especially hard. I'm high-strung and independent. I like people, but don't like being crowded, physically close or confined. Being born a free spirit as some of us are, confinement is hell. This was obviously not a conducive environment for my happiness or comfort. Lol.

Needless to say, I was very unhappy. Although being denied food in the beginning, I still couldn't eat and felt my body wasting away. Slim as I am, I normally eat like a horse. I eat all the time and worship my food. I could also feel my soul wasting away. I really didn't know how long I could last there without going insane or having a complete physical breakdown.

I was a wreck feeling alone and lost in this desolate predicament. Thank goodness these three compassionate women had my back. I was and am eternally grateful. Two Muslim girls, Sonya and Alaïa, and one French hooker, Carmine, were my unlikely saviors. My empathy for them and their tender affection toward me made all the difference in making me feel somewhat human again.

The guards physically mistreated me and were verbally abusive without any reason. It wasn't necessary for them to shove me into the cell like they were throwing the garbage out. The gendarme from the airport had left me in the "care" of the jail staff. As bad as the gendarmes were, they were sweet puppies compared to the staff at the Nice Women's Prison and I would soon learn what deeper pain and humiliation were.

When I almost lost consciousness and pitched towards the floor, Carmine was quick enough to catch me. She's the reason I still have a face. The three girls then laid me on one of the lower bunks and waited until I sort of came back to life. It became obvious these ladies had all done prison time previously and were familiar with the protocol. Sonya was in for dealing heroin with her boyfriend and was five months pregnant. Alaïa had bitten off her mother-in-law's finger in a knockdown drag out fight. (Talk about a family squabble.) Carmine was a sweet prostitute for the most part. She was stopped for speeding by a policeman, then got out of the car and beat him up.

They huddled around me like mother hens tending to a wounded member of their flock. When I was able to focus again, they sat me up and offered me a cigarette, which of course I declined because I've never smoked. I was still grateful for their kind offer. They sat on either side of me and Sonya held my hand as she tried to understand my predicament.

CHAPTER 4

I WAS OBVIOUSLY AN ODD DUCK IN MY DESIGNER slacks and blouse with a silk scarf tied over my tangle of blond hair. I definitely didn't look like usual jailhouse fare and didn't look like someone who should be there at all. The women didn't hesitate asking me what the hell I was doing there. They were as curious as they were kind.

"What is it, chérie?" Sonya asked as she took my hand and held it tightly. "What did you do?"

"That's just it," I said looking deep into her dark brown eyes and at that moment thinking I had never seen eyes that were warmer or more sympathetic and kind. "I don't know. I don't know what I did."

And with that, I put my head into my hands, broke down and began to cry...really, really cry. I finally let out the sobs I had held back for the past few days. The girls didn't mind and held my hands while patiently waiting until I exhausted myself.

My mind was swirling and wondering how I was going to get out of there. I kept thinking when I would see my wonderful daughter, TK (The Kid), again who was in Uruguay with her father. What had I done that was so wrong? Did I really deserve this?

Being able to find the presence of mind, obviously, I realized it was connected with Jacques. At the time, I believed Jacques' legal status was clear, but later discovered this to be false and he was a fugitive in France. I hadn't done anything wrong. It was just cruel fate being Jacques' wife under French spousal law. When you're married in France, each partner is responsible for whatever the other one did. Lucky me. I cried.

The two Muslim girls and the lovely French prostitute patted me on the shoulder, smiled and waited until I was ready to tell them my side of the story.

Since I was in such a state of shock, I'm not sure what I was able to communicate to them about what had occurred. Unbeknownst to me, they already knew more about my incarceration than I did. It was all over the television broadcasts, radio and newspapers. That's when my cellmates decided to handle me with extra special care. Sonya knew I needed their protection. As I was gaining notoriety on TV news with photos and videos being aired regularly, the girls didn't let on that I was on the tube at first. They would turn it off or change the channel for my sake after I returned to the cell following further interrogations. They immediately sensed how fragile I was and thought it best to shield me from additional damage the news would inflict.

In my mind, I was attempting to make sense of where I was and what had happened to put me there. My thoughts wandered, but the reality remained. I was now in a prison.

CHAPTER 5

WHEN I WAS MARRIED TO JACQUES, WE REFUR-
bished 12,000 square feet of Napoleon III's summer palace in Nice
as our official residence. It was called the Palais de La Préfecture or just La
Préfecture. This palace had also been the former royal residence of the monarchs of Sardinia, or the Dukes of Savoy as they were also known. It's located
in the old city flower market across from the sea and is a grand 150,000
square foot building with a personal space for the President of the French
Riviera, Jacques.

But, for now, my reality was prison. Unable to relax in the bunk, I had
a terrible sleepless night with a mattress as hard as rocks and the rank odors
refusing to subside. I couldn't sleep standing up either and shuffled around
the cell even though there wasn't any room.

Finally, Carmine, the prostitute slipped down from the upper bunk
which was across from mine and looked me in the eye. She said in French,
with a kind but firm voice, "Dear, even people in jail have to sleep. You're
making things worse for yourself. You have to accept you're here and can't
change that, but you can fight it. You just have to think how you are going to
fight and what you can do to help yourself now."

Her words encouraged me. She was right. I wasn't going to allow them
to oppress me and was determined to be hopeful. My thoughts continuously
drifted to where my lawyer was and what was being done to obtain my release.
I was certain Lilou and Jackye who had been at the airport to pick me up had

contacted him. With that, I laid on my bunk and finally fell into an exhausted, much needed and welcomed sleep.

I was still frightened when I awoke, being undeniably miserable. I felt weak and unprepared for the day ahead considering my physical and emotional state. At least I mustered the confidence to believe I had the strength to stand up to the coming events.

Time seemed to move at a snail's pace. So much had changed in the past two days. Everything I had assumed as normal in my life was no longer. We were served some kind of disgusting gruel for lunch, which had been jammed through a narrow slit in the door. I couldn't eat anything and probably wouldn't have eaten this slop even if I was hungry. I thought the cuisine in a French prison should have been better. Lol.

After lunch, it was "rec" time. Time to move to the courtyard and get our daily dose of exercise. I was still so new here and intimidated by the surroundings. I would have preferred to just stay in my cell behind a safely locked door and let the other girls go. I really didn't want to exercise because my adrenaline was still pumping with my heart beating uncontrollably too fast. The exercise was mandatory, however, and only consisted of walking in a circle around the yard. Prisoners were required to go to rec time. If I didn't comply, the guards would grab and drag me outside whether I liked it or not.

So we went outside…Sonya, Alaïa, Carmine and me. The area was a large square shaped dirt courtyard. Dust was rising up from all the feet shuffling about, but at least I could see the sky and feel the sun. I must admit I did welcome the sun. The rays felt glorious embracing me with their warmth. The gorgeous sunlight didn't free me, but made me feel better for a moment. It was a tiny instant before the gravity of my situation would once again settle in.

My three cellmates clustered around to protect me. The yard was full of thirty mean-looking females who were staring at me. Everyone was moving in a slow circle around the open area. We had to keep walking in one direction because that was the rule so the guards could control the women easier. Attempting to avoid eye contact, I could feel all the circling eyes upon me.

I only glanced at the bodies moving in the circling procession and saw the prisoners were in jailhouse wear or rough work clothes. Talk about uncomfortable. I was still wearing the same outfit I wore at the Nice Airport. It was a bit sticky after three days and I was definitely out of place.

CHAPTER 6

THE COURTYARD SCENE REMINDED ME OF THE classic film *Midnight Express*, with the downtrodden prisoners shuffling in a circle in the dusty courtyard. They were the sullen faces of lost girls counting their remaining time without freedom. Aside from their vacant eyes, I noticed these faces became distracted by something very unique in their presence…Me.

Several of the prisoners were young women who started to come towards me. Without speaking, I could feel Sonya, Alaïa and Carmine tighten around my body. They assumed the role of my de facto bodyguards and would defend me if necessary. There was a problem though. There were only three of them and at least thirty other women in the yard. As the onlookers continued to advance, their appearance was not difficult to distinguish. They were tough and quite capable of crushing anyone they didn't like.

I looked around desperately. There wasn't a guard in sight. There had been one in the corner when we came in, but I couldn't locate her now. My paranoia and panic set in, especially not having any idea how I could have offended these women who I was about to meet. It didn't appear they were approaching me to sit and have tea.

All of a sudden, one of them shouted, "Madame Médecin!" They ran towards me with their arms outstretched and smiles emerging from grim faces. I suddenly realized these were fans. They knew me. These girls from the streets and the poor districts were the people of Nice who loved me because I had worked so hard to help them. They knew I cared about them. While campaigning for Jacques, I sought support from not only the highest echelon of politicians, but with common people on the streets of Nice. I had worked with street vendors, small shop owners and, yes, prostitutes too like Carmine. They loved me because I loved them. I never looked down on them like many people did. They were my equal as women, but unfortunately had fallen on hard times.

I was the First Lady of Nice and it was my personal commitment to improve the living standard of the Niçois citizens. I became known as "La Comtesse de Coeur" (The Countess with a Heart). People said I had the common touch. The truth was I didn't have any touch. I just liked people and put forth my best efforts to help those truly in need. I did what I could. Politics, ideology, and class differences were not my measure of people. I was just an advocate for the needs of the good citizens of Nice.

The girls were close to me now. I thought I might recognize a face or two. Their dark hair, bright eyes, the mix of French, Italian, Corsican and Arab blood made up this eclectic group. I'd seen these faces before and cared for them. Although I had been gone from Nice for six years since 1991 when Jacques and I were forced to flee for our lives, these women were still our supporters and hadn't forgotten us.

They ran up surrounding me, laughing, giggling, smiling, and extending their arms. They wanted my autograph. "Madame Médecin!" they cried, "Madame Médecin, give us your autograph. Please. Please. Sign your name on our arms." They pulled newspapers, magazines, pages torn from books and even candy bar wrappers from their jail suits imploring me to give them my signature.

They were so glad to see me, like an old friend had returned to them from their past. In Jacques' and my absence, a new socialist regime had seized power in Nice. Truth be told, despite their typical hypocrisy about loving their citizens, the common folks were not doing well under this new socialist administration. They were truly 100% better off and respected more by Jacques and me, the capitalists.

I was touched and tears formed. The girls were jostling around me with their arms out. I couldn't believe it and grabbed every scrap of paper, torn page and candy wrapper I could reach, scribbling my name across each one. My hand was shaking, and my signature was rough. It didn't matter. My cell-mates just stood and watched, clapping their hands and smiling wildly. I was amazed, grateful and tremendously relieved at this outpouring of affection.

CHAPTER 7

HOW DIFFERENTLY THE GIRLS APPEARED TO ME now since they were friends and not a threat. It just shows how much misguided expectations can warp perceptions and how fear can twist the mind.

This was entirely too much laughter and fun for a prison yard. Of course, after a few moments several female guards came rushing out including the bitch that enjoyed physically probing my body. The guards ran straight into the crowd, brushing the girls aside and knocking several of them down. They were coming for me. Evidently, the guards thought this was my entire fault being responsible for the disturbance in the prison yard.

The girls wouldn't let them get near me. These women from Nice were on my side. They clustered around my body protecting me. Now, I had more than just my three cellmates. In solidarity, the group shielded me as best as they could from the guards.

I so appreciated them, but realized they could get in trouble for defending me against the guards. I couldn't let it happen. I pushed through the girls and made my way up to one of the guards. I explained this was MY fault. I had caused the disturbance and the girls were not to blame. I would take the blame.

"Take me back to my cell!" I yelled.

Well, that surprised the bitches! They couldn't argue with my demand, so they grabbed me by the shirtsleeves and hauled me back to my so-called accommodations. I knew the guards weren't going to harm me. Not with thirty highly agitated, very upset Niçoise females behind me! Sonya, Carmine and Alaïa followed me back to the cell. We were shoved inside with the heavy iron door slamming shut. The four of us cellmates began to laugh so hard we cried until we sobered up with the reality we were still behind bars.

"Oh fuck!" Carmine cried. "You are something else, Madame Médecin. I've never seen anything like that. Talk about putting those guards in their place!"

But the day wasn't finished yet, and the excitement wasn't over.

A guard suddenly appeared to say the American Consul had come to see me. It's about fucking time! At last, I was going to get to the bottom of this. I followed the guard down the corridor to the waiting room. Once more, as I entered the room, I was body searched for contraband as if I was hiding something somewhere. The guards had regained their composure after the debacle in the yard and needed to reassert their control. They wanted to let me know who was boss. I braced myself as the woman guard circled around me, patting here and there, picking at my pants and puffing out the sleeves of my shirt.

She touched my breasts, my hips and my touché. How could I have hidden anything as I was coming from my cell? I had been thoroughly searched at the Nice Airport as well as each new detention stop.

I had had enough. I lost it. I was extremely angry and yelled at this creepy woman to stop touching me in places she had previously examined. I didn't care at that point because this intrusion on my body had to stop now. I shouted, "Get away from me! Get your fucking hands off me! You've searched my entire body four times today and there's nothing left to look for!"

She jerked back, looking like she had just received the shock of her life. She hissed at me and backed away snarling. As events continued to unfold, I understood my predicament was not good as the rough treatment only escalated. Since the Socialists were now in power, their influence was torturing me from the prison administration down to the guards. Of course, it was political to make an example of me because I was Madame Jacques Médecin.

CHAPTER 8

ONCE I REALIZED MY PREDICAMENT WAS STILL part of a political reprisal, I remembered years earlier how relentless the Socialists had been in their pursuit to destroy Jacques. One of his greatest fears was any attempt to arrest him on charges as part of a plot to overthrow him. He was afraid an example would be made of him. This was founded on the fact he was pro-death penalty and might soon share accommodations with criminals not in favor of that policy. Jacques was a conservative and ran a tight ship. Some people outside of Nice resented this. Now that a socialist regime had the power in France, it was payback time for whoever was on the right. Jacques wasn't in France, but I was, and I became acutely aware their wrath would be forced on me in Jacques' absence. I hate politics. It brings out the worst in people, no matter what side you are on.

It all started years prior with the French politician and economist, Raymond Barre, initiating a smear campaign against Jacques in an attempt to dethrone and replace him on the Côte d'Azur. Jacques wielded all the power in his long held positions. Jealousy and greed with a lust for power drove others to great lengths to diminish him and us. This vicious campaign continued from the Left once Francois Mitterand became President of France in 1981. With the Niçois, and especially the Médecinists continuing to voice solid support for Jacques even after his exile, the leftist media continued their brutal attacks.

The leftist media saw an opportunity to further exploit their platform. They had not only kicked us to the gutter, but continued to stomp on me by cramming broadcasts and media articles with lies surrounding my arrest and imprisonment.

When I finally met with the American Consul, he told me the American government couldn't risk a problem with France because the case was too high profile. But, they would closely watch me as the events unfolded. I shouted at the Consul, "DO NOT EVEN THINK OF CONTACTING ME AGAIN! This is how you treat me? Fuck you! And thank you very much for not protecting an American citizen, especially as I promoted and supported American interests as The First Lady of Nice and the French Riviera. Oh, and did I mention I was the only American woman other than Grace Kelly to be presented with the Grand Humanitarian Award by the French government for my benevolent contributions."

Of course, I was subjected to another body search before returning to my cell. Thirty minutes passed and my lawyers arrived. I was led back to the body scan room once again. MERDE!

I was finally relieved to see the two men who were representing me and learned why I was arrested. They informed me that I was being charged for Jacques' crimes as crazy as it sounded. This entire frightening experience and mistreatment was not for anything I had personally done, but for what Jacques had allegedly done.

It was and still is Napoleonic Law. The spouse is responsible for the crimes of his or her mate. Two hundred years of this antiquated, biased, unreasonable ruling and, now, I was in jail because of it.

It was August 1991, when Jacques fled Nice, incredulously ending up in Uruguay and not in Argentina, which had been his first choice. President Carlos Menem had denied him at the last minute to enter the country. President Menem would be campaigning for re-election and didn't want to incite an international media calamity. A friendly informant in the Socialist Party disclosed to Jacques that he was about to be charged with money laundering through the Nice Opera House. "It was all political," he said. Being a strong, outspoken conservative in a socialist country with his family ruling the Côte d'Azur for over a century, he knew he wouldn't receive a fair trial and was realistically aware and genuinely fearful of being in jail, even for a short time.

"I will never come out alive," he said. "Too many enemies on both sides."

CHAPTER 9

T HE FRENCH RIVIERA WAS THE MOST COVETED
region in France, and Jacques was "The Boss." He had a heartfelt passion to make Nice a shining city, the glory town of the entire French Riviera.
Jacques Médecin ruled it with total devotion to his Niçois constituents. Most
importantly, he succeeded in accomplishing his goals for Nice, and consistently earned the respect and support of the popular vote. Unbelievably he
kept every promise he made, making him an anomaly among politicians. He
was and is still today dearly beloved and missed by the Niçois. Jacques kept
everything clean, secure and safe. At the time, he had great prestige as the
most respected and accomplished mayor in France. Even Mitterrand, the
socialist president, praised Jacques in an interview as being the best mayor
in France.

Within three days and a flurry of events following Jacques' departure,
TK and I escaped. We made a hasty retreat on the non-stop Pan Am flight
from Nice to New York. Once again, the socialist informant provided fore-
warning through our Press Secretary that our daughter and I were to be held
under house arrest at the Préfecture until Jacques' returned.

Thank goodness, a few years earlier, Jacques had negotiated a contract
with the President of Pan American World Airways to establish a direct
non-stop route between Nice and New York. It was a great opportunity for
both cities regarding tourism, cultural exchanges and, of course, commerce.
Fortunately, this also enabled my daughter and me to escape by the skin of

our teeth. Our Press Secretary, Jean Oltra, called the airline president and said it was urgent we were on that flight. Room was made for us, but I was still fearful with anticipation there would be an encounter with U.S. Immigration and Customs. I had grabbed whatever personal valuables I could seize, given the quick departure. We were planning to unite with Jacques in Uruguay, but were subsequently prevented from joining him.

In 1994 Jacques was extradited from Uruguay to France. He was brought to trial and convicted of embezzlement and fraud, then sent to prison in Grenoble. His Niçois Mafia was ready to do whatever it took to get him out. They were part of the fabric of Nice's history, woven from many generations. Their presence was seamless as everyone was aware of and accepted them. It was understood they were the men protecting Jacques. Max, our fixer, was on top of it. I knew they'd pull whatever strings they could to free their mayor.

Jacques was released a year later in 1995, but that was the extent of my knowledge until after my arrest. Our relationship was definitely strained after his release and our level of communication had much to be desired. Legal details were omitted from our conversations. Since he was living back in Uruguay after his release, I just assumed everything was okay. Prior to my arrest, I didn't know he had been restricted to Nice on appeal, but had escaped. He was no fool. Not until after they arrested me did I learn he had escaped again through Italy back to Uruguay. There, he would remain until his death.

CHAPTER 10

OK, LET'S GO BACK TO WHY I WAS IN JAIL, BACK to the book's title, *Arrested*, and how all of this came to be. Let me explain. Following a not so celebratory departure from France in 1991, I struggled to reconstruct my life being back in the United States. In France, I was beloved and accustomed to being celebrated and revered, but then had to escape my adoptive country feeling like a criminal.

Life was moving on with many other challenges. I was living in Los Angeles and traveling back and forth to Uruguay to see TK. Through this horrendous ordeal, Jacques and I became separated. Although our lives had transformed drastically, I believed we were completely dedicated to our daughter's safety and well-being. At least, I was.

I longed to go back to France to see old friends after many years. Lilou Dini, my former chief of staff, had invited me to the grand opening of her new restaurant in Nice. It would be fun to go. This was February of 1997 and I had no trepidations about returning to France. I thought it would be safe even being aware of Napoleonic Law, which I mentioned. Again, the spouse is responsible for whatever the partner did even if they were not complicit. However, at the time, I was under the impression that Jacques' case had been resolved since he had returned to live in Uruguay and was completely unaware he had escaped while awaiting his second trial in Nice.

Jacques was repeatedly under political attack. Threats were widespread, but he had taken precautions to protect me. I never had a bank account in

France. We never had a joint bank account nor did we own property together in France or elsewhere. His business affairs and mine had always and consistently been separate. I had done nothing illegal and honestly believed that because I was a U.S. citizen my native country would surely protect me. So, I decided to visit my friends in France. It was, as they say, a fateful decision because when the shit hit the fan the American government abandoned me.

On my way to France, I stopped in England to visit an old friend in Bath. Trevor Mound was my dear and beloved buddy who had formerly been the British Consul in Marseille. We became very close from the time he first arrived in France in 1987, ten years earlier. Jacques had held a luncheon for him and his delegation as a welcome to Nice. This helped them understand the lay of the land. In other words, Trevor was quickly made aware of the hierarchy and who had the power. We sat next to one another at the luncheon, and I uncontrollably started to cry. Jacques and I had quarreled that morning, but this was the first time I ever broke down at an official gathering. Trev was so kind and empathetic and said he couldn't stand to see me so upset. From that day forward we were cherished confidants, lasting until his death from lung cancer. Sadly, he smoked like a chimney. He has a special place in my heart. To this day, Trevor is one of the men I have most deeply respected. There are two important reasons for this. He had a profound and innate compassion for helping people and his remarkable intelligence was off the charts. Her Majesty The Queen had appointed him to reopen the British Consulate in Shanghai after it had been closed for decades. He spoke four Asian languages, plus French, Spanish, German and Italian.

After a wonderful visit, I left Trevor and Bath to catch my flight to Nice. I truly thought it was safe for me to go. There were no financial ties between Jacques and me. What could happen? Perhaps I should have given it a little more thought.

Anyway, it would be wonderful to see Lilou and Jackye. I boarded the plane in London and headed for Nice with only happy thoughts and positive emotions. There was no sense of foreboding, and I didn't feel any bad vibes, as I usually would have felt if there was a concern. I'm finely tuned-in and wired to something I can't explain, but am typically connected to something electric in the universe. When bad things are on the horizon, when evil winds blow, I can generally feel it. I just know, but not this time. When I needed my antennas the most they seemed to have disappeared and there weren't any signals. Therefore, the following events are history.

Everything was fine upon my arrival in Nice. Although I passed through Immigration, the name change on the addendum in the back of my passport apparently triggered their interest. By the time I entered the baggage claim area, I was met with a flurry of national police, arrested, and then thrown in the airport jail. What a mind fuck! I had no idea of what or why this was happening. To make matters worse, the gendarme stuck it to me more because of who I was and especially because I was American. I wasn't even able to make a phone call.

The next day I was transferred to the Nice Women's Prison and by that time I knew I was in a world of trouble. The French legal system is brutal once you become entrapped and extremely difficult to get out. I now realized that Jacques' enemies were out to get me and they might succeed. What could I do? What could my lawyers do?

The only thing I could think was to contact my Sagittarius friend, Jacques Chirac, the

President of France. We had been not just friends, but sympathetic buddies. Our birthdays were two days apart with mine on the 27th of November and Chirac was the 29th. I knew he would help me if only my lawyers could reach him. Otherwise, I was going to rot in a French prison cell.

BOOK TWO

Influences of
My Early Years

CHAPTER 11

I WAS BORN ILENE JOY GRAHAM AT CEDARS-SINAI
Hospital in Los Angeles, California on November 27th, 1948. My father
was Jack and my mother was Elaine. Both Jack and Elaine were exceedingly
attractive people who thought they had fallen in love. Dad was 5'11" with
black hair and turquoise eyes. He resembled Cary Grant. Mom was 5'7", slim
and had long black wavy hair. She exuded elegance.

I was raised in a relatively normal environment, a typical existence.
Well, for Beverly Hills anyway. My father was the accountant and business manager for his Uncle John Factor, also known as Jack Factor, a very
wealthy businessman. Not until high school was I truly able to gain a real
understanding of Uncle Jack's activities and Dad's role in his business. Uncle
Jack was very close with my father and always looked out for his well-being
as he grew up. After my paternal grandfather passed, Uncle Jack assumed
the father figure for my dad. Since my father was extremely bright and so
much more than Jack's own sons, he became Uncle Jack's right hand man
in business. As a result, Dad became responsible for Uncle Jack's finances
and was always extremely protective of all his interests. Although my family
lived in Beverly Hills, growing up with my Uncle Jack and Aunt Rella was
an introduction to over the top extreme taste and opulent luxury. This was a
lifestyle I wanted even more of. Why not? I was totally fascinated with their
lavish parties and A-List guests, which included high-powered politicians
and celebrities of the day.

Our family went to Las Vegas every summer for one month in the late 50s and early 60s. This was a result of Dad preparing all of the accounting and annual reviews for the Stardust Hotel that was owned (in name) by my Aunt Rella. The history of my Granduncle John Factor has been written in several books, but I can attest only to my own first-hand knowledge. Also, one must understand growing up in Beverly Hills with so much notoriety, stories of its residents was common knowledge. My family was no exception as I came to learn. Although my family name was Graham, I was singled out as another "Factor" in high school. Dad had changed our name while we lived in Canada due to anti-Semitism. There were several Factors (cousins) that preceded me at Beverly Hills High. With that recognition, I heard all the stories previously unbeknownst to me about my Uncle Jack as well as Uncle Max. Uncle Jack was also known as "Jake the Barber" in other circles that involved ties to the Chicago underworld. My family never directly shared any of these details with me, especially because my father was always vigilant and very protective. My father emphasized that "Jake" was definitely not a permissive name to ever be used in any reference to my uncle. As it turns out, my legacy of this "underworld" was actually quite intriguing and exciting to me.

I had an interesting childhood. I was seven when we moved back to the States after living in Canada for 4 ½ years. There were four grammar schools in the district that sent their graduates on to the oh-so-famous Beverly Hills High: Hawthorne, El Rodeo, Beverly Vista and Horace Mann. I went to Hawthorne. I didn't like grade school and liked high school less, but that didn't prevent me from trying to excel at it. My four years at BH High were good and bad. Good, because I seemed to be elected to things that I ran for. I was Sophomore Princess, head junior varsity cheerleader, voted most popular girl in my senior class and senior campus couple with Howard Erenberg.

It also was great fun to be one of three girls who were sponsored by the school to go to special off-campus modeling lessons, which led to an enjoyable modeling career.

So much for having to love something to be good at it. I simply modeled because the opportunities presented themselves and they were easy for me at the time. I liked the attention. Who wouldn't? A harbinger of things to come, I suppose. High school was good because I met Howard Erenberg, my first and only puppy love and a bit more. He was the most handsome boy in school at six feet with pitch-black hair, a beautiful athletic body, deep dark brown eyes and quite shy with a kind of cowboy allure which did not fit in at Beverly High. We discovered first attraction, lust, and sex. "Howie," as I called him, and I were voted "Campus Couple" our senior year. Unhappily, that's when things started to go downhill. I thought we would go to the same college and tie the knot after. We ended up going to separate colleges and grew apart. We still remain friends today and he owns a ranch outside of Los Angeles. It wasn't a surprise to me because he was always a cowboy at heart.

CHAPTER 12

G ROWING UP WHILE ATTENDING BEVERLY HILLS
schools was a typically normal existence for me. I was accustomed to being raised amongst the glitz and glamor of BH and neighboring Hollywood. Being in the bubble, I really didn't know anything other than this lifestyle. The only issue I had was being confronted by the snotty attitude of many who subscribed to that way of life. It was the 1960's and the economy was prospering. Movie studios in L.A. were continuing to roll out box office blockbusters and TV was really making it big. It was commonplace being in school with friends and other kids whose parents were famous movie and TV personalities. It all seemed normal.

At Hawthorne Elementary I became friends with Van Johnson's daughter, Schuyler, who was in the 7th grade with me. (Van Johnson was a popular and attractive actor who starred in *The Caine Mutiny*, *Brigadoon* and *In the Good Old Summertime*.) Poor Schuyler got pregnant in the 7th grade when she was just twelve. I never asked who the father was and she never told me. Being afraid to face her parents, she ran away from her home to mine wanting to hide immediately after getting the news. When they realized where she was they picked her up and that was the last time I saw her.

Developing into a teenager in the 60's, I became more aware of the nuances of life in Beverly Hills and venturing into neighboring Hollywood. There was the drama, the dysfunction, and the shallowness. It was also crazy, wonderfully intriguing, and fabulous at its best. "Never be bored." That's my motto. I certainly liked it enough to be drawn in. Maybe I needed all of this energy and excitement because I was now at the age where my mind and body started to awaken.

My hormones were raging and I craved excitement. By the time I was in 9th grade, I was developing into a young woman with extremely long legs. Both boys and men found my natural smile attractive, innocent and alluring. I didn't want to be innocent, but still had to learn to deal with this sudden new interest from the opposite sex. Sure, I thought I had it more or less together. Although I had a high confidence level by the time I was sixteen, I still lacked the true wisdom that comes with experience.

I began to realize men were watching me. Although somewhat flustered by the attention, I was flattered. It scared me a little, but of course I liked the excitement too. What female wouldn't? Being attractive holds some sort of influence, but it can also make one vulnerable to uncomfortable situations.

At sixteen, I had already found my path that would be my destiny—an independent female with newly discovered confidence. I craved freedom of mind and body without restrictions or limitations.

I was still just a high school girl and really knew nothing about sex, love, lovemaking, men's bodies or even my own body. I wasn't yet familiar with its feelings, commands and urges. I felt men's lust and sometimes my own, surprising me with odd sensations when least expected. I didn't really start to understand it until my first awakening.

It all started with Howard, who awakened that desire.

CHAPTER 13

BEFORE DISCOVERING SEX, ALL I CARED ABOUT were sports, riding horses and swimming. I was outdoorsy and athletic, a proficient rider. I loved to gallop at breakneck speed, reining the horse sharply around taking considerable risks. I rode horses at several day camps my parents sent me to during the summer. Dad had Tennessee Walkers. We rode English style, but my preference was a western saddle. The excitement of cowboys and rodeos had appealed to me from an early age. Interest in risk taking and impending peril has somehow been innate in my DNA. I am willing to take it to the limit for something I believe in or desire. I insist on my pleasures, yes, but more importantly, I stand up for my principles.

I was basically a cowgirl at heart. When I was ten I truly wanted to be a cowgirl on a big ranch somewhere, so I acquired the full cowgirl accouterment with cowboy hat, cowboy boots, a calfskin vest and a kerchief around my neck to pull up over my nose if the dust on the trail got too thick, ha ha. As mentioned, my father loved Tennessee Walkers and we had three of them. Big Red was Dad's favorite, and I rode him with ease even though he was seventeen hands tall. He was gentle and steady.

It was the 60's and I was a rebel, never accepting the rules if I couldn't understand them. If something isn't logical, I cannot relate. Many rules are created to be followed while lacking a clear and reasonable explanation. This is unacceptable to me. For someone imposing the rules, they must at least provide a logical rationale so I'm able to better understand them. Clear and consistent thinking is important to me. It was as true then as it remains today. That was what would eventually make being in the Nice Women's Prison so infuriating. There was no logic for me to wrap my head around.

High School came and went after our 1966 graduation. At Beverly Hills High there was a predominant social criteria of who had the best car in the parking lot, who was in the "In Crowd," who was dating who, and whose mother or father were succeeding in the entertainment industry. It wasn't exactly the most altruistic of goals, but that was the shallowness of growing up in Beverly Hills, which I came to understand many years later.

Now real life could begin, so I thought. And you know what? I was right. My Real Life did begin.

CHAPTER 14

I WAS OUT OF HIGH SCHOOL NOW, SO I WAS OF marrying age. At least, that was what Uncle Jack thought.

Uncle Jack loved me and spoiled me rotten even though I was only his niece, a grandniece at that. He also was of the opinion that he had the right to boss me around. He didn't. I wouldn't do what he told me if I didn't want to. He assumed I should dutifully accept whatever my "beloved uncle" wanted me to do. For instance, he had in his mind I should marry Harry Korshak. Harry was the eldest son of his dear friend and lawyer, Sidney Korshak. Uncle Jack was actually quite insistent about it. He was a tough man to butt heads with, but I had his blood and was tough and hard headed as well.

Harry was kind of cute. I won't say he wasn't, but he looked like Art Garfunkel with frizzy hair. He was sweet, but we were just friends. I wasn't attracted to him and we were too young to marry anyway. I was nineteen and he was a few years older. I saw him as a nice boy and truth be told, I have never been attracted to nice boys. At least in my early years, I craved more excitement. Just look at whom I dated and married.

Nevertheless, Harry's father was the real thing, a dominant figure in his own right and not to be lightly dismissed. You had to say "No" to Sidney in a nice way, if you said no at all. This was also the case with my Uncle Jack. Sidney was a highly successful lawyer and "fixer" protecting the interests of the Italian Cosa Nostra as well as the Jewish Mafia. "A finger in both pies," as Uncle Jack would say. He was also a specialist at representing large U.S. corporations in labor negotiations. An extremely influential man, he counted celebrities and heads of entertainment among his close friends, as well as many politicians. The FBI once named him as the world's most powerful lawyer.

Uncle Jack and Sidney insisted it would bring the families even closer if Harry and I tied the knot. In other words, the two men were willing to do a little selling of the family bloodline to secure the family business. Blending these two bloodlines would have brought immense clout to them and what they believed to be their social status. It wasn't that Jack and Sidney believed they were doing anything out of the ordinary, it's that business and family were deeply intertwined. That is the way things were done in the family and it was important to have willing participants. However, I was not a willing participant.

From a strictly profitable point of view, it made sense. I had to admit for Harry and me to join forces to produce Factor/Korshak kidlets would have been a great move. Uncle Jack would have been very happy to have the families bonded. It would extend his realm and would be a royal marriage of the gangster sort. I wasn't however about to marry anyone I didn't want to marry. Not even for Uncle Jack.

There was also another consideration. I had a fiancé. Greg McKay was the promoter at the Kaleidoscope Theater on Sunset Boulevard, which was a very popular venue for the leading American and British rock groups. The groups would hang at the club after the concerts and party. Of course, I was there to join them and PARTY. Those were some wild times. I was nineteen and we partied hardy with Canned Heat, Jefferson Airplane, Sly and the Family Stone, and the Byrds among others. It was a hangout for musicians like the Beatles, Rolling Stones, and Joplin even if they weren't on the playbill.

Uncle Jack easily solved the problem of Greg by sending Dad, Mom, brother and me on a two-week cruise to the Mexican Riviera. He got rid of Greg before we returned from the cruise. My uncle told me to give him the engagement ring and he'd make sure Greg got it back. Suffice to say, I never heard from him again and was fine with the decision. He was not a good guy.

CHAPTER 15

I T WAS TIME FOR ME TO DISCOVER THE WORLD. A born adventurer and risk-taker even from an early age, I have always appreciated the opportunity to travel. By the time I was nineteen, my hunger for knowledge became motivated through my travel experiences. The map of my travels eventually unfolded into a journey of a lifetime, as I will soon share with you. I thrived on learning about diverse cultures, their languages and art. I will forever be extremely passionate about experiencing the world. As someone who was curious about other cultural perspectives, I sought avenues and destinations of interest whether at home or abroad.

We had regular hangouts along the Sunset Strip and Hollywood Boulevard while growing up. The iconic Whiskey a Go Go was a favorite. It was one of the hottest clubs on the Strip. During the 60's Rock'n Roll was on a meteoric rise and Los Angeles was the "Mecca of Music." Adding Jimi Hendrix to the Whiskey with a whole lot of shaking and gyrating going on and you get one very interesting cocktail.

My best friend at the time, Shari Barman, who would later become one of the founders of The Virginia Slims Women's Tennis Tournament, had a crush on Jimi. One night he happened to be a surprise guest after Sam & Dave. He was decked out in a fantastically wild outfit with a multi-shaded purple cape, deep dark purple velvet boots and tight spandex purple pants that made everything visible. He sported a huge musketeer shaped purple chapeau (hat) with a rolled brim and a large white feather protruding from the headband.

After Jimi played his set he left the stage to mingle with the young, wild and crazy audience. I was talking with some people when Shari came to me and said, "I want you to meet someone." It was Jimi. He was talking to a small group when Shari joined them and asked him if she could introduce him to a friend of hers. She pulled me away from my people, introduced us and that's when the three of us started to click. We were laughing and very "highpy," as I call it. (High and Happy = HIGHPY) Jimi asked if we wanted to join him in his suite for a drink. Shari and I looked at one another and simultaneously said, "YES!"

We met him at the Chateau Marmont, an iconic hotel on the Sunset Strip, and followed him into the suite/living room where he offered us a joint and champagne. We talked and talked for almost an hour until Jimi and Shari disappeared into the bedroom.

I was sleepy but followed them a few minutes later. I knew how Shari felt about him so I wasn't too surprised. Shari was my height; 5'9" with dark brown hair and a very athletic build from being a tennis pro. She was a handsome female with light brownish green eyes and rather shy. But not when it came to this, obviously.

I got on the bed and we were all kissing and rolling around. Then I passed out for a bit. It was late. Shari and I hugged and kissed the "Man" goodnight and thanked him for an incredibly memorable evening. I found out that night Mr. Hendrix and I were born on the same day, November 27th…both Sagittariuses! No wonder we clicked. Sag's are wild risk-takers.

CHAPTER 16

ND THEN ALONG CAME BERT (HUSBAND #1). I
met Bert Poncher, my first husband, when I had just turned twenty-one. He was sixteen years my senior, six feet tall, a dark and swarthy com-
plexion, handsome in a rugged manly way and always dressed to the nines.
At the time I was modeling at Haggerty's, which was an upscale women's
department store on Wilshire Boulevard near Rodeo Drive.

A few times each week I would walk to meet my dear friend Richard
Mylon for lunch or coffee. Richard worked at Mr. Guy's Men's Store, which
was not far from Haggerty's. He was the younger brother of one of my best
childhood school friends, Robin Mylon. On one of these particular days I
was walking north on Rodeo Drive to meet Richard. There was a group of
men who saw me strolling on the opposite side of the street. I glanced and
noticed a beautiful Jaguar 2+2 parked in front of the Beverly Rodeo Hotel.
Four men were standing next to the car and apparently thought I was glancing
at them when one of the men called out to me, "Come over here, beautiful!"

I laughed and yelled back, "If you want me, come get me!" And that's
exactly what he did. I told Richard we'd meet up later as the man ran across
the street, introduced himself, and escorted me back to the car and their
group. One of them asked me to have a drink at the hotel bar and I replied,
"Why Not?"

We all went inside the hotel which was very sheik with the "in" crowd,
yet comfy in a laid back way. It was a neighborhood hangout for Beverly

Hills locals and hip visitors. One of the men who happened to be the most dapper, sat next to me and asked how I knew his employee (the man who had called shouted out and brought me over to the car). I said I had never met him before. His face lit up while he introduced himself and asked, "Will you have dinner with me tomorrow night?" That was Bert.

I liked him because he was a gentleman. He was also quite attractive and sexy. "Yes, that would be nice," and gave him my number and address. I was living in my parents' home at the time and they happened to be out of town for a few days. I waited until the next evening. He was punctual. I came down the stairs in slinky hip-hugger bell-bottoms with a flowing tunic top and my hair down instead of up, as it had been when we met the day before. I answered the front door and greeted him with a big smile. His face lit up once again. It was Friday night and we went to Ted's at the Beach on Pacific Coast Highway. While waiting for our table, we sat down at the bar and started to talk. By the time the table was ready, Bert said he was smitten and asked me to marry him. Well, that didn't take long. After he made his proposal, I stared at him somewhat taken aback.

I told him that we should get to know one another first, ya think? So, we started dating and I felt very comfortable with him. He seemed to fit my ideal man-type. I wanted to get out of my parents' home to have more freedom and some experience living with a man before I went on my "Quest." I was preparing myself to be ready when the ultimate man of my dreams would appear. Call it a course in practical husbanding.

I asked him what he did for a living. He had recently started his own automotive rep company after first working for his cousin, Lenny Poncher. Lenny had the top auto rep company in the U.S. at the time. Bert was a solid businessman and outright successful. Following our divorce, his company became one of the largest reps in the country. I don't think there was any connection between those two things; our divorce, and his success, I mean.

So, we were married with Elvis officiating. First, we eloped to Las Vegas with my parents as our witnesses for a quick ceremony in an Elvis Presley wedding chapel. What a hoot! Of course, we stayed at the Stardust Hotel (my Uncle Jack and his partners built it) and had a fabulous time. When we returned my mother planned a large wedding reception with 300 guests, which would take place at the Beverly Hills Hotel in August, five months after the Vegas ceremony. The reception was a beautiful event with white and pink flower arrangements and delicious chicken, steak or fish entrees. The wedding cake was three layers of white vanilla with dark chocolate ganache in between the layers and white frosting. It was a wonderful celebration and the next day Bert and I were off to London for our honeymoon. We had a lot of fun together and traveling was our drug. Bert's business required constant traveling and I was "all in."

There was only one problem with our marriage. I wasn't in love, not even from the beginning. Who really understands the depth of true love at the tender young age of twenty-one? I was honest and told him I would leave before I was thirty and did just that at twenty-five years old.

CHAPTER 17

MY FAMILY HISTORY INCLUDES MY GRANDUNCLE Max Factor Sr., the cosmetic mogul, who was largely responsible for pioneering the modern day cosmetics industry in the United States. Together with his son, Max, Jr., the term "make-up" was coined. He created the first cover up foundation for cinema in Hollywood called "Flexible Greasepaint," which was the first makeup used for a screen test of *Cleopatra*. His famous quote was "You are not born glamorous. Glamor is created." After Max Sr.'s death in 1938, his son Frank Factor assumed the name of Max Factor Jr. and he was my Uncle Max. My uncle followed in the legendary footsteps of his father and together they developed "Pan-Cake," the first commercially available foundation. Uncle Max later developed "Pan-Stik" which was a foundation based on the ever-popular Pan-Cake. It was unique as a roll-on, akin to applying lipstick. He went on to revolutionize the cosmetics industry with hugely successful lipstick and mascara products, just to name two.

The Factor clan is still a legend in Hollywood and my name would have opened some doors in Los Angeles had I ever wanted to use it to my advantage, but I never did. From my teenage years in high school I forged my own path, although I wasn't always quite sure where it would take me. My quest was to find what the world had to offer. I was eager to pursue almost anything that captured my interest. As a voluptuary who lived by her five senses, I was a pleasure seeker and as previously mentioned a few times, a risk-taker. To me, there was nothing better.

I loved my family and was close to them. Like my Uncle Max, they were, well, unique. Max Sr.'s half brother was my other Granduncle John Factor, who I previously mentioned. He was also known as "Jake the Barber" in certain circles. Uncle Jack (as I called him), was a Prohibition-era gangster, associated with the likes of Al Capone, Arnold Rothstein, and Jimmy Hoffa, as I later learned. He gained quite a reputation as he lived and enjoyed life to the fullest. He was an exceptionally clever person who stood his ground and was well respected among his associates. My father once said to me, "You're just like your Uncle Jack, wild and fearless." Dad, being his right-hand man, knew Uncle Jack's personality very well and apparently recognized some of the same traits in me. I had an extraordinary father who was always there if I needed him. As protector for Uncle Jack, Dad had earned the exclusive responsibility to manage his finances and legal matters.

Uncle Jack became one of the principal owners of the Stardust Hotel in Las Vegas starting in 1955. Our family spent seven summers there while my father worked on financial statements. During the early 1960's, although still too young to be in a casino, I accompanied my uncle as his "good luck charm." While I may have been young, I could clearly see he was losing thousands of dollars at the tables.

Dad was always busy with his work for weeks at a time when we were there. We fried in the sun at the pool by day and at night went to headlining hotel shows with always the best seats in the house. Uncle Jack had many close Italian and Jewish friends, so there were always fabulous dinners and extravagant parties. It was a very glamorous and exciting time with the "Rat Pack" regularly performing. My impressions as a young teenager of these high-powered men and their lifestyle were fun, sexy, and dangerous. I was definitely intrigued and fascinated. That's when I realized this was the type of man and lifestyle I really was attracted to. They did not take crap from anyone. These important men were incredibly generous, a masculine trait lost today.

Uncle Jack was one of those men and my father was committed to watching over him. Growing up, Dad never spoke about my uncle's business activities or his associates. It was not until my Aunt Rella's funeral in 1969, while riding in the same limousine with Uncle Jack that he shared his first-hand recollection of his kidnapping and the name Roger Touhy. As I learned, my uncle had been a close friend with Al Capone. Through this association, an "arranged" kidnapping of my uncle was accomplished in 1938. Not the actual, but alleged perpetrator Roger Touhy, an Irish-American Mob boss from Chicago, was framed for ordering his kidnapping while behind bars. Touhy, not an associate of Capone's, was murdered by the Mob the minute he stepped out of prison because he swore to have my uncle killed. The purpose of the kidnapping was to buy time for my uncle to avoid extradition back to England where he had been sentenced in absentia and not to be accused in Touhy's demise.

Uncle Jack had previously committed the largest stock swindle in European history. The victims of the swindle included members of the Royal Family. While the kidnapping plot was successful, he continued to deal with legal issues through the years. In an effort to dismiss these concerns, he became the largest contributor to John F. Kennedy's 1960 presidential campaign. In an unusual move, mostly because it was not at the end of a presidential term, Uncle Jack received the best present...that of a presidential pardon by JFK on Christmas Day in 1962.

All I can say is this; that ride in the limo with Uncle Jack was an eye opener. He never mentioned another word about those events after that day, but I was able to fill in many of the blanks on my own as a result of that revealing discussion. With my romantic eyes gaining wisdom as I grew older, I saw Dad was like brother Tom Hagen in *The Godfather*, ensuring every deal was legitimate.

Have you noticed by now that the three most important men in my life were all J's—and with almost the same name—my father Jack, my Uncle Jack, and my late husband Jacques (Jack) Médecin? I find that an intriguing coincidence.

CHAPTER 19

I T WAS 1970 AND ABOUT THIS TIME I DISCOVERED needlepoint. This was a life skill that became very important to my well-being, especially in later years.

I am an artist to the core and will design anything. Homes, clothing, jewelry…anything. Designing and stitching needlepoint is an art I grew to love.

I was 21 and married to Bert when I met a lady at the checkout stand in the grocery store. She was carrying the most intricately designed needlepoint purse. I complimented her purse and asked where she bought it. We introduced ourselves and I met Gloria. When she told me she made it herself, I was astonished. I asked if there was any way she could teach me the stitches so I could make one too. She said she'd never given lessons before, but if I was really serious she'd help me.

I was not only serious. I craved this and would go to her home twice a week. She taught me the standard needlepoint stitches, and also "bargello," upright flat stitches laid in mathematical patterns. This intricate skill added a third texture to my projects, and the results were complex and beautiful. I was enthralled and loved what I was learning and creating. After months of diligent effort, my purse was completed. It was colorful, attractive, and intriguing because each tiny panel was a different stitch symbolizing significant items I cherished. You might say each panel was a memory I had woven into time. Gloria was so impressed with my learning skills and was thrilled with my work. Excitedly, she told me about an upcoming fair and felt my work was worthy of one of the three prize-winning categories. We entered my newly created treasure and waited for the day the winners were announced. I was very nervous. They started with the third runner up, then second runner up. Then, of course, there was a long pause before the winner was announced. I had hoped to place, but figured it was over for me now. No way could I imagine that I'd win first prize. NO WAY! OMG!

Was I wrong! My name was called as my purse was placed on the highest podium with my fellow winning contestants. I was ecstatic because the only thing I ever won was a candy bar at the Encino Theater when I was nine. Now I believed I could do more and was motivated by my next project, which was a vest. Gloria again helped me, and I learned how to attach the template to the canvas. This was an even bigger task, but my enthusiasm drove me to finish it in no time. The vest was entered in another contest...and who'd a thunk it. My vest won first prize again! I was definitely hooked. I had won two first place awards, and it spurred me on to create more elaborate and unique designs.

I didn't realize then how important needlepoint would become in my life. I'm left-handed and thought it would be fun to teach needlepoint to other left-handed people. There was a little antique store on Santa Monica Boulevard in Beverly Hills called The Staircase. Upstairs was a section devoted to needlepoint. Patti Reagan, the daughter of President and Nancy Reagan, worked downstairs, and I was hired two days a week to teach my new and obsessive craft to a left-handed group. The other days were dedicated to the right-handers.

It was the early 70's, when then Governor and Mrs. Reagan came to visit Patti. They were so nice. I was appalled at the way Patti spoke about them after they'd left, revealing personal information that should not have been divulged in public. I admired the Governor and Mrs. Reagan for their grace and charm. I agreed with their politics too, but as it turned out, I didn't respect their daughter at all. She was snotty, rude to her parents, and most other people.

Eventually, I left the Staircase and began designing and making needlepoint pillows, selling a few of my finished products even though I really didn't want to part with them. I never intended to sell my pillows, but friends or acquaintances insisted on buying a few. I still have a nice collection of my designs today, some of which are over 50 years old.

CHAPTER 20

I KNEW I WAS NOT "IN LOVE" WITH BERT BECAUSE I honestly didn't recognize those feelings at that time in my life. He was my first step experiencing an adult relationship. Let's call it an apprenticeship. I wanted to be confident and ready when I found the "True Love" of my life as I mentioned. There's no better way of learning something than having the real experience. When Bert asked me to marry him, I said I would leave him before I was 30. He told me I would fall in love with him in time and wasn't concerned.

We shared many of the same interests such as travel, party, food, sex and shopping. He had great style and was a sharp dresser. We were a dynamite looking couple and looked like we belonged together, leaving people all the more shocked when we divorced.

For me, just sharing the same interests wasn't enough. I wasn't in love and I was bored. I was just too young. Also, my having grown up with exciting accomplished men around me like my father and uncles made me critical and picky about men. I hadn't yet found a man who measured up to all my expectations. Someone who completely excited, thrilled, and fulfilled me. That all changed when I met Jacques.

We had good times together, Bert and I. We had fun until it wasn't fun anymore and it became time to part ways. Then the car accident happened. It was horrendous. A woman on Sunset Boulevard made a left-hand turn from the right-hand lane, approaching me from the opposite direction, barreling through a red light and broadsided my driver's door. The car did a complete rollover due to the severe impact. Even though I was wearing a seatbelt, I smashed my head on the console. My life seemed to race in front of me. I had a clear thought that if I made it out of there in one piece, I would continue my quest to find the love of my life. My face was a bit bloody and an ambulance arrived and rushed me to the hospital.

At the hospital, the doctor told me I would feel even worse and would hit a low point after a couple of days. I had a concussion and my neck was twisted. As I awoke on the second day, my whole body was in spasm from the aftershock. The nurses gave me an injection to help lessen the pain, but I knew it was going to be a long recovery. I was scheduled for physical therapy three times a week and someone would have to drive me to the hospital. Bert couldn't do it because he was busy working. But I had—well—a rescuer. Stuart Deutch, a friend of Bert's who had recently been released from prison for embezzling 14 million dollars from a Florida bank. He had nothing pressing to do, so Stuart said he'd love to be my chauffeur.

I had met Stuart at one of the wild parties Bert and I gave. We hosted many parties. Bert asked if he could invite his friend Stuart, who had just arrived back in town. I said sure. When I was introduced to him, I was favorably impressed. His rough look appealed to me. Black shirt, leather jacket and leather pants. When we sat down to talk he showed me his right leg where he'd stuffed a .38 revolver. Now, that's sexy.

We got along famously and that's how he became my driver. He took me to the physical therapist three times a week.

CHAPTER 21

BERT COULDN'T SAY I DIDN'T WARN HIM. I TOLD him right at the beginning when he proposed to me that I would leave him. He didn't believe me, but it would have been better for him if he had. I don't lie.

We had been married for five years. It was 1974, and it was time for me to go. I was 25 and took half of the wedding gifts, which my family had given to us. I took my personal belongings and left. The note I wrote Bert should have reminded him of what I had communicated from our first date. He would come home one day and I wouldn't be there. Again, I don't lie.

Was this a bit hard-hearted? Well, perhaps. I was convinced my destiny was headed in a different direction than the last five years. I had to follow my gut instincts and longed to be free of all constraints. It was my life to live and I wanted to experience what this grand world had in store. The explosions waiting around the corner were wild and improbable. Somehow, these inevitable events would change my life and make me the Queen of the French Riviera, the darling of the Côte d'Azur, and would lead me to new heights and awarenesses. Little did I know that eventually my life would be in jeopardy.

CHAPTER 22

AFTER I DIVORCED BERT, STUART AND I HAD A ball. Now, he not only was my chauffeur, but an exciting companion to play with around the world. Whatever I wanted, he would provide. We were in San Francisco visiting Jimmy Fratianno, aka "Jimmy the Weasel," an alleged hitman for the Italian Mafia, when they started discussing robbing jewelry stores. I just sat and listened. It sounded dangerous and exciting, and it was. Later, I understood danger is not the same thing as excitement. That was a lesson yet to be learned.

I told Stu one night that I was craving a really good pineapple. The following morning he booked us tickets to Hawaii for the weekend and I had the sweetest pineapple ever. That's the kind of guy he was.

We were in Atlanta and went for a stroll from our hotel passing by expensive clothing and jewelry stores. I stopped in front of a shop and admired the most beautiful red cape in the window. I told Stuart I loved it. We kept strolling and then returned to the hotel.

Upon entering our room I saw a gift-wrapped package on the bed. He looked at me smiling. "It's yours baby. Open it." How he did it I don't know, but there it was…my red cape. That was Stuart. He was wild in a very quiet way. He'd sit, listen and not say much, but when he did say something, it was relevant.

Back in L.A., the jewelry heist plans were progressing. The target was Lion d'Oro, a high-end jewelry shop on Bedford Drive in Beverly Hills. Stuart had his 3-man team. Jimmy the Weasel Fratianno would fence the stolen goods. Jimmy the Whip, a proficient cat burglar would be the smash and grab guy. He had recently been released from prison and was also an ex-jockey. Jim was very thin and stood 5'2". Apparently, he was better at the burglary business than being a jockey. They also had a getaway driver and were ready to roll. The heist would take place in three days. Before the day arrived, there was a glitch. The driver bailed and it was down to the wire. Stuart was on the phone with Fratianno discussing what to do.

Who could they trust? Guess who? They said they needed me to cover. I silently thought, Holy Shit! They were serious. I mulled it over and decided to follow my life motto, Why Not? When one is young, fear is far from the equation. At least, that was true in my case. I was excited, nervous and riveted. But I was ready and have to admit, I loved it. The adrenaline. The thrill. The danger.

The day arrived. I slowly drove Stuart and Jimmy the Whip to the shop on Bedford. I drove a nondescript gray Chevy sedan, which we hoped would not bring attention. I went slow and easy, though my mind was racing 100 miles an hour and my foot wanted to stomp on the gas. We definitely didn't want to be stopped on the way to the robbery or back. My heart was pounding so hard, I thought my chest would burst.

We arrived. I parked the car across the street from the shop. They were well dressed and nothing was amiss except for the facemasks and pistols, which were hidden under their clothes. Everything was happening so quickly now. Before I knew it, they jumped out of the car and ran across the street to the shop. I can't believe I did it when I look back on this today, but I did.

I watched as they entered the door and the rest was described to me afterwards. Upon entering the store with masks on, they said the clerk split for the back room. They proceeded smashing the glass cases and threw everything into black bags running as quickly as they could back to the car. The Whip threw the bags in the trunk. Stu jumped in front and said, "Hit it!" and I did.

The bags were full of diamonds, rubies, sapphires and emeralds in expensive settings including necklaces, rings, watches, brooches, and bracelets. It was an exclusive, independent jewelry store in Beverly Hills that made similar quality pieces compared to *Cartier* and *Van Cleef and Arpel*.

I drove as fast as I could within the speed limit so as not to attract attention and dropped them off at Stuart's penthouse. They hid the bags of jewels under a floorboard in the closet. I changed cars and went to my apartment to wait for them to contact me. I knew that Jimmy the Weasel was going to fence the jewels with his contacts. There was nothing else to do but wait. I think it took a day for my heart to stop racing.

Two days went by and not a word. Then, Jimmy the Weasel called me from San Francisco. "Listen to me very carefully," he said. "The Feds were tipped off by a snitch. Stuart is going to be arrested. Someone has it in for him. Some bastard ratted him out. They didn't mark Jim the Whip, but they probably will, so he's gone into hiding and will contact you when he feels it's safe. Your phone might be tapped because they know you're Stuart's girlfriend. They don't know who drove the car. Get up to the fucking penthouse ASAP before they raid it, grab the jewels and hide them. The Feds plan on visiting you at 7:00 in the morning. Just remember, you know nothing."

He hung up. Panic set in. I drove to the penthouse. I was totally freaked out. I kept looking in my rearview mirror all the way. I was sure I was being followed. Every car that got too close to me looked like a police car. I saw one patrol car with Los Angeles County painted on the side, a red flasher on top, moving through the intersection. It wasn't even close to me, but I almost passed out. This was when I learned that danger and risk were not always fun and definitely not a healthy adrenaline rush.

I got to the penthouse, walked around the complex looking for anything suspicious and prayed I wasn't being followed. Nothing yet. I went to the top floor and slipped in the door still looking for any signs. No one was there. I pried open the floorboard, grabbed the two large bags and left.

I was responsible for the jewels and knew they had to be hidden. I called a good, loyal friend named Carole and asked her to come to my place at once. She dropped what she was doing and rushed right over. "The Weasel" told me after the Feds left I had to somehow make the bags permanently disappear.

"Carole," I said, "I don't want you to ask me any questions right now, but I'm going to give you two big heavy bags after the Feds leave. Take them to your place and hide them until you hear from me. In the meantime, I need you to spend the night to be here as my witness when they arrive." She didn't say a word, just nodded. Her eyes became huge, glossy and looked nervous, but she didn't ask any questions.

The next morning at exactly 7:00 am the doorbell rang. Two large FBI Agents in dark suits and close-cropped haircuts were standing in the doorway. They entered and started to question me. I said I knew nothing, but they persisted. They were getting miffed. They wanted to know why my friend was there. I told them I wanted to make sure I had a witness in case they became disrespectful.

They weren't expecting that answer. They scowled at me, twisted their faces into a grimace and said I would be contacted again and left. Carole was staring at me in complete shock. I sat her down and explained what I could, not telling her what was in the bags. She said she didn't want to hear more and whatever I needed, she was by my side. This was a very, very good friend. She left with the bags until I could decide what I was going to do.

Jimmy the Whip knocked on my door a couple of days later because he was afraid to use the phone. The penthouse was off limits. This was my own apartment I had rented the year before. He told me Stuart was in L.A. County Jail. As it turned out, he remained in County for one year before being transferred to Chino State Men's Prison.

The next day I got a call telling me I was to appear before a grand jury to testify. I immediately contacted a lawyer friend, a man who I had worked for during the summer months when I was out of school. His name was Irving

Shimer. He was a tall imposing figure with a very serious demeanor. He was a no-nonsense man, well respected by his peers. I trusted him. Irv was brilliant and later became a judge in the Los Angeles Superior Court for sixteen years. He assured me that he would be with me every step of the way and he was.

I wanted to call Jimmy the Weasel in San Francisco, but had to do it from a safe phone. I went to a phone booth (yes, a phone booth, non-existent today) and dialed his number. He said he'd been waiting to hear from me. I told him about the grand jury. He said, "I'm not worried about you. Take the Fifth and you know nothing." Although feeling a bit overwhelmed, I understood and hung up.

The day of my grand jury appearance came. Irv and I drove to the courthouse together. As we entered the building, there was a swarm of photographers waving cameras and popping flashbulbs and pleading "Miss Graham, Miss Graham, this way!" They wanted to get a full face shot for the newspapers. I hadn't expected this nor was I ready for it. Why? Apparently, the press found out I was Jake the Barber's niece and wanted to make an example of me.

Irv stood 6'4" and was very strong. He grabbed one of the photographer's cameras and threw it on the ground and shouted, "That's enough. No photos. Now leave at once!" They knew he wasn't joking and high-tailed it out of the building.

Irv told me the same thing Jimmy the Weasel had. Take the 5th on every question and don't volunteer a word. As we entered the courtroom, it was a big somber space, very grim and very intimidating. The judge entered and assumed his place behind the bench and, yes, there were twelve people in the jury box. It was frightening and unsettling. I was called to the witness stand and the questioning began. I was stoic and answered as I had been advised, saying nothing. I took the 5th. The prosecutor who was asking the questions seemed frustrated, but Irv was there to protect me and we finally left after what seemed hours on the stand. They hadn't learned anything from me. Irv was and still is one of my celebrated heroes.

CHAPTER 23

STUART WAS IN JAIL. FUN MOMENTS WITH HIM POP into my mind now and then. Especially the pineapple in Hawaii and the red cape on the bed in Atlanta. I savor those memories for an instant and then brush them away. I knew I had to keep moving to forge ahead in my quest. If I stayed true to it, I hoped to find my dream. Miraculously, I did.

My friendship with Jimmy the Whip ended when he had a heart attack and died. It was unexpected and left me feeling alone and without an ally.

Life as I knew it was about to change in ways I could not even fathom. I am a dreamer and push life to the limits, but I couldn't have imagined what was to come. I was nervous and anxious, and sensed something was changing. Surprisingly, needlepoint was my savior and helped me get through it. My hobby, focusing on creating something of value took on a bigger role, drew my mind away from my worries and helped me while I was waiting, waiting, waiting.

It was worth it when it finally arrived, and it was mind-blowing.

CHAPTER 24

I WAS IN A BAD WAY FOLLOWING THE EVENTS SUR-
rounding Stuart, finding my life filled with worry and anxiety. I was a
nervous wreck just trying to get through one day at a time. I called Roger, a
friend of Bert's, and told him I had something extremely important to discuss.
He invited me to lunch in the marina. I knew I had to somehow dispose of
the jewels and had an idea. Stuart was in county jail and I devised a plan.
Roger had a boat in Marina Del Rey. During lunch, I told him I needed to
go out on his craft and insisted he not ask me any questions. He was curious
but kindly replied, "Of course."

The next day we met on the dock and he helped me on board with my
bags. We sailed far enough away not to be noticed by anyone. I told Roger
to just steer and look straight ahead. Meanwhile, I dumped the loot at the
bottom of the ocean floor. I brought a bottle of Dom Perignon with me. I
don't like the taste of alcohol, but figured I'd better do something to drown
my tears. I know Roger enjoyed it better than I did. He never asked me about
my cargo and to this day the jewels haven't surfaced. That was almost fifty
years ago. Go figure.

During the same lunch with Roger, he said he knew someone who was
selling high-end wholesale women's apparel from a rented office in Beverly
Hills and thought I would like to see the merchandise. We went after lunch.
The guy's name was Michael and he was also a music promoter who staged
headliners in the Beverly Hilton Ballroom. He also promoted rock concerts.

Michael immediately started fawning over me and invited me to dinner. He definitely wasn't my type, but continued to pursue me. When I came down with a cold, he brought over two huge platters of BBQ ribs and chicken. Food is definitely a way to my heart. He nursed me back to health and announced we were going to Acapulco to relax.

If only I had said no. But I was still feeling fragile after all the scary incidents with the jewelry, so I thought, Why Not?

After my divorce from Bert, my brother Richard (five years five days younger than me) decided we should share this cool penthouse apartment in Brentwood, California together.

I was feeling very good about this decision. My brother and I were close and we settled into that really neat place for just four months. Unfortunately when I was in Mexico, Bro called to tell me our building had been sold and the new owners wanted to live in our unit. I broke down and started to cry. I told Michael I just couldn't handle another move. I was mentally and emotionally drained. Facing a new move and having to decide immediately what I needed to do about my life felt very daunting. Michael told me not to worry about anything.

"Marry me?" he pleaded. "I'll handle the move so you won't have to lift a finger."

It seemed like a way out and I told him the truth. "I don't love you," I said. "I'm not even sure I like you and don't want to marry you."

He quickly replied, "Try it for a year and if you want out after, I'll let you go." It seemed like a solution at the moment. BIG MISTAKE, but I allowed the marriage to take place anyway which only lasted a few months.

Michael set everything up for the wedding the following day. I bowed out for a minute to go to the ladies room to catch my breath and wonder what the hell I was doing. I knew this was hasty and took a look at myself in the mirror and teared up. Then, out from one of the bathroom stalls appears my friend Shari Barman…in Acapulco! What a surprise! (Yes, my friend who had been with Jimi Hendrix and me.) We looked at one another and started to scream. Talk about a coincidence! She immediately knew something was wrong. I explained as much as I could in ten minutes.

"Holy Shit!" she shouted. I asked her to stand up for me at the ceremony. I needed moral support. She and I both knew this was temporary, but I was still a wreck. I wasn't sure what the future would hold because I wasn't going in the direction of my dreams. Shari was with the pro tennis player, Rosie Casals, and they both attended the wedding.

Back home, Michael moved me into his condo on Maple Drive in Beverly Hills and every night he cooked up a storm. I was enjoying his cuisine immensely, but a few nights later there were strange phone calls and inconsistencies in his explanations of them. Then one night these tough guys showed up at the condo and dragged him into the hall for a private conversation. I was becoming more and more uncomfortable with my circumstances. I knew it was time for me to leave, ASAP. I got myself an apartment in Brentwood and was gone before he arrived home the following day. I asked my friend Carole to move in with me. I paid the rent and she helped with household chores. It was a good deal for both of us.

Michael kept coming over to my new place, begging me to come back and tried to beat down my front door. I had to get a restraining order against him. I had been with him for three and a half months and decided to get an annulment. It was quite a lot of trouble, but I got out. That mistake was over.

Following my departure, the future for Michael was not good. He cheated the Italian Mafia—not a smart thing to do—stealing money from concerts they had sponsored. I heard many years later when I was in Nice, they beat him to a pulp in his garage and he was on dialysis for a year. An old acquaintance somehow got my private phone number and called to inform me what had happened to him.

I received a phone call two years later from the same person, telling me this time the Mob put a gun in Michael's mouth and blew his head off in the garage.

I have one comment to make on that subject which is, he deserved it. He had talked me into investing in a Led Zeppelin concert, which was supposedly canceled due to the band being ill and I never saw my money again. Being young and naïve, I lost that money and paid the price. I only had myself to blame for allowing him into my life. Consequences are not always pleasant.

CHAPTER 25

I T WAS 1976, AND LIFE WENT ON. CAROLE AND I settled into a routine at the apartment. I went to work modeling, she kept the place clean and kept me well fed. I was starting to feel my passion for life returning. Carole had a friend living on a ranch in Arcadia, near Pasadena, who had invited her to a party. Carole asked if she could bring me.

When we arrived at the house it was incredibly warm, comfy and inviting. Our hostess' name was Corky Dunn. She and her brother Kirk ran a family ranch in the Pasadena Hills. Corky opened the door to welcome us. I shook her hand and took to her at once. I felt nurtured just being in her presence. Kirk was late. When he finally arrived, we were introduced and there was an immediate spark. He was handsome, six feet, incredibly fit, and sweet as his sister, so we started to date. Corky and I became really close. Kirk was patient with me. I told him that I needed time to make any intimate decisions. He asked if I would like to move to the ranch and get away from my hectic (Lol) life to get my head clear. I said yes, and he gave me my own room.

He was one of the most understanding and kindest men I have ever known. Kirk gave me space. I really started to heal with his and Corky's help. I was young and realized the need for my spirituality to evolve. They both taught me the meaning of love with their unconditional care and my hope was to become a more self-sufficient person.

It was time to regroup. I felt like I had fallen out of a tornado with my life spinning around after my time with Bert. I invoked the Fifth with Stuart, and then came the four-month insanity of the Mexican wedding disaster. Kirk, the gentleman that he was, gave me time to consider his marriage proposal. All of this occurred within a year.

Corky and I became best friends and remain so to this day, forty-seven years later. She was solid as a rock, being there for me when I needed to cry or vent. Her kind and gentle nature enabled me to grasp fantastic advice she often gave me about love and life. She was and is an incredible teacher. In fact, her lifelong occupation was a high school teacher. She had been awarded "Teacher of the Year" more than once, and was even a candidate for the national award. Many of her students still recognize and cherish her mentorship to this day.

I was still modeling. Corky asked me because of my background if I would like to teach a class at her high school. It would be a class to help young girls gain more confidence, learn how to dress and how to present themselves on job interviews, etc. I loved the idea and Corky helped me with the exam for my teaching certificate. We met with the principal and they set up an elective course for my program.

I was so excited! I had never taught before, but the course content was natural to me. I designed a program that I hoped would not only be helpful, but fun. The turnout for the class was a bit overwhelming as I was surprised to see how many students showed up. Even a few boys wanted to take the course, but I had to turn them away. The program was specifically for teenage girls ranging from fifteen to eighteen years old with a limit of twenty students. I began the first day by introducing myself and proceeded to take Polaroid photos of each girl. I spoke individually with them, as I wanted to understand their goals and aspirations.

Four of them wanted to be in entertainment. Some wanted to be career women and many wanted to find husbands. Our first task was to evaluate their level of self-esteem. We delved into their family background in an attempt to reconcile any lingering issues from their childhood that had never been addressed. It was imperative for them to recognize these concerns in order to move forward. Otherwise, it would be vastly difficult to gain the confidence required to succeed, no matter what path they chose for themselves. Concurrently, we addressed their physical needs to improve their diets and start an exercise program.

I taught them about colors that would complement their skin and hair, which would enhance the look they wanted to achieve. They learned better posture, how to walk, how to give a firm handshake, and to stress the point when speaking with someone to look them directly in the eyes. They learned about hairstyles and plastic surgery if necessary.

We bonded. We cried together. We laughed. It was one of the most gratifying and rewarding experiences of my life. I was able to help these young women along their dream path. It prepared me for my future. Of course, I couldn't have known it at the time.

At the end of the semester, I had the young ladies invite their family and friends to the school gym to witness the incredible results of their efforts. Each girl came down the red carpet strutting her stuff and was videotaped in their glory. They entered with hard-earned confidence, proudly showing their new hairstyles, unique wardrobe items, admirable weight loss, and wonderful fresh outlook, knowing they had prepared themselves for future goals. The crowd was ecstatic.

We compared the Polaroids from when they first entered the class to the videos of their graduation. Rivers of happy tears were abundant. Many congratulations were offered for their achievements. There were many proud people that day, especially me.

Four of my young ladies became successful in the modeling field and acting. My career ladies got the jobs they wanted. My other girls found the husbands they wanted and we all kept in touch for many years. They were all so beautiful. I was on a high to see them happy and successful. For myself, it was also an incredible lesson. The real feeling of accomplishment that I experienced opened up a part of me I hadn't discovered until then.

CHAPTER 26

I T WAS SEPTEMBER 23ᴿᴰ, 1976. AS I WILL EXPLAIN later, 9/23 became a significant date. I was still living with Kirk and Corky in Arcadia. I had a job modeling jewelry with *Frances Klein*, one of the top antique jewelry dealers in L.A., and drove into town for a photo shoot. Following the shoot I walked over to the Brighton Cafe in Beverly Hills, on Brighton Way between Camden and Bedford Drive, to have a quick bite with a male friend. I mention the date and place because two miracles happened to me in the same area thirty-two years apart. Two miracles that utterly changed my life. I was enjoying a meatloaf sandwich with mayo on rye toast. They were famous for their meatloaf.

After about twenty minutes of great conversation with my lunch partner, who should stroll by but Duny Cashin. There was a striking looking gentleman with him. Duny was more than a party friend. I had grown up around him. He and I and our group of eight cohorts would get together every Thursday at the Beverly Hills Hotel Cafe, downstairs from the Polo Lounge, to plan the weekend's debaucheries. He was a scammer and a rascal, but I liked him and he was fun. He'd been a nurse and companion to my Aunt Milly, Max Factor's wife, after her strokes. Milly's brother, Hal King, who was Duny's ex-lover and famed make-up artist, passionately hated him. But that's another story…

Here Duny was with this impossibly rugged debonair man standing beside him. The man didn't look American. Perhaps French, maybe Italian, but I couldn't be sure. He had on a light summer suit with a bright blue tie. He wore the suit casually, in that effortless way American men hadn't achieved, but European men often do. He just seemed to ooze confidence, charm and a worldly manner. He was suave and he was marvelous, even standing still, doing nothing. He was amazing.

His perfectly shaped mustache with black and silvery hair made him look more continental and even more a man of the world. I felt his power. I didn't know what sort of power, but he had it. He was both a playboy and a gentleman; I could see it at once. I caught all that in a glance.

Duny looked in the window, waved and barged in to embrace me. He came up to my table and leaned down to give me a hug. "Darling," he asked, "where have you been? I haven't heard from you in three months."

The alluring man entered with him, but seemed to be moving on a higher, smoother plane than Duny.

I hugged Duny, but was really looking over his shoulder at the man behind him. Although he had just been dragged into this restaurant to stand in front of people he didn't know, he seemed perfectly calm and at ease.

Duny asked me how I was and what I was doing. "Still modeling," I said, "and teaching a course at Temple City High School."

"Oh good," Duny said, "You're much too beautiful not to be using your brain and modeling too. But why haven't I seen you?"

"I'm laying low," I said.

The man behind him had eased forward. He was smiling at me and was purposely inserting himself into the scene. He looked at me and stepped forward.

"Oh my!" Duny said, "Excuse my manners. Ilene, darling, this is my friend Jacques Médecin. Jacques, this is Max's niece, Ilene. Everyone calls her i."

The man took the final step towards me. He leaned forward slightly as his smile broadened. "I'm charmed," he said, "It's a pleasure."

I stood up to shake his hand and that was when the world, meaning my world, changed forever!

An electrical current ran through our arms from our first touch. A "coup de 'foudre," Jacques called it, and it was a lightning bolt! I looked at him and knew my life was about to change. Even if I never saw him again, the thought was clear in my mind that I would not accept anyone less than Jacques in my life from that moment on.

He smiled and said, "You must come shopping with us." Without hesitation, I put money on the table, told my male buddy I was going to leave and headed up Rodeo Drive with the two of them. I suggested Mr. Guy's, one of the best men's shops in Beverly Hills.

My friend, Richard Mylon, was their top salesman. He was delighted to see us and to meet Jacques. Of course, he gave us the very best treatment.

Jacques told him what he needed and tried on a few things. At the checkout counter he was purchasing a bathing suit for the hotel pool, a light pair of pale blue slacks and a light colored t-shirt. He asked me to stand by him. He leaned into me and my knees buckled. Whoa! Did he feel that same rush? He must have felt something because he asked me out for dinner that night.

I was busy that evening and couldn't break my engagement. He asked me out for the next night. I accepted and rearranged my schedule for the following day.

When we had first met at the café I was wearing my hair in a topknot with big Elton John glasses, gauzy cream-colored pants and a matching top. I had on these very high 4-inch platform sandals, which were covered by my long pants. When I stood up, Jacques who was 6' 2", was surprised. I was his height in my shoes and weighed 110 pounds. So when I went to meet him at the Beverly Hills Polo Lounge the night of our date, my look was quite different. I had told Kirk I was going to town to have dinner with my Uncle Max.

I did love Uncle Max. He really liked me, even though I was family. In other words, Uncle Max didn't have any pleasant words to describe our family.

He was a busy man and was constantly being chased after and bothered by the most self-centered, narcissistic, needy people in the world. This is how he described the Factor clan. I was grateful he always found time for me. He knew I didn't need anything from him.

CHAPTER 27

I WALKED INTO THE POLO LOUNGE WEARING MY long blond hair down, a sexy black pant-dress, a touch of make-up and a smidgen of tasteful jewelry. I knew Dino, the maître'd, and we gave each other a hug. I eagerly asked him if anyone was looking for me. He said that a very distinguished foreigner was in the back. Dino escorted me towards the booth. Jacques didn't recognize me with my hair down. When he realized it was me, he stood up and rushed over, apologizing for not standing up immediately to greet me.

Then he double French-kissed my cheeks and tugged my hair. I asked, "Why did you do that?"

He laughed and told me that French women have such thin hair that he thought I was sporting a wig.

I giggled and blurted out, "No, it's all mine."

We sat down and I asked, "So, what do you do for a living?" He threw his head back and laughed.

"I'm the Mayor of Nice, France, member of French Parliament, President of the French Riviera, Minister of Tourism and a Medici Count," saying all this in one long breath.

I looked at him square in the eye and replied, "You're a politician. I don't like politicians."

He heartily laughed again. He was so impressed I didn't know who he was. I loved his massive, thick hands. He reminded me of one of my favorite

Italian actors, Rossano Brazzi. He was in a dark blue single-button down *Christian Dior* suit complemented by a *Turnbull & Asser* white and blue pin-striped shirt with white collar and cuffs. He knew how to dress. His stature and warmth also reminded me of my maternal grandfather, beloved Papa Sam, who always let the family know I was his first and favorite grandchild.

Papa had protected and spoiled me not only with gifts, but also with his intense and deep love. As his first grandchild, he always stated I was his number one and favorite. I wanted the same feeling from a partner. Could this be the man?

We laughed, we talked about deep feelings, and then he asked me what my goals were in life and quickly segued into telling me he was married. I hadn't even considered that.

When this was revealed, I knew our fabulous encounter would not continue. At least it couldn't be anything long lasting and enduring.

I wasn't into dating married men. We left the Polo Lounge to have dinner at a newer hip restaurant on Canon Drive and Little Santa Monica, named "The Saloon." We were seated right away. Jacques took my hands from across the table and kissed my palms. I thought that was one of the most romantic gestures I'd ever experienced.

He asked me if I knew the significance of the gesture. I said I didn't believe I did. He explained, "When a man kisses the inside of a woman's hand it shows the utmost respect, and that's what I have for you."

I was enchanted with this incredible man. I heard bells ringing in my head. My adrenaline was racing and felt surrounded by shimmering bright lights. We stared at each other during the entire meal. When we finished he asked me to come to his room for an after-dinner drink. For me, that would be diet Pepsi.

My stomach reacts against alcohol. My grandmother Belle didn't like the taste of it, but might have a grasshopper, a very sweet drink, once a year for her birthday. She liked a sip of beer occasionally. I was the only one in the family like her. The rest absolutely enjoyed their libations. Everyone knows I don't drink, which will come up later in the story.

While waiting for the valet to bring up my car after dinner, he suddenly turned me around to face him, pulling me close and started passionately kissing me. That was our first kiss and it truly changed my life forever.

Our bodies literally melted into one another, and I almost fainted from the chemistry. I'd never felt anything like this before and was stunned. He asked me again if I would go back with him to his hotel room. I said yes.

In the room we sat on the bed and talked a little more. Then he slowly started removing my clothes and his. I was there for him heart, mind, body and soul. He gushed, "My God, you're gorgeous." I swooned. He took me in his arms and made the most tender and passionate love to me. I had never experienced that kind of connection before.

CHAPTER 28

H E OPENED UP AND TOLD ME WHY HE FLEW TO L.A. He was attempting to recover from a recent mental and physical breakdown that he experienced after a session of Parliament in Paris. He said he was so exhausted and overwhelmed with his personal and public life that he just broke down crying. As I came to learn his personality, one would never identify Jacques with a man who could ever break down. He told me his soul was empty and he had never experienced real love. Jacques felt he had never been loved just for him, but only for what he represented as a figurehead.

At the end of the evening I actually began to cry as I felt his pain and my desire to comfort him. He held me tightly. He asked me if he'd done something wrong and I said, "No, No, No. I'm just sad that I will most likely never see you again because you're married." I also knew in my heart that I would never settle for any man less than him. I had heard about Frenchmen and their affairs and would not accept being his mistress. Even though it was the most wonderful night of my life, I sadly thought it would be the only one with him. I knew he was leaving for France the next morning. I gave him my silk stockings saying these words, "Take them as a souvenir and think of me from time to time."

He looked at me in astonishment. "How could you possibly think we'll never see one another again?"

"Because I'm realistic," I answered him. "But it's fine because at least I know what I want in my life now."

I told him I had to leave and thanked him for the most romantic encounter I had ever experienced and knew I would never forget him. I decided not to give him my phone number because I knew he was not available and we could never be together. However, that marvelous night would stay with me always.

Of course Duny had my phone number, but I didn't want Jacques to call me. I knew that this relationship couldn't go anywhere.

That was Saturday the 24th of September. He was flying back the next morning to Paris, arriving there at night, which would be morning for me. There was a nine-hour time difference between France and California. My phone rang at 10 AM the next day. "Good morning, Beautiful."

His voice was deep and thrilling over the phone. I have to admit it sent a ripple of excitement through me. Duny obviously gave him my phone number, but I was still surprised he called.

He said, "I'm flying to the U.S. next week with one of my assistants. Nice is a sister city with Dallas. Please meet me at the Beverly Hills Hotel. We'll have dinner the night before and leave the next morning for Texas."

I needed to see Jacques again and find out why he wanted to rendezvous so quickly. I would be there.

I told Kirk I had a modeling job in Dallas, leaving L.A. Thursday and coming back Monday.

I met Jacques at the Beverly Hills Hotel again, but this time for another reason. We decided to order room service and ate on the bed. The following morning we woke up early and rushed to the airport. Jacques' assistant at the Ministry was Jean-Paul Claustre. He was waiting for us. Jacques had confided in him about our "coup de 'foudre." He scrutinized me from head to toe when we were introduced. The three of us boarded the plane and waited for takeoff. I was nibbling on cheese and crackers and certainly was not thinking that my world was about to explode.

Jacques turned to me and said, "I've made up my mind. I am going to get a divorce, quit my political career and marry you."

"What?!" The cheese and crackers I had been munching on spewed like a volcano out of my mouth onto the back of the seat in front of me. "But you don't know me!"

He replied, "I know all I need to know about you. Take your time, but not too much time. I want you."

Well, I started to shake and became cognizant this was not just a fling. If I answered yes, it would be a decision that would change my life forever. That was a massive understatement.

CHAPTER 29

JACQUES HAD PLANNED ANOTHER POLITICAL TRIP a few weeks later so we could be together. We would again meet at the Beverly Hills Hotel and fly out the next morning for Tahiti, where we would spend two weeks getting to know one another better.

Typically as my life would have it, there was an unusual incident that took place on our flight. Two armed men suddenly burst from the rear of the plane and raced to the front, moving past First Class to the cockpit door. They tried to subdue a passenger who was pounding on the door attempting to force his way in. He was a big burly man, probably 6'1" and around 240 pounds, Caucasian, with drab brown hair cut very short, and a stocky build. Not good. Jacques jumped up and joined the two guards. They finally subdued the man with the help of a medic who gave him a sedative shot to calm him down. He slumped to the ground and passed out. I thought to myself that must have been quite a dose. He was handcuffed and dragged, disappearing somewhere to the rear of the plane. Great, what a way to start our love affair.

When we arrived at the airport in Tahiti, we were whisked away to our hotel in a Jeep limo driven by the resort manager. We had our own hideaway away from everyone. It was a romantic bungalow with a real thatched roof. I scanned the premises and noticed there was no television or radio. Oh no, I thought. Just us with no distractions. This will either be an incredible experience or turn out to be a disastrous one.

Arriving in the afternoon, we napped until dinner arrived by way of room service. Our conversation continued through the night until morning. We certainly were on a roll.

Jacques rented a yacht on the fourth day, complete with a captain to take us out to sea and show us rainbow-colored coves. How romantic. I felt my Walt Disney fairytale dreams coming true. We went into the galley and Jacques started to peel me a pomelo, a delicious Tahitian fruit originally from Asia that tasted like citrus and melon.

He put each slice that he had cut with precision into my mouth with his gentle fingers and asked, "How do you like the taste of this exotic fruit, ma Chérie?" He had me melting. I gazed at Jacques with each juicy pomelo sliding into my mouth. My beloved grandfather Papa Sam used to feed me like that when I was a little girl. I realized that we both shared the same incredible passion for eating. So here was another man who loved cooking, eating, and savoring tasty food just like my Papa.

Afterwards, we went to the stern of the yacht. Jacques was standing at the back railing, and I was in a chair close to the cabin under a canopy. All of a sudden we hit a large wave. Jacques stumbled and I thought he was going to fall overboard and get ripped to shreds by the propeller.

At that precise moment I had an epiphany that I would lose the love of my life if he fell overboard. My whole aura altered. Jacques looked at me asking, "Are you alright?" He told me that the expression on my face had dramatically changed.

I said, "Yes, and I've made a decision. I will tell you about it when we get back to our little grass shack on the island."

I just had to come back down to earth. I needed a minute to understand what had happened to me. I never before had this undeniable awakening, like a crystal clear light bulb going off in my brain letting me know for the first time in my life I was truly falling in love.

Arriving at our shack, I hugged him and stepped back. I stared deeply into his eyes and said, "The expression you saw on my face was the realization of physically experiencing this enormous bolt of light rearranging my aura. I had an epiphany and suddenly knew I was in love with you, and yes, I will marry you."

I kept looking at him waiting for his reaction. We finally understood in both our languages the significance of what I had just told him. He took me in his arms and broke down and cried, bending me back over his thigh, hungrily kissing me. When we got into bed that night, Jacques said we had to start making plans for our future.

I didn't have a clue as to what this future would be. I knew it would be challenging and that Jacques would have to get a divorce, hopefully convincing his wife, Claude, to agree. In France, a divorce requires mutual consent. Otherwise, there's no divorce. Jacques was positive she'd grant it to him. He was wrong.

It was December 1976, and the plan was that I would join Jacques in Paris after the New Year, which was three weeks away. I wanted to be alone during Christmas and New Year to get myself mentally and physically prepared for my new unknown life. I only felt like being with Dad and his wife for Christmas dinner.

Jacques and I were either on the phone or writing letters back and forth every day. His letters were at least ten pages long, pouring out his guts and opening up his heart to me. It was wonderful and beautiful, the power of his love and the amazing things he wrote.

I wrote him back explaining a bit of my previous life, telling him I was feeling emotions I had never felt before and had only dreamt of until meeting him. I was opening my heart to him as well. Jacques wrote it was like a lightning bolt striking when we met. He believed we were twins in our past lives, but separated after birth to finally reunite in this life.

Whatever he told me, I believed or wanted to believe. It was beyond magical. I lived for romance and still do.

I arrived after the New Year in Paris, during the coldest winter they had experienced in 100 years, so I was told.

My mother had taken me shopping before I left L.A. She bought me a glorious wardrobe of perfect outfits for my new life. She was the only person who believed Jacques would get a divorce and marry me. Everyone else thought I was a fool because Frenchmen never get divorced and certainly a man in Jacques' position would never marry a young American female almost twenty-one years his junior. We had a struggle ahead of us and both knew it. I never doubted how much we loved one another and that was what kept me sane through a long, long uncomfortable ordeal yet to come.

Don and I

*Trevor Mound and I, as hostess of
Grace Kelly Floral Competition*

*Howard and I at Beverly Hills
HS Sophomore Dance*

Sheik Tayeb and I in Dubai

Donald and I

Alain and I

David Niven and I

Alvio

Lilou Dini and I in Florence

My bodyguard Jean Claude,
Marcel Dini and Dora

My sexy husband

Beau, Belle and I

Wedding Ceremony in Udaipur

Beau and I

Beau and I at Taj Mahal

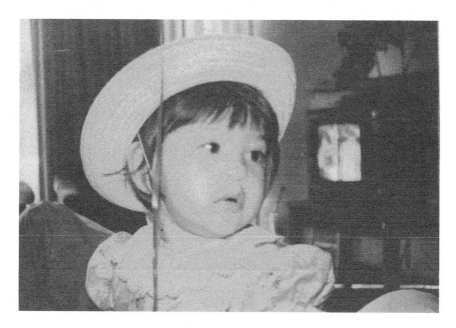

Baby Tara, my helper

My wonderful in-laws, Michio and Rose

Pregnant in Dubai

Riding my camel in Dubai

Guy La Roche promotion in Japan

Japanese welcome parade for Jacques and I

Petting baby elephant on reserve of President Bongo of Gabon

My friend in Nepal

Chiang Mai, Thailand

Fabulous Sikh Temple in Amritsar

Welcoming me at Lake Palace, Udaipur

Rat Temple

My precious White Rat

Trish and I in Udaipur

My dear friend and guide,
Lax, at Lake Palace

Trish and I on our elephant in Jaipur

My dear friend and guide, Selvan, in Delhi

My first husband, Bert Poncher

Dora from Hungary, Nana, and I

My Jackye in Nice

My 4th husband, Lee Rich, and Michael Crichton

My bodyguards at political rally

My one and only Corky

My beloved Papa Sam

My elegant Mom and Nana Belle

*Brother-in-law
and Sister-in-law,
Joyce and Dennis
(From my 1st marriage)*

Baby brother, Lichude

My Wonderful Dad

My precious daughter, TK

My second official duty

My first official duty

40th Birthday Dress by Valentino

Modeling on the Côte d'Azur

Max Gilli, our fixer

Christmas Poster

Ilene Graham wearing an exquisite diamond brooch and matching earrings. The set contains over 30 carats of diamonds. It is early Victorian (circa 1840) and magnificently crafted. Notice the art deco bronze in the background. At Frances Klein Antique Jewelry, Beverly Hills.

GUCCI, HEAD TO TOE—Ilene Patcher, left, mod...

*Modeling for Frances Klein
in Beverly Hills*

*First Gucci staff model
in Beverly Hills*

Brève rencontre entre Sophia Loren et un jeune admirateur dans la salle du « Gaumont Palace », où la grande comédienne assistait, aux côtés du député-maire de Nice et de Mme Jacques Médecin, à la présentation du film d'Ettore Scola, « Une journée particulière ».
(Photo Jacques Gargano)

With Sophia Loren in Nice

Charles Aznavour   _Deputy Mayor Estrosi_

With Baby Doc in Haiti

Greeting Red Chinese Minister in Paris

Princess Caroline and Prince Rainier at the Acropolis

My Sag Buddy, Jacques Chirac

Dancing at the Acropolis with the American 6th Fleet Band

Chanel advertisement at the Acropolis

With Jeanne Moreau at Italian Film Festival in Nice

With Sergio Leone at Italian Film Festival in Nice

Ken and Laurel, my support system

Baby Cousin, Jillian

For our reality show

Denny and my adopted Big Sis

Grand Humanitarian Award

Cannes Film Festival with Bobbi Bresee

BOOK THREE

Life in

the Fishbowl

CHAPTER 30

I T WAS 1977, A NEW YEAR AND A NEW LIFE. I WAS
in France with Jacques, but it wasn't a bed of roses. Life was beautiful,
wonderful and difficult at the same time because of his prominence. We were
in love, but no one could know about us. I couldn't be seen in public with him
and basically was still in hiding because he was married, and the Mayoral
election was coming up. It was a challenging time.

I had to lay very low. I lived at the Georges V Hotel in Paris for six
weeks, hidden away while Jacques campaigned for re-election. Concurrently,
during the past two and a half years, he also served as Minister of Tourism
under President Valery Giscard d'Estaing. Although he was serving the
country as a national minister, it didn't help his preferred local political base
in Nice. The Niçois were resentful because he wasn't spending enough time
with them and their city. Jacques had to make a choice and prove to them
that he was back in full force as their Mayor.

Therefore, I was kept secretly in Paris while he campaigned in Nice.
During those six weeks he flew back and forth from Nice to join me. He had
some official duties in Morocco coming up and told me that we were going to
relax, recharge, and get some sun. Of the many ever-changing events at this
time, this was one more experience that didn't turn out as planned.

We took a private government plane to Morocco, and stayed at the La
Mamounia Hotel in Marrakech. That's where I met the Countess d'Villier,

supposedly an old friend of Jacques. While I wasn't aware of it at the time, she was one of the villains in this tale and not a woman to be trusted.

She swept into the pool area one day, sashaying up to Jacques, bending down while he was relaxing on his chaise lounge to give him a big double kiss. Of course, this was the first time I had ever seen her, but she certainly didn't bother to introduce herself. How rude. Jacques was startled and a little taken back. He introduced us and started telling her about the problem of having to hide me for a few more days until the election was over. He said he was afraid someone would find out about me if he kept me at a hotel and that would not be a good thing.

D'Villier smiled coyly at him and purred, "Why don't you two stay at my home in Cannes? I'll watch over Ilene while you're gone." Boy, did she watch over me. That's when she started to sabotage Jacques and my relationship. I'll explain further in a moment.

Jacques had to fly back to Paris for a sudden meeting at the Ministry. It was important and mandatory. He told d'Villier to take care of me until he returned the next night. We had been invited to the Prince of Morocco's palace for dinner and Jacques wanted her to go with me to make sure I was properly escorted. He told her to take me shopping for an evening gown.

We went to a lovely boutique near the hotel and I chose the most beautiful sapphire blue caftan with an all-colored rhinestone V-neck collar. It would be the perfect attire for the dinner. I was looking forward to meeting the Prince and seeing the palace. We were picked up by one of the Prince's limos and arrived promptly on time. The dining room was covered in huge luxurious colorful pillows seating three or four guests with hookahs next to each one. Beautiful floor candelabras and huge silver platters shimmered, presenting Moroccan delights such as citrus chicken, couscous, vegetables of all kinds, and sugary desserts. The servants were dressed in wild hues of sapphire, pink, lime green, salmon and pale yellow. Their outfits were the perfect accouterment to the dazzling decor of the room and the delicious food.

I thoroughly enjoyed myself and couldn't wait for Jacques to return and tell him everything. He arrived the next afternoon and we flew back to Nice in his Minister's private plane. Then I was whisked off to d'Villier's home in Cannes. Jacques couldn't spend the nights with me yet, but we would have dinner every evening. He'd been campaigning all day from seven in the morning into the night.

That first night we dined at her villa. The next day she took me to lunch and showed me around Cannes. The following day she notified me that we were going to have lunch in her large dining room instead of going out. I found it unusual the entire table was formally set. Maybe she just wants to honor me and show respect, I thought. Ha. Foolish me. We sat at one end having salads and cheese. We had a light conversation and then she started in. This became a lecture and a reprimand, not a light lunch between new friends.

Standing up suddenly, she began to tell me I knew nothing about French etiquette because I was just an American. She said, "Most Americans are like wild Indians who don't know how to set a formal French table and it would be essential if you are to become Jacques' wife."

This wicked woman didn't really believe our marriage would ever come about. She told me that she was more suited to be the First Lady with all of her contacts, titles and status. She seemed certain that I was just a fling. Her vile nature emerged when she sniped, "Jacques needs someone by his side that knows how to handle political life, and you are too young, inexperienced and American."

I was so shocked I couldn't say a word. I told her I wasn't feeling well and went back to my room. I started to shake and cry. Was Jacques in on this to get rid of me? My mind was overwrought with panic. Here I in a foreign country, all alone, while trusting this man with my life and love. Everyone at home was telling me I was a fool because he would never marry me and jeopardize his position. I sat on the bed and sobbed. Was I a fool?

Happily, Jacques arrived at just this moment. When he entered the bedroom he grabbed me in his arms and kissed me, but I was standoffish. I was hurt, angry, unsure, and insecure at that moment. He didn't react to that at first, but would hold his response for later. He had a way of hiding his feelings until striking back, strategizing the unexpected moment at the most inappropriate time. I would soon learn this tactic, which was a behavior of his revenge.

We went downstairs to meet Countess d'V. The three of us were heading to dinner at a small offbeat restaurant to avoid the public eye. Little did I suspect this would be my introduction to Jacques' jealousy.

We drove in a tiny car with d'Villier sitting in the backseat. Jacques parked and we walked down the road to the bistro. We were seated in a corner in the back of the restaurant. Jacques sat across from me. D'Villier was next to me. Jacques asked me what I wanted to eat. I said I didn't care and he should order for me. Suddenly, he slammed the menu down and started screaming at me.

"I know why you pushed me away earlier! I saw the young man who parked his car across from ours outside the restaurant. He was looking at you and you were looking back at him! I know you think I'm too old and would prefer to be with him!"

I was so taken aback by his spontaneous insanity I couldn't believe what I had just heard. Talk about being insecure. There was never any male across the street that I noticed. I pushed the table into his stomach and ran out of the restaurant in a hysterical state. I didn't know where I was or where I was running. I just kept running down and down a spiraling road to a trashy, abandoned looking area where homeless men were sleeping. I found a corner in the back, crouched down into a fetal position and rocked and cried. I didn't know what to do.

I don't know how much time passed, but Jacques appeared looking frantic and cried out, "BABY! There you are!" He lifted me into his arms with tears in his eyes. "I love you! What is going on?"

Jacques got me in the car with d'V in the back. Not a word was spoken. When we got back to the villa, he grabbed my hand and led me to the bedroom. "Don't ever run from me again," he pleaded. "What is happening?"

I was still crying, but managed to stifle my tears enough to tell him in detail what d'Villier had said and done to me. I told him I didn't see a man looking at me because I only had eyes for him.

He told me to pack my bags at once. "We are leaving!" He went to find the bitch, as he called her and heard him raging at her. He told her never to come near me or to ever contact him again.

We left immediately and went to the Meridien Hotel in Nice. He checked me into a suite where I stayed until the election was over, which was just a week away.

CHAPTER 31

JACQUES WOULD SNEAK INTO THE HOTEL TO SEE me twice a day, once for lunch and then for dinner. We would order room service and cuddle and talk and cuddle some more.

He came for lunch one day and swept me into his arms madly kissing me. We threw off our clothes and started to make intense, passionate love. All of a sudden the door opened and the housekeeper came in. In France, I found, the service people never knocked even if there was a "Do Not Disturb" sign hanging on the door.

Well, she was not expecting to see her Mayor naked with an equally naked young woman. Jacques flew off me, dragging me to the floor with him, practically under the bed. His bodyguards were down the hall guarding the main entrances, not thinking about checking the service access on the floor.

She shrieked and ran out. I'm sure that made her day. We were laughing hysterically. It became a precious memory, but later there was another incident that was not so funny.

I wasn't allowed to leave the hotel, so I mused, why not get a massage? I went to the spa on the top floor of the hotel and chose the avocado detox bath with a Swedish treatment. A tall funny looking man told me to undress and get into the tub. I soaked for a while and then he came back and started hosing me down.

His eyes seemed to be ogling me. I got onto the massage table and he slowly kneaded my neck and shoulders. He stopped massaging and I wasn't quite sure what he was doing. Suddenly, he jumped on top of my back while shoving his pants down. I was already nervous about the entire circumstance of being concealed from the public because of the election. All I wanted was a relaxing massage.

He was trying to force himself on me or in me, and I kicked him so hard he fell off the table. I wrapped the sheet around me, screaming at him not caring whether he understood me or not.

"How dare you, you imbecile! If this is the custom in France, you can shove it! And, I will not tip you!"

I quickly put my clothes on and ran back to the room. Still in shock at what had just occurred, I wasn't sure if I should tell Jacques, already having experienced his temper. Would he blame me? So when he came for dinner, my words had to be weighed. After a moment of contemplation, I decided it would be wiser to tell him. I told him exactly what happened and he really flipped out. Thank goodness he didn't blame me and immediately left the room. After a while, "J" returned announcing there would no longer be a problem and "No, that was not a normal French massage!"

"Baby," he pled, "Please stay in the room until after the results of the election."

I said, "No problem." To my knowledge, that man was never seen in Nice again or for that matter in France. Don't mess with the Mayor.

We were joined at the hip, Jacques and I, invariably holding onto each other and laughing. I gave him a younger viewpoint on life and an American perspective on how to have fun and he loved it. We were twenty-one years apart and my goal in life was to enjoy it to the fullest. "J" definitely needed to lighten up and have more fun. We still had to get through the election and he promised me, win or lose, he would tell Claude that he wanted a divorce after the results came in.

I knew we both needed to relax after the outcome because this particular election was so crucial and the stress level was at a peak. Although Jacques had promised to quit politics for me, I realized it was impossible, as he needed to reaffirm his steadfast commitment to the Niçois. They were unhappy with the amount of time he spent in national politics with the French Parliament and as Minister of Tourism. The Niçois felt it was distracting him from local affairs. This election was paramount for him and I soon understood politics was in his blood. He would never quit or back down. He confided in me, "I'm worried I have not spent enough time in my city because of very intense ministry duties." Jacques was aware that he had neglected his constituents and this truly bothered him. As for me, I had enough of being hidden during this pre-election process. It was time to do some private traveling, make love, and laugh all around the world.

He was fascinated by my innocent heart and spirit. J told me that I had saved his life. He was miserable in his marriage and being with me made him want to live again. I gave him the strength to get over his nervous breakdown, which he was going through when we met.

All we had to do was get through the election, finalize his divorce and then we would be so happy together. I believed him and was looking forward to it.

CHAPTER 32

J ACQUES WON THE ELECTION IN 1977, BUT IT WAS
a knockdown, drag-out battle. It made him realize the Mayor's office was
more important to him than any other position he held. Nice meant everything to him. Jacques was Niçois by birth and these were his roots and people.
Since he was no longer going to be Minister, he was able to dedicate his life
once more to Nice and the French Riviera, of which he was President. His
constituents were ecstatic. They wanted their beloved Mayor "Jacquou" back
and were relieved to know he would resign as Minister of Tourism. Jacquou
was an affectionate name given to him by the Niçois.

Now it was time to tell his wife Claude that he wanted a divorce. Jacques
thought she wouldn't contest it because they hadn't shared a bed in fourteen
years and effectively didn't have a relationship. The relationship was nothing
more than polite hellos and goodbyes. He told me she never helped to support
his political career and wasn't a wife to him in any way. She was a dreadful
mother to Martine, his eldest daughter who was six years younger than me.

He went to their home to talk to Claude. I waited for him to return with
good news she would be agreeable. I was nervous, but expected that he knew
Claude and everything would work out. NOT EVEN CLOSE!

Jacques recounted they were on the stairwell in their house when he
told her. Claude was a few steps above him and went berserk. She flew down
the stairs attacking and jumping on top of him. He threw her off and told her

to calm herself. She threatened him and that's when Jacques left. He definitely did not have her consent.

So, the news was not good. Adding further insult to injury, Claude hired a communist lawyer just to spite Jacques and all hell broke loose. She should have known better than to cross him. He quickly held a news conference to introduce me to the press as his fiancée. The media said it was the biggest scandal since the days of the Kings and Queens. Jacques was the last scion of a century old political dynasty. He was no ordinary politician. What politician would think of divorcing his French wife to marry a young American girl? It was too crazy, too racy of a story, too juicy and scandalous. The press went wild with it.

Claude started spreading rumors I was a high-paid prostitute. The newspapers went crazy over her accusations. French journalists flew to Beverly Hills and tracked down my Uncle Max Factor to see if they could get anything unseemly and nasty about me out of him. That was outrageous and dishonorable on so many levels. They also contacted my modeling agencies to see if I had done any porn photos. Of course, they found NOTHING!

This was my first real experience with biased media. All the liberal press cared about was finding dirt to smear and they didn't care one bit how it would impact me. They didn't care if they destroyed lives and reputations with their lying exaggerations. Leftist newspapers were as irresponsible as tabloid journalists, being committed to their own agenda. To this day I have no respect for the media, less than zero.

It was an epic outrage and with our relationship now out in the open the paparazzi wouldn't leave us alone. They snapped pictures and hounded us wherever we went. I couldn't go outside without facing a blizzard of flashbulbs and sleazy reporters screaming and throwing questions at me. It was awful.

The press especially loved that I was an heiress (so they claimed) to the Max Factor cosmetic fortune, that branch of my family. Of course, everyone knew about Max Factor. It was a billion dollar brand. I did think it was interesting they never got around to mentioning my gangster Uncle

Jack. You would think that would have made good press too, linking Jacques' "Ladylove" to a Chicago Capo. Maybe the French press corps decided they'd just leave it for the time being. Who knows?

And just to set the record straight, I did not inherit a vast fortune or any fortune from the Factors. My Uncle Max told me after meeting Jacques that he wanted to leave me something special because I made it on my own without leeching from the family. But you know families, typically, when it comes to money. They get tangled up in their internal bickering, squabbling and backstabbing. Unfortunately, many families epitomize jealousy and greed when it comes time to inherit. When your family is in the big-time beauty business (Uncle Max) as well as casino & investments (Uncle Jack), let's say the backstabbing is pretty extreme. You have to watch your back in the Factor clan. Many of the offspring think their shit doesn't stink. Well, it does.

CHAPTER 33

I T TOOK MORE THAN TWO YEARS TO GET CLAUDE to finally consent to the divorce. It was 1979 and what a terrible drawn-out fight it became.

During that time, I was still learning French. It's true that sometimes ignorance is bliss. Thank goodness I didn't comprehend the full extent of what was being written about me.

Following the initial press explosion, the relentless pressure of the screaming paparazzi wherever we went and all of Claude's false accusations, things finally cooled down. As much as they dug into my life, nothing bad or awful had been discovered about me. After we were married, my credibility was no longer in question. All of a sudden I was admired. The press started to call me the other famous American lady on the Riviera and compared me to Princess Grace of Monaco. What a change in the tune they were whistling now.

There was even more irony. France presented me with the Grand Humanitarian Prize years later. What an unexpected and remarkable honor. Princess Grace was my predecessor in receiving the award, and we were the only two American women to have received that honor, even to this day.

I thought of that from the top bunk of my jail cell, wondering how the French could be so hypocritical, treating me so shamefully. Oh well, as I have said, "Politics and the media."

CHAPTER 34

CLAUDE FINALLY GAVE UP. JACQUES LAID DOWN the law and told her if she didn't sign the divorce papers he wouldn't give her a dime. Since money was all she cared about, she finally acquiesced.

During those years while we were waiting and hoping for the divorce, Jacques and I were alone together as much as possible. We were blindly in love. We'd go on little getaways and "J" (one of my nicknames for him) would show me around France, Switzerland, Italy, England, Morocco, and then we would spend Christmas in Los Angeles, as well as six weeks during the summer. He loved being away from the limelight and I took him to my favorite haunts. I even took him to Pink's Hot Dog stand on La Brea and Melrose in Hollywood. They were famous for their chili. He had an iron stomach, but after eating a chili dog his digestion was a little challenged. I, of course, downed two. It's still my favorite chili in the world.

Throughout those times in Nice while waiting for his divorce, I went everywhere with Jacques except to official engagements. I'd sit in the limo for hours with the Niçois Mafia guarding me while I did my needlepoint. This is what I meant earlier in the story when I said needlepoint became so important to me. I can't believe how many pillows I made while waiting and waiting for Jacques. I loved having this time to pursue my art.

Perhaps I should say a word about the Niçois Mafia. Most of these people had been with Jacque's father, Jean Médecin, before Jacques came into power. All total, Jacques and his father ruled Nice for over sixty years.

The Mafia were loyal to the core and central to Nice's history and personality. They stood by Jacques' side to protect him and the good Niçois population. We got along extremely well. Since my uncle was in the Mob and Dad was his consigliere, it felt familiar to me. They adopted me as their only female cohort.

My entire being revolved around Jacques and that's how it was for many years. He slowly molded me into his image, and I was fine with it.

I was his Barbie doll. He loved to buy me clothes and jewelry. I looked very young for my age, so in the early photos I appear more staid and reserved because that's how Jacques wanted to dress me. Wonderful wardrobe, but subdued. He didn't want me to appear quite so young. After some years, I chose my own designers and wore my hair down instead of in a chignon. I was more daring. I let my imagination run.

He dressed me in the French designers Dana, Nina Ricci and Christian Dior. My own choices became Yves St. Laurent and Chanel, when Lagerfeld started designing for them. As my tastes expanded, I fell in love with Valentino, Versace, and other Italian designers as well.

My favorite shop in Nice was a high fashion boutique in the walking zone called "Pink." Madame Pink was ecstatic whenever I would come in. She asked me one time if I would model her choicest inventory in a photo shoot for an advertising brochure showcasing the top European designers she carried. Since I enjoyed modeling and hadn't done any for some time, I was more than happy to oblige. Madame Pink was so grateful and gave me a few of the outfits after the shoot. I was thrilled.

I wore Elton John-type glasses, designed by Emanuel Kahn, in many different colors to match my wardrobe and they became my trademark. The press would always shout at me, "Madame Médecin, take off your glasses, we want to see your beautiful eyes." I was so shy in the beginning, it was my way of hiding my emotions and nerves. Eventually, I took off my glasses and only wore them when necessary as I was feeling more comfortable in my role.

CHAPTER 35

THE OUTRAGEOUS FRENZY EVENTUALLY CALMED down. Reporters warmed up to me, not that I ever warmed to them. From then on I got great press until we had to escape France fifteen years later. Of course, they blamed me for Jacques' downfall because I was American. They said I had "turned his head" with my influence to make him do what he did. Let me say this in my defense. Jacques did what he wanted to do, period. No one could make him do anything unless it was his idea. He called his own shots. Having weathered the press attacks and having put "Le Scandale" behind us, we became the "*Golden Couple*," especially across Europe.

We finally began our new, out in the open "normal" public life. I started inviting friends to keep me company at several official functions. Prior to getting married I had developed close friendships with some of Jacques' personal buddies who were not friendly with Claude. People like Jackye and Phillipe Bonello, Odette and Jacques Seassal, Sandrine and George Marguerita, the Giordangassins and a few others. All I can say is "Thank Ganesh" for Jackye. She became my mentor, best friend and the godmother of our daughter (to come).

I didn't speak a word of French when I arrived in Nice and only had eight lessons with a British/French teacher who came to our house. She taught me some essentials to get me started, and then I was on my own. I continued to learn and became quite fluent and a damn good speaker of French, if I do say so myself. I was immersed in the life of Nice and in the nitty-gritty on-the-ground politics with Jacques. I learned the common language as well as formal French. I picked up the real mother tongue, including slang, by years of conversing with people in the streets.

That's how to learn French. I had a friend who studied the language for eight years in high school and college. When she first came to visit me, she couldn't understand what people were saying. It took her years of visiting before she was able to somewhat converse and understand the everyday practical lingo.

To live in a country is the only way to truly get all the nuances of the language. Jackye and I used sign language, photographs and patience to communicate with one another during our first get-together until I was able to somewhat speak. To this day, she remains my true loyal friend and soul sister. I love this woman beyond. She's been with me through thick and thin and vice versa. Her husband, Phillipe, had been imprisoned in Switzerland, but was released to die at home because he was very ill. He had been arrested in Geneva for absconding with funds from a heart valve company he co-founded. The money came from business contacts he had in Nice. His story was a sad one, but she still loved him and was happy to have him home. He died peacefully in Nice under her love and care. She has always been an inspiration for me and we are in contact by phone at least once a month. I luv my Jackye.

CHAPTER 36

F INALLY, THE TIME HAD COME WHEN JACQUES
and I could start planning the wedding. We both wanted to have a civil
ceremony with just our closest friends, his daughter Martine and her best
friend Nicole (whose family were loyal Médecinists).

Following the ceremony at City Hall, we planned a huge reception at
the Grand Negresco Hotel on the Promenade des Anglais for over 800 of
Jacques' political friends and our personal friends. It had taken over two years
to get the divorce and this would be an incredible event. Jacques was putting
his political position and reputation at risk to marry a young American.

Jacques' First Deputy Mayor Francis Giordan would officiate. My personal designer, Dana, who was introduced to me by Jacques, had outdone
himself with an off-white alpaca mixed wool jacket and skirt. It was marvelous; it was a fairytale ensemble, which was just what I had dreamt of. I wore
gold shoes to match the gold piping on the suit, accompanied by simple gold
hoop earrings and, of course, my marquise diamond engagement ring from
Jacques designed by Alexander Reza. Alex was a friend whose family had
escaped Russia to Nice before WWII. Alex's father was a personal jeweler to
the Czars. He was able to bring his inventory and precious stones with him
when they escaped, but nothing else. Alex had inherited from his father the
highest quality stones including enormous sapphires, diamonds, emeralds,
rubies and more. His incredibly rare necklaces, rings, bracelets and brooches
were fit for the Royalty of Europe.

Indeed, the ring was a wish come true. When I was very young, not yet in my teens, I fantasized about the perfect engagement ring. It would be a marquise cut diamond center stone surrounded by small round white diamonds in an eighteen-carat yellow gold setting. When Jacques took me to Reza's office in Paris, Alex brought out cases and cases of rings and loose stones. I saw this beautiful champagne diamond and said this was the one I wanted, not even thinking at the time of my childhood dream. Alex said he would design the ring for me. I agreed and couldn't wait to wear it. One month later he called to say it was finished. I sat on the couch as Jacques and Alex were talking and then Jacques stood in front of me, opened the box and put the ring on my finger.

All of a sudden I felt a rush and a flush. This ring was exactly what I had envisioned when I was a young girl and started to cry and scream with deep emotion.

The two men were so surprised by my reaction, but ecstatic to see me beyond moved. I will never forget that moment of recognition, shock and excitement. I still feel the same way today about that moment. One day my wonderful daughter will have the ring as a keepsake of her father's and my love.

Wherever we went there were reporters asking questions. We were out in the open now, so everyone was anxious to meet me. Jacques told our inner circle not to mention to anyone when the wedding ceremony would take place. I really wanted it to be private because I was shy, vulnerable and frankly a little scared. None of my family would be there for this event. They did fly in for the reception a few months later.

It was finally our wedding day…a magical one. The limo picked us up and we headed to City Hall for the civil ceremony. There were throngs of people and press as we pulled up.

Jacques and I looked at each other in disbelief.

Who leaked our special moment? I was not pleased, but when we exited the car everyone started to clap and cheer. Inside the chambers, every seat was filled. Our inner circle of friends was seated in the front row. Martine and Nicole were our witnesses and sat with Jacques and me. Francis, the first Deputy Mayor, gave a beautiful speech and pronounced us man and wife. Of course, I cried. The paparazzi went wild as we left City Hall.

The Mayor was finally divorced and had married his young American bride. I know there were many bets against it actually happening. I endured the skeptics up my ass for all the time prior to Jacques' press conference. Now they wanted to be close friends. What hypocrites.

The entire population of Nice wanted to know me. I was an American and now, their First Lady. Of course, that was after saying "I do" and became Madame Médecin. I never ever forgot who my original allies were when I first arrived in France and eventually included them in as much of my political life as possible. We had so much fun together while they assisted me along the way, helping me to better understand the culture.

CHAPTER 37

WE HAD DECIDED ON HAITI FOR OUR HONEY-moon. The Haitian President Jean-Claude Duvalier wanted to collaborate with Jacques on a cultural exchange. He was called "Baby Doc" and took over his father "Papa Doc's" position after he passed away.

We stayed on the Presidential grounds in a lovely house. Ernst Garnier was one of Baby Doc's personal servants and was assigned to us. He and I became close and were very fond of one another. I said to Jacques I would love to have him come back to Nice as our personal butler.

Ernst was on top of all my needs. I would only mention something to him once and it would be done. Although we were very friendly, he was afraid of Jacques.

Jokingly, J said to Baby Doc how much I liked Ernst and wished he could live and work for us. Baby Doc said he would let him go because it would be a privilege for his servant to work for the Mayor and Mayoress of Nice.

I spoke with Ernst and asked if he would like that. He replied, "Madame Médecin, I would be honored to work for you. I'm ready to leave when you are." The three of us flew back to France after our two-week honeymoon and that's how Ernst came to be with me.

I loved Haiti. It was warm and colorful. The people were so sweet and welcoming even though their quality of life was less than the best, to say the least. Their lush vegetation produced some of the best mangoes and papayas

I'd ever eaten. The Haitians expressed themselves with bold colors in wonderful drawings and fabulous paintings of landscapes and daily life. My new husband was a collector of anything beautiful or practical, not that the two are necessarily related. We came back with over 700 paintings. Did I ever mention excess? I began to realize Jacques was over the top in everything he did. Most of those paintings along with most of our personal belongings eventually disappeared except for three remaining ones that I was lucky enough to retain.

CHAPTER 38

MY MARRIAGE TO JACQUES CAME WITH POLIT-
ical duties. Being First Lady was my job. I was still learning French
and not yet near fluent. This led to some interesting moments.

One night we were invited to the Malacarnes home for dinner, which
was a tight group including the Niçois Mafia and other political friends.
The Malacarnes were Corsican and they had the best private beach on the
Mediterranean. It was imperative for them to serve great food and they did.
Certain families rented sections of the beach and only the more exclusive
ones from Nice had any chance of getting that special stretch of sand.

When I wanted to go to the beach, Jacques told me to use only the
Corsican one. I wasn't allowed to go topless there or anywhere, nor would
I. Later, I learned the reason for my going to that particular beach. Jacques
wanted to have me monitored and the Malacarnes would keep an eye on me
when we were apart. I didn't realize until later what a tight rein he had on
me. Not only did I have my bodyguards escorting me everywhere, but also
Jacques always had backup with other people covertly watching both the
bodyguards and me.

So at this dinner I wanted to impress everyone with my language progress. I'm left-handed and I kept bumping elbows with my dinner partner. I
spoke up loud enough for everyone to hear because I was bragging—well,
showing off my new mastery of French, ha ha.

"Je suis a gauche," I said. "Je suis désole."

Everyone gasped and looked at Jacques. I had actually said, "I am a leftist. I'm sorry."

Jacques threw his head back and laughed. He explained in French, "My wife is learning our language and is left-handed and was sorry to keep bumping you." They loved it. I meant to say "Je suis gaucher." I felt like a fool and never made that mistake again.

That wasn't my last slip of the tongue. The fire department bought a new fireboat and asked if they could name it after me. I answered, of course they could and was extremely flattered. This was going to be my first public inauguration and all I had to do was crack a bottle of champagne on the bow of the vessel. Jacques stood next to me with all the cameras clicking as I tried at least ten times to break the bottle. I couldn't do it. It wasn't happening. Jacques finally took the bottle from me and smashed it with no effort.

He asked me to say a little something. I took the microphone, full of my newly acquired confidence and proudly stated, "Je suis la Reine du Pompier." Correctly, I should have said, "Je suis la Marraine du Pompier." Pompier means fireman or fire department. Pompier is also the slang word for giving a blowjob!

Well, the crowd burst into laughter and Jacques grabbed the mike from me. Again, he said I was learning French and it was not what I meant to say. I suddenly became more and more popular. Gee, I wonder why? I was certainly different from French First Ladies and they loved it.

I was surprised a couple of days after the ceremony when Lilou, my Chief of Staff, came to me with requests to appear at several different inaugurations and functions. I thought, why not? Isn't that what a First Lady does? I looked through all the cards and chose one to attend. It was a lower school function in a part of town that wasn't familiar to me. My bodyguard, Daniel, was very surprised we were heading for this location, but said nothing. I dressed as a cowgirl with a Stetson hat and cowgirl boots. I was winging it as I entered the school and started shaking hands and hugging the children. I spoke to them in my broken French and relayed fun stories about the Wild

West in American history. They were so happy to have me there and were thrilled I acknowledged them.

After I got home and Jacques arrived a few hours later, he was ecstatic to have found out I had ventured into the communist section of the city and won them over. He never ever would have agreed to me going if he knew since it was an unsafe area and typically didn't garner support from its voters. I was shocked. I had no idea who they were. I was just trying to help J.

As it turned out, my first duty and visit to the school influenced the next Mayoral Election. The communists voted for him and helped us win on the first round. There were two rounds. The first one being a runoff with a slew of candidates. Then the two candidates with the most votes would run against each other in the second round to win the Mayor's Office. A candidate had to have over 50% of the vote to win the whole thing on the first ballot. Thanks to my school visit, Jacques was over the 50% mark. When the results were posted, the crowd hoisted us on their shoulders as they shouted "Jacques Médecin, Ilene Médecin, Médecin, Médecin!" It was a glorious moment and I was deeply thrilled and amazed by the incredible emotions and spirit displayed by his loyal followers.

CHAPTER 39

J ACQUES MÉDECIN WAS AN EXTRAORDINARY POL-
itician with a long list of titles, posts and official names with way too many
responsibilities. He rattled them off for me that night at the Polo Lounge, our
first real date, but I will repeat them again. He was Mayor of Nice, member
of French Parliament, and Ancient Minister of Tourism appointed by the
President of France, Valery Giscard-D'Estaing. Also, President of the Alpes-
Maritimes (presiding over the Côte d'Azur), and a Medici Count descended
from the House of Medicis of Florence, Italy. That was my husband. Yes, I
was proud of him. Very proud not only of his titles, but of his many accomplishments for the French people. He definitely was not a typical politician.

Prior to his political career, Jacques had an extraordinary war record.
He had fought during WWII, escaping the Germans in Nice at the age of 14
by hiding in the mountains and fighting with 200 Jewish partisans for two
and a half long years. He was a hero of the Resistance and a boy who chose
to become a man risking his life when he was barely old enough to shave. He
had an amazing resume, but this experience left profound scars on his life.

I didn't have a clue about French politics when I married Jacques and
certainly not international politics. I was thrust onto this stage and had to
perform delicate diplomacy. Luckily, my modeling experience actually helped
me because I was used to being in front of people and making quick wardrobe
changes. Talk about a hectic schedule. Thank goodness I was young and had
enough energy to tackle all of those changes every day and night, attending

a variety of events. There were ceremonial inaugurations, and christenings of boats, trains and airplanes. There were ribbon-cuttings and festival events to open. I was appointed President of Honor for all the English-speaking groups living on the Riviera. I was also sent to meet foreign presidents and dignitaries from around the world, representing not only France, but as an American on behalf of the United States. Now there were two American women representing American interests on the Côte d'Azur.

CHAPTER 40

I SLOWLY GREW INTO MY ROLE AS FIRST LADY. MY first official appearance was by accident as I previously mentioned at the communist school. That's when J proudly said, "You are incredible! The buzz is all over town how Madame Ilene Médecin went into a Communist school dressed like a cowgirl hugging and kissing all the kids!"

Jacques said that he would never have sent me into that neighborhood because I was an American. He couldn't be sure of their reaction. Now, the people were telling everyone how honored and grateful they were that I came and they loved my cowgirl clothes and me. No one could believe I did it. I was just being me.

My popularity was increasing due to the fact I was interacting with people on grassroots levels. There was no judgment about who they were, what party they were affiliated with or what their station was in life. I loved campaigning in the red light district and having tea with many of the "Girls of the Night." One of the ladies loved the perfume I was wearing, so the next day I sent my driver over to deliver a bottle for her. All the "Night Ladies" quickly heard the story of the perfume. Our girls voted for us 100% when Election Day came around.

I was on a roll and politics, surprisingly enough, became my forte'. Who'd a thunk it?

CHAPTER 41

MY FIRST EXPERIENCE PARTICIPATING IN AN election was a huge success and I was thrilled. From that point on, I sincerely believed that politics was my bag. Being a hero for the people had been a touching experience and was a tremendous rush.

I was profoundly evolving in ways that helped guide my future. When you deal with the public on a daily basis for over fifteen years, you learn who is telling the truth and who sincerely needs help. After dealing with multitudes of people, it becomes easier to figure out who is lying. These invaluable experiences changed my opinions on many subjects and I gained an enormous amount of knowledge that has helped me throughout my life.

CHAPTER 42

MARRYING JACQUES, I ALSO ACQUIRED INSTANT family obligations. My stepdaughter, Martine, was having an affair with a policeman named Daniel Veron. Due to the prominence of my new position, I was required to have personal protection and had to choose a bodyguard. Their official duties were to drive and protect me. Martine or "Steppy" as I called my stepdaughter, asked me to get her father to consider Daniel for my personal protection. While he was a municipal policeman, he wasn't in the official chauffeurs' pool. She said he would never let anything happen to me and knew the city backwards and forwards. So Jacques finally acquiesced and I hired Daniel. It was unprecedented for a municipal policeman to work as a mayoral driver/bodyguard. The official chauffeurs, as they were called, had specialized training in personal protection.

Martine's birthday was just a day after mine, November 28th. Sagittarius people in general are fun loving, independent, Peter Pan-like characters who never seem to grow up. Martine and I had that in common. We became close. Her mother, Claude, kicked her out of the house when she said she wanted to meet me. She worshiped her father and didn't have a good relationship with her mother, so she was on our side from the get-go. She lived with us for a while and then Jacques got her an apartment. Daniel was married and not going to get a divorce, so he and Martine eventually broke up. He remained with me for many years as my driver until he betrayed me later on, which is coming up.

CHAPTER 43

ONCE I WAS "OFFICIAL," THE INVITATIONS CAME in droves. Lilou went every evening around 5 PM to City Hall. One of my secretaries gave her printed cards with my schedule of events for the following day and night. There was a master list of obligations to attend, plus personal choices that I felt would help gain votes. We were always campaigning as politicians do. I was enjoying my unique experiences and learning day by day how to deal with different cultures, languages, personalities and motives. I was working at ground level and in the trenches with real people who needed help. However, there were a large number of phonies attempting to manipulate me, wanting to selfishly obtain material things like money, property, and personal items they felt they were entitled to from Jacques and me. I regularly gave speeches in French and English. I was the honorary godmother to every English-speaking group in Nice, as well as hospitals, daycare centers and theatrical clubs. You name it, I was on top of it, aware, and working for and with the people.

Nice was not used to having a First Lady who was so active and participating in events. Jacques' former wife didn't want to do anything to help him while she sat home and played cards all day. It was a very rare occasion when she even accompanied him to a gala. She was Parisian and didn't care for the Niçois, nor did they care for her. On the other hand, they and the Niçois Mafia gratefully embraced me. They started referring to me as their own American Princess, in deference to Princess Grace Kelly.

Jeff Robinson, an American journalist living in France, interviewed me for an article in the International Herald Tribune. The title was "The Model and the Mayor." Grace Kelly and Prince Rainier of Monaco had been dubbed "The Actress and the Prince" when they got engaged. Jeff thought his title would define me and suggest similarities between Grace and me. It also emphasized the fact that Grace and I were both Americans.

After a few minutes, he was surprised at how casual I was during the interview. He commented that he really liked me and it was mutual, so we became friends. He lived in London for many years and is a famous author of crime thrillers. Super guy. He always wrote nice things about me. No wonder I liked him. He's now living back in New York.

Daniel and I were always zipping around the city while I was attacking my duties with fervor. Unbeknownst to me at the time, he had a second job reporting all my daily activities to Max. Max Gilli was Jacques' right-hand man and alleged "cleaner." Of course, he would report all this information to Jacques.

I was being spied on all the time each and every day, but wasn't aware. My later knowledge of this fact became extraordinarily important for my survival during the last few years before we escaped France to live in political exile in Uruguay.

CHAPTER 44

NICE IS BOTH WONDERFUL AND BEAUTIFUL. IT'S unique because, in its heart, it's both French and Italian. Even though Nice is in France, due to its geographic proximity and roots with Italy, Nice identifies more with Italian culture than French.

Napoleon III was the first elected President of France, from 1848 to 1852. When he couldn't be re-elected constitutionally, he seized power and became the Emperor of France from 1852 to 1870. I'm mentioning a little history so you will understand why Nice is a tale of two cultures. Nice, which was on the border between Italy and France, had to take a vote when Italy unified in 1861. It was a monumental choice whether to join Italy or France. The people chose France because Napoleon III was the leader in Europe at the time and they thought it would be more beneficial and prosperous for their economy. The roots of the Niçois people are Italian and they are a proud distinctive culture.

During the 19th Century, Nice became popular as a beach resort and was one of the first cities in Europe to have a purely tourist-based economy. Queen Victoria loved to spend her winters here along with many aristocrats relaxing in the mild climate. In the late 1800's, Nice became the fastest growing city in Europe, opening up to the rest of the continent. During the early 1900s, artists and writers such as Cezanne, Van Gogh, Matisse, Hemingway, F. Scott and Zelda Fitzgerald, Aldous Huxley and Thomas Mann flocked to Nice for inspiration as well as the beautiful scenery and luminous light.

The first gambling casino opened in 1927. Jazz also established itself in Nice in the late 20's. This musical tradition is carried on even today. Each year, Nice sponsored an international jazz festival where the top musicians would gather and play. It was a grand event and so much fun listening to these talented people jam together.

France was invaded by Nazi Germany in 1941 and Nice was incorporated into Vichy France, which was under the control of the Germans. Later, as Italy became an ally of Germany, the Italians occupied Nice. In 1944, Allied forces landed on the Côte d'Azur and the region was liberated.

CHAPTER 45

I WAS FEELING INCREASINGLY MORE CONFIDENT about being in public as a politician's wife. I certainly became more comfortable in my role as the accolades came pouring in. Lol. The amount of adoration and praise I was receiving was unbelievable. It was actually surreal when men would bow and women would curtsy in my favor. I really enjoyed being out and among the people. Who wouldn't? I still hid my shyness behind my huge ivory Emmanuel Kahn glasses that looked like they were from Elton John's collection. It became effortless for me. How hard is it to shake hands and be nice to people?

Unfortunately, I had a lot to learn. The future would teach me that politics wasn't as rewarding and fulfilling as I had envisioned. In fact, just the opposite. It's the lowest form of hypocrisy where power and greed is a staple and is the most ominous profession to be in. My life has been in jeopardy more than a few times because of it.

CHAPTER 46

MY AGENDA WAS ALWAYS FULL WITH OFFICIAL dinners, balls, political meetings and cultural exchanges. I dealt with very powerful and prominent people from around the globe. It was incredibly interesting of course as new worlds were opening up to me. It was sometimes fun, but not always. Life is always tense and stressful in these high circles.

When it came to being famous, no one on the French Riviera was more famous than Prince Rainier and Princess Grace of Monaco, the former Grace Kelly. Just in case any readers are too young to know, the Princess had been an iconic Hollywood movie star with roles in a long string of highly acclaimed pictures like *High Society, Rear Window, High Noon* and of course the Hitchcock classic, *To Catch a Thief*, which happened to be filmed in Cannes and Nice. She shared the screen with Hollywood's most famous dashing and handsome leading men like Gary Cooper, Cary Grant, Jimmy Stewart and Clark Gable. She gave up her successful film career to marry Prince Rainier in what everyone felt was the all-time fairytale marriage and romance. The princess got her prince who was a true prince. That was the way the whole world looked at it and they lived happily ever after. That was not entirely true, and I will get to that.

Of course, I had to meet Grace, her Highness the Princess, because Jacques and Rainier were the two "Monarchs," as it were, of the Riviera, and because Grace Kelly and I were both Americans, which made our lives singular and unique. We both played significant roles in a non-American setting and were very much in the public eye. We were two American women who had traveled far to find their "Prince Charming" and settled abroad, you could say.

Jacques and Rainier were close, both as heads of adjoining governments and personal friends. They were both confident, rugged, and sexy men. The press and the public loved them. They were also men who did not lack ego, vanity, or pride.

It's no surprise that it wasn't long before the invitation came for Jacques and me to attend a Grand Prix dinner in Monaco being hosted by Grace and Rainier. This would be my introduction to the Princess. I was excited and just a little nervous. I had gained more confidence by this time with my political triumphs working alongside the public. I was looking forward to the evening and meeting the Princess who I had always admired from afar.

Jacques prepped me and told me I had to curtsy, take Grace's hand and say, "I am honored to meet you your Royal Highness." Oh my, I thought. I had never even considered doing that for anyone. It's not an American custom. So, I had to take special lessons to be perfect with my dip and bowing before we attended the event.

The night arrived. Was I prepared enough with my curtsy to please Grace? We would see. We were greeted at the entry to the Palace by valets and ushered into a private room where Rainier was waiting for Grace to appear. I made myself ready for our formal introduction. I stood quietly next to Jacques in anticipation. Grace entered wearing a Christian Dior gray and silver dotted patterned dress, which ironically was made from the same fabric Dior had chosen for me in a blouse and skirt ensemble. But, that was another style and another outfit. This night I was dressed in Nina Ricci, a long black billowy off-the-shoulder chiffon gown with matching heels and purse.

I was immediately surprised. This was not the gorgeous regal princess I was expecting. She had not aged well and seemed off-kilter. Her crown was askew and her hair was not well coiffed. Who was attending to her? No one with any style or brains, apparently. She was on the chunky side and had seemingly been drinking. I immediately knew she wasn't focused on her present surroundings.

She was still the Princess and I needed to curtsy. We were introduced. I dipped, kissed her hand and repeated my lines, "I'm honored to meet you, your Royal Highness."

She smiled and said "Pleased to meet you Madame Médecin. "Apparently, my curtsy was a success. The lessons were worth it.

It seemed dreamlike, but I had pulled it off. We were then escorted to a large room where the guests were mingling before dinner. Robert de Balkany, the husband of the Princess of Italy, and Philippe Junot, Rainier and Grace's son-in-law (soon to be divorced, was married to their daughter, Princess Caroline) were gabbing together, so Jacques brought me over to be introduced. We were all at ease and it was going well. The men and I were having a fun conversation when Jacques said he had to go to the loo (British slang for toilet or bathroom). He said to Robert, "I'm leaving you with a gift. Take care of my wife while I'm gone, but do not open the present."

Philippe drifted away to another conversation and Robert escorted me to a luxurious burgundy velvet bench on the side of the room. He kept telling me how beautiful I was and didn't stop with the compliments. I started feeling uneasy and realized this was not just friendly banter. All of a sudden he stood in front of me and said, "How much money will it take for you to have sex with me?" I was so taken aback I couldn't make a decent response for a moment. That was when I started to catch on to the true decadence of European aristocracy. I sat up very straight and blasted him, "How dare you! You won't ever have enough money to bed me! I love my husband and won't tell him about this incident because he'll kill you."

When Jacques came back he looked at me and said, "You're pale. Is everything alright? Robert, did you take care of my Madame Médecin?"

Robert glanced at me, and I said, "Everything is fine, he just told me an off-colored joke." Jacques said he hoped it wasn't too off-colored.

I didn't see Robert again until many years later. He ended up finally having enough money, lol, and that story will be shared later.

Back to our evening in Monaco, it was time for dinner. The doors opened to a lovely ballroom with individual round tables and beautiful flower centerpieces with the usual golden gilt. I was seated at Princess Grace's table and Jacques at Prince Rainier's.

Grace was very gracious and turned to me and said, "Madame Médecin, I hear very good things about you. The public says you are very accessible, you are a real person, and very nice. I'm glad to have you here representing America."

I thanked her profusely for her kind words. I was seated next to another Royal named the Prince de Polignac. He whisked me onto the dance floor and we laughed, twirled and had a great time dishing about the pomp and circumstance, which the other Royals took so seriously. It was apparent he was gay. I would have liked to see him again, but he disappeared after dinner, not to appear at any other Monaco event.

After we left the gala, Jacques told me Prince Rainier had given me an incredible compliment. He told Jacques, "You know, your wife reminds me of Grace when she was young and we were first married." I was so surprised and thrilled. That was one of the greatest compliments of my life.

When Princess Caroline and Philippe Junot decided to marry, Princess Grace was adamantly against it. He was a well-known playboy, seventeen years Caroline's senior. Grace didn't feel he was the right man for her daughter and a family struggle ensued. As it turned out, Grace was right and the marriage floundered. It was a disaster and they divorced.

The story I'm going to tell you is one Jacques recounted to me when we were first invited to the Grand Prix dinner in Monaco. This was after Princess Caroline and Junot had announced they were going to divorce. Until then, Jacques and I had been deemed the biggest scandal regarding a French politician in 100 years. Who would think of jeopardizing their career and status by getting divorced and marrying a young American? I became known as the other American lady on the French Riviera. Only Jacques had been invited to Junot and Caroline's wedding because Princess Grace said she didn't want our scandalous beginnings to overshadow the event. Therefore, I was not included in the invitation and Jacques respectfully declined.

Since Caroline and Philippe were going to be divorced, I was finally included in all official invitations—like the Grand Prix dinner. Gee, thanks. Protocol, protocol. The press, which was always sensationalizing our lives and distorting the truth to increase circulation, loved to keep writing about us whether it was good or bad.

Jacques shared some early history (before we were together) about his friendship with the Prince. He said Rainier, Robert de Balkany, the husband of the Princess of Italy, Thierry Roussel, soon to be married to Christina Onassis, and Philippe Junot would meet in a huge penthouse in Paris to have parties with beautiful women and let loose. Jacques said he, Robert, and Philippe were joking around one night when Robert said to Philippe, "I bet you can't marry a Princess." Philippe answered, "I bet I can." So he won the bet, but not for long. He and Caroline were married in 1978 and it only lasted until 1980.

I saw Prince Rainier many times after the Grand Prix dinner and we developed great rapport over the years. We were enjoying ourselves one evening as I read the lines in his hand like a real palmist and told him a little bit about his future. He was a Gemini and was marveled by my intuition and insightful predictions knowing I had studied with Daniel, his daughter Caroline's astrologer.

I became good at reading horoscopes and also studied Chinese astrology. It was all for amusement and everyone seemed entertained. The French are big on Tarot cards, psychics, astrology and mediums. I fit right in. I found all the mystic practices fascinating and applied my astrology knowledge when meeting new diplomats, royals, heads of state, etc.

I wanted to be prepared when meeting new and important people and would analyze their horoscope in advance. It might sound odd, but it helped me to best approach them to communicate. Most of them were pleasantly surprised. I was definitely a unique and more relaxed First Lady than they had ever met.

CHAPTER 47

J ACQUES OPENED UP ENTIRELY NEW AND EXOTIC
worlds to me. I had never been to the Middle East and found it incredibly
fascinating. Nice had business there, so we went. The experience brought back
memories as I relived scenes from of one of my favorite epic films, *Lawrence
of Arabia*. As a teenager, I had the opportunity to attend the Oscars when
the film took home seven awards. To my surprise, I was introduced to Omar
Sharif and was stunned when he kissed me on the cheek. This was after I told
him I thought he was so handsome.

Our first trip was to Dubai in 1980, making stops in Israel, Cyprus
and Athens. We traveled regularly to Dubai, usually for weeks at a time. A
consortium of sheiks from the United Arab Emirates wanted to build an
exhibition center and hotel in Nice. Naturally, Jacques was happy to meet
with them. We were invited to Dubai to meet with Sheik Ahmed Baker,
who was the head of the group. He had a younger brother, Tayeb, who (as
it turned out) was disturbingly handsome with pitch-black hair and Steve
McQueen looks. The sheiks were already major builders and construction
magnates. They didn't lack for funding and had just finished building the
most exquisite hotel in Dubai called the Jebel Ali. They opened it just for us
as their first exclusive guests. It was like a "soft opening" being fully staffed,
but we were the only guests. They had a French chef, German management,
and a very formal British maître d'. The lobby was like a king's throne room.
There were two large elevators with beautiful rugs, changed daily with a new

design for each day of the week. We had the most beautiful suite with all gold fixtures and Roger & Gallet creams, soaps, perfumes and potpourri. To this day, whenever I spray on Roger & Gallet perfume (a touch of lime and musk, always sexy and enticing), I'm transported back to Dubai.

We developed good relations with the sheiks. I was the only woman allowed to attend the all-male dinners and gatherings. I wore a dish-dash, which is a loose floor-length garment with long sleeves. They're really quite comfortable. I had them made for me in an Arab marketplace, which is called a souk. I wasn't required to wear a headscarf.

As "Royal Guests," we were accorded the highest level of honor and respect. Anything we desired was provided. While they are semi-nomadic and descend from the oldest inhabitants of the Arabian Desert, I was greatly impressed by the sheiks acquired taste for ultimate luxury.

We were on the Persian Gulf and the Jebel Ali was on the beach. The waters were pale blue, calm and crystal clear. Ahmed had opened the hotel solely for our stay with all the plush amenities. Everything was so well refined with all details superbly crafted. They had succeeded in creating both luxury and comfort.

The dining room reminded me of the elegant Louis XV restaurant at the *Hôtel de Paris* in Monaco. They had decorated it in a pale blue and white palette in concert with the calming color of the ocean. Ornate silver candelabras dressed each table with sparkling French crystal glasses and sterling silver cutlery. Of course, they hired a top French Michelin Star chef who created sumptuous meals from breakfast to dinner. Special food and ingredients were flown in from around the globe.

We were given the Presidential Suite on the top floor, which was around 800 square feet and adorned with real gold-plated faucets and fixtures. It was exquisite and I was in heaven. They had created the leading edge of luxury for the time that exceeded any grand five-star hotel in the world and Ahmed had opened it just for us as his exclusive guests. Other than being fully staffed, Jacques, Jean Oltra, our press secretary, and myself were the only guests.

We were invited to dinner the next evening with all the surrounding sheiks. The last one to arrive was very late, so we commenced the meal without him. Finally, halfway through, he appeared. This man was in a very jolly mood and it showed on his face. Following his apology for tardiness, he then proceeded to describe in detail what had gone on the night before. This sheik had a medium-sized fiefdom (the domain of a feudal lord) and began to share his story.

Adjacent to his land was another sheik who had a slightly smaller fiefdom and a daughter. The two sheiks agreed they would unite their states by the first sheik (with the larger fiefdom) marrying the daughter of the second sheik (with the smaller fiefdom). The first sheik would give the wedding party in his grand dining hall. The ceremonies proceeded. The entire family of the new bride had been invited to this grand event and were wined and dined to excess. At the end of the extravagant meal, the sheik had his personal assassins swoop in and cut off all their heads! Except for his new bride.

He said to her, "You are either with me or with your family. All the land is mine now. It's your choice. You can lay with them or be my wife." She decided to remain his wife.

All the sheiks spoke English, so I was hearing this first-hand and the hairs on my arms stood up. Everyone around the table clapped. This was not a joke. He was serious and they applauded him. I was shocked and horrified. My facial expressions betrayed my feelings and Jacques put his hand on my thigh and started to squeeze hard. He whispered in my ear as I was shaking and tried to compose myself, "Do not show your feelings and keep it together." I pulled it off, but that savage story remains permanently embedded in my brain.

I was getting quite a practical education being deeply immersed in this type of schooling, learning about cultures around the world and their own unique way of thinking and behaving. Is it any wonder I felt so isolated because of my broadened awareness when I finally returned to the U.S. to live? It's difficult for people to understand harsh realities in other parts of the world if they haven't experienced it. The contradiction is amazing because what is considered perfectly normal in one culture is a true abomination in another. I was a first-hand witness to these conflicting cultural practices.

The following day we were driven to another hotel of Sheik Ahmed's that was 45 minutes away. He had a Cadillac limo pick us up as part of a caravan of limos escorting us to one of their other grand hotels where they hosted a fabulous party in our honor with the local Bedouins. It was simpler, but still luxurious. That night a dinner was planned on the seaward side of the building.

It was as if I had stepped into a scene from *The Arabian Nights*. On the sweeping grounds of the hotel, there were several enormous canopies erected on the sand, under which huge colorful cushions and intricate hand-woven carpets were placed. There were hookahs at each pillow, which seated four people with low-styled tables filled with a large assortment of hors d'oeuvres including dried fruits and a variety of nuts. The vibrant color and design of the textiles were a pleasure to the senses.

As Bedouins are known for their hospitality, sumptuous local cuisine was served on gleaming silver platters heaped high with lamb kabobs and basmati rice wrapped in grape leaves, accompanied by delicious honey-dripping desserts. The aromas and tastes were absolutely splendid.

After dinner Ahmed came to sit by my side. He had a gentle, easy voice—elegant yet commanding. His English was immaculate, naturally.

"Madame Médecin, what is your favorite stone?"

I looked at him in amusement and said, "Diamond of course." He smiled and escorted me outside the tent to an area where a bonfire had been lit. More Bedouins surrounded the pit in colorful dress, dancing, smiling and swaying to the music. A small group of men were playing Turkish Mizmar flutes—an exotic, enchanting sound. I joined them and was soon whirling and laughing and having quite a unique time.

The Bedouins in bright colorful costumes came in to cavort around a huge bonfire. There was an old man with a skinny wooden stick who put out his hand and led me down from the feast to dance with the group. I was in my element, swaying and twirling with my new friends who were grabbing my hands and spinning me around.

When they finished, the leathery old man took me back to my pillow and presented me with his camel stick. He told me through a translator that he had it since he was a young boy and because I was so nice to him, he wanted me to accept it for my own personal luck. There was something special about my encounter with this man. I connected with his peaceful aura in a way I can only describe as mystical. I was so touched our eyes teared up and I gave him a hug. That cherished moment will always be with me. I believed the power of the stick later saved me from almost certain death. Its symbolism gave me the strength to carry on through all the frightening challenges that were to come.

We spent the following day at the pool which was just steps away from the gorgeous waters of the Persian Gulf. Everything was perfect; the weather was beautiful, the water was warm…a very quiet and relaxing day.

The next day we had lunch in an open-air restaurant serving fresh fish and several types of salads. Leaving the hotel, Ahmed wanted to show me the Gold Souk and Spice Souk, traditional markets in Diera, in eastern Dubai. First, the Spice Souk. It was an olfactory wonder, an orgasm for the nose. I was fascinated with all fragrances from a zillion spices and the way they were organized and displayed in colorful rows. Next stop, the Gold Souk.

Now, that blew my mind. Row upon row of stalls selling gold necklaces, bracelets, rings, earrings and little art objects. You could buy just gold pieces or ones with precious and semi-precious stones. Sheik Ahmed took me to one of his special stalls and in Arabic told the man what he wanted. His friend said it would be ready the day after. The next day around 4 PM when I came back from the pool, a box was sitting on the bed.

I opened it and there was a gold necklace inside encrusted with tiny rubies and diamonds. The placement of the jewels formed a script—it was writing with my named spelled out in Arabic. I sat back on the pillow and let out a gasp. I was so touched.

Ahmed was so wonderful to me during the entire trip and I knew this was a memory that would warm my heart forever. He had pitch-black hair, a sweet smiling face with rosy cheeks and stood around 5' 11." All the men wore traditional dish dash ankle-length cotton kaftans, usually with long sleeves even during the hot summers.

Then, there was his younger brother Tayeb who I thought was around my age, but never dared ask. He was the epitome of a gorgeous Arab sheik. He was around my height with black hair, brown bedroom eyes and so handsome he made all the girls swoon, including me, which I decided to keep to myself. I've seen recent photos of him on the Internet and even with age he's still as gorgeous as ever. We had a good rapport and I wished we could have had a friendship, but alas that was not in the cards.

It was a good business trip for the Côte d'Azur and good for Jacques, politically speaking. Ahmed and the sheiks became allies of Jacques' and were soon developing a new hotel and convention center in Nice. I had now succeeded in international relations and diplomacy as well (or so Jacques told me).

CHAPTER 48

I HAD BRIEFLY MENTIONED WE HAD STOPPED IN Israel on our way to Dubai. The purpose for our visit was for Jacques to meet with the regional heads of Israel. We needed their influence with the Jewish population in France to vote against Mitterand, the Socialist Candidate for President.

It's not an easy thing to travel from Israel to an Arab country. Since we couldn't have Israeli stamps on our regular passports when we entered the Emirates, Jacques and I were issued diplomatic ones.

Israel was quite an eye opener. I knew we would be visiting the Wailing Wall, so I had a short list ready to place in a good crevice to be blessed in the Holy Land. I had some very, very specific wishes and especially meaningful ones for Jacques and myself.

When we arrived Teddy Kollek, the Mayor of Jerusalem, and two colleagues welcomed us and escorted us to The King David Hotel. Apparently, this was where they hosted visiting dignitaries. We had the Presidential Suite on the top floor. It was comfortable, but with no frills.

The next day we were off to meet an official group to visit the Yad Vashem Museum of the Holocaust. It had been established August 19, 1953 as the official memorial to the victims and was closed to the public during our visit. The mayors and their wives from Israel's largest cities were there to honor us. After being formally introduced, we boarded a large bus and reached our destination around two in the afternoon. Along the way our guides excelled at explaining the interesting history of the surrounding area.

The last mural in the museum depicted a ship of Jews leaving their homeland in Europe bound for America. They were seeking refuge from the Nazis. I stood there transfixed and became very emotional. Franklin Delano Roosevelt was the President of the United States at that time and had turned them away.

As I was reflecting on the significance of this mural, the wife of the Mayor of Netanya came next to me and started to scream.

"You, you Americans turned our people away and we will never forgive you!" I was stunned that a Mayoress would have the nerve not only to speak to me like that but yell at me. This was unacceptable. I won't mention her name, but I have never allowed anyone to treat me with such disrespect.

I turned to her and said, "Number one, I was not born at the time. Number two, if Israel is alive today it is because of the support of the United States. You are out of line, and I suggest you never come near me again!" She was flustered by my response and rapidly retreated to the back of the bus.

Jacques saw that I was terribly upset and I shared what had occurred. He said he'd have a talk with Teddy to explain his wife's appalling aggression toward me was unfounded and to have him keep her away from both of us.

As I was taking my seat on the bus, I saw her sneering at me and so I sneered back. We were to have an official dinner with the entire delegation that evening. They dine early in Israel, so we were seated at 6 PM. The Netanya Mayoress and her husband were late. Shortly after being seated near me at the big round table, she started to foam at the mouth and her head fell into her plate. An ambulance arrived and away they sped to the ER. We later learned she had been so agitated by our previous conflict that she had a diabetic seizure.

Normally, I'm a very compassionate and empathetic person, but in this case I wasn't. My experience in Israel was not as rewarding as I had hoped.

The next day all of the mayors were to meet us without their spouses. The woman's husband approached me to profusely apologize, saying she had been out of sorts for a few days, but realized that was no excuse. Other members of the group came up and conveyed their remorse at what had happened and acknowledged without the aid of Americans they would not exist.

To make matters more complicated, it was Friday the Jewish Sabbath— Shabbat. Elevators were not allowed to run on the Sabbath. Only one tiny service elevator was in use. The hotel staff typically used it, but we commandeered it instead of plodding thirty-eight floors to the penthouse. It stopped at every floor going up and down.

That night we had room service. Israeli food in those days was not very good. It seemed there was sugar in every dish I ordered. Even the gefilte fish was made with too much sugar.

The next night the delegation met us in the hotel dining room for our last meal. There were two separate and distinct sections in the restaurant. The meat section was across the room from the dairy section. We were seated on the "meat" side. I ordered a brisket, which was very tough and not too tasty. Since living in France, I was used to having cheese towards the end of the main course. I asked the waiter for the cheese menu. He told me he wouldn't serve me because I was in the meat section. That was enough for me to hear and told him how it was.

I said, "You are serving foreigners in an international hotel. I respect your culture, but I demand you respect mine." I stood up and went to the milk side, sat by myself and told the waiter, "Now bring me my cheese."

Everyone looked at me in astonishment. Jacques smiled and said, "That's my wife. She's very fair in her judgements and I stand with her." They smiled and acknowledged I had a point. That was 1980. Though I've not returned since, I've heard the food has vastly improved.

Following Jerusalem, our next stop was the island of Cyprus where we stayed a couple of nights. We were on the Greek side. The island is divided into Greek and Turkish sections. I liked Cyprus. The food was delicious in the hotel and restaurants. In the hotel dining room, we were served Koupepia, the official cuisine of Cyprus. It's made of grape leaves stuffed with rice and minced pork or beef. All the food was so yummy I would return just to eat.

From Cyprus we flew to Athens where I had one of the tastiest and healthiest meals I've ever eaten. We dined at the port where we consumed fresh seafood, Feta cheese and Greek olive oil with a great assortment of olives. My mouth still waters when I remember that lunch. The domestic olive oil in Greece, mind you, not exported; to me is the best olive oil I have ever had.

Our regular passports were then exchanged for our diplomatic passports (the non-Israeli stamped ones). As Ahmed sent a private jet to pick us up in Greece, my Arabian Nights journey began.

CHAPTER 49

IT WAS ON THAT FIRST TRIP TO ISRAEL AT THE
Wailing Wall when I made my personal request, but I had to wait for the
second trip to Dubai for my prayers to be answered.

At the Wall I had inserted a piece of paper into the ancient stones with
my written wishes. That's the tradition. I asked to be pregnant within six
months with a healthy baby girl who looked like Jacques, had his stamina
with blue or green eyes and my body type. I figured as long as I was there...
how often does one get to the Wailing Wall? I asked for three pieces of jewelry
I had admired at Faberge when we were in Paris. I thought if none of that
happens in six months, I won't think about it anymore.

Well, guess what? I can honestly say you can pray for anything and
place your handwritten wishes in the small crevices. Yes, they will come
true. I'm convinced that the Wailing Wall has special powers of the Universe.

Back in France, Jacques had to report to the central government on
what had politically transpired from our trip.

CHAPTER 50

WE HAD BEEN SHOPPING IN PARIS WEEKS before the Middle East tour and I was touched by the fact J loved to spoil me. We passed by Faberge and strolled in. I focused on three pieces that caught my eye, but I wasn't going to say anything. Jacques asked if I wanted something. I told him I wanted to think about it because I noticed a few pieces I liked.

After returning to Nice from our trip, we had to leave a few days later for Paris because Jacques had to attend a parliament session as well as report the findings from our trip. When his meetings were finished, we went to lunch and he tenderly took my face in his large hands and said, "Let's go to Faberge." I didn't hesitate. After arriving at the showroom, the manager removed the three pieces I had selected for viewing in a private room. Without a pause, J said, "Which one do you want?"

"I really love the enamel bracelet, but I really love the gold pineapple, and also the enameled egg." I said, "You choose."

He said to the salesman, "Giftwrap all three pieces please." Wow, I wasn't expecting that! I realized one of my wishes had come true three-fold. The jewelry was just a secondary and superficial desire of course. There was a greater stronger wish, one that came from my soul.

CHAPTER 51

THE POLITICAL AND BUSINESS WORLDS WERE essentially one in the same. It was all about who you knew and their financial resources because that is what reaped the power and influence. There were functions upon functions, and I was obligated to attend them all. The personal became the political and the political became the personal. It was an endless parade of lunches, brunches, coffee stops, quick breakfasts, balls, formal dinners, ribbon cutting events and, at every one of them, I was either hosting or was the person of honor. I was constantly busy greeting people, delivering speeches, helping peoples' promises come true, and always switched "on" and forever working by Jacques' side. It was sometimes exhausting, but always fascinating and exciting.

On one special occasion there was the dinner with Madame Gould, where the diamonds were pulsating like a starlit night and emeralds and rubies were so huge they almost covered the entire finger, earlobe, wrist and neck. It was quite the dinner and yet, not so unusual for the lifestyle on the French Riviera.

Jacques came to me with a special invitation from Madame Florence Gould, who was the widow of Frank Jay Gould, the son of the robber baron and American railroad magnate Jay Gould. He told me it was important that we go because she had been in love with his father, Jean Médecin, and they had a history. Jacques said she loved him too because he reminded her of his father and she was a big financial supporter to his campaigns. When she was young Florence loved to sunbathe, but didn't like the rocks on the French Riviera beaches. So, she had her husband change the rocks to sand at her special bathing place in Juan-les-Pins, a jet set beach next to Antibes, which her husband created for her. When you have that kind of money, you can do those sorts of things.

Jacques said his mother picked up a gun one time to pay a visit to Madame Gould, threatening to shoot her if she didn't stay away from her husband. Fortunately, Jacques arrived in time to prevent any further escalation between the ladies and escorted his mother home. Jean, his father, then ended the relationship.

I was told that there would be some very heavy hitters invited to the dinner. These were men and women with old, old money from royal lineages and famous marriages who were mostly in their 80's. Who, you ask was so old, so revered and so rich? Well, the Aga Khan, for one.

We arrived at La Vigie, Gould's little palace-by-the-sea. The villa was huge, gilded, splendid and tasteful as I expected it would be. We were greeted at the colonnaded front entry and escorted in by liverymen in tight black pants, high boots and red tailed jackets. The servants had a jockey-like look. A lot of these people were very "horsey." The Aga Khan, in particular, owned some of the finest thoroughbreds in the world and had an enormous breeding farm in Normandy.

As we entered the vestibule, I was astonished by such a vast collection of the most coveted and expensive art in the world. It was a private museum gallery. Virtually every known master's work was hanging on the walls. Every inch of wall was filled with Rembrandt, Van Gogh, Matisse, Picasso, Chagall, and I could go on. It was like stepping into another wild world with centuries of art, color, mastery and skill, all packed into one high-ceilinged room.

The decor was a mix of styles. The look of the home boasted a lot of Louis XIV style surrounded by an eclectic selection of antiques that were just astounding. The magnificent pieces were spread almost at random throughout all of the rooms. Madame Gould told me to call her Florence and proudly gave me a tour even of her bedroom. White and pale blue satins, embroidered pillows in Italian and French flavor, all with a total feminine flair.

We entered the grand dining room. It was a small and select group. The Aga Khan's mother, Joan, was at the table accompanied by ten other distinguished figures, who were a mix of French and Middle Eastern jet-setting aristocrats of the era. They had many titles, honorifics and surnames. When we were introduced, I realized by far I was the youngest one in attendance. Of course, I realized I was dining with a group whose type of hierarchy would soon be extinct. I felt honored to be fraternizing with these incredibly fascinating people, mostly women. To this day, I realize how much I learned simply from chatting during that meal.

They were very well educated and worldly. The only feature more impressive was their jewelry as I mentioned, regarding the size of the stones. I have been around the finest high-end jewelry. I modeled jewelry for Frances Klein on Beverly and Rodeo Drive, and my own family has had some incredible pieces, but the jewelry on display this particular evening equaled and even surpassed the British Crown Jewels. I'm not easily impressed when it comes to sparkles and carats, but I was definitely impressed. I had never seen anything like this jewelry before that night. This was a collection to rank with the Indian Maharajas and the Romanov crown jewels.

Madame Gould wore natural pearls the size of golf balls around her neck with a diamond clasp to match. She was wearing a D-flawless, non-fluorescent, 60-carat ice-white diamond ring and a one-carat each diamond, emerald-cut wedding eternity band with the same fabulous quality stones. The ruby and diamond necklaces, the rings, bracelets, emerald and sapphire pieces worn around the room were huge and way beyond dazzling. I was so impressed with her jewelry and curious that I asked many details about her pieces. She recognized I was not a novice and was amused by my youth and direct questions. Madame appreciated my straightforward attitude and said it was refreshing.

The dinner table was gilded, shimmering and vibrant with diamond sparkling light. It was set with Lalique crystal, gold tableware and serving pieces. The menu was typically eclectic haute cuisine; smoked salmon, caviar, baby chicken with cream sauce, green vegetables, and île de flottante (floating island) for dessert. I never quite got into French haute cuisine, which didn't bother Jacques. He thought my wholesome Americanness was charming and would say, "Have another hot dog ma chérie and some buttery popcorn. I love your casual California style." But I did enjoy the cuisine that night. The Dom Perignon and Cristal flowed easily of course, plus the rarest of after dinner liqueurs. Unfortunately, or perhaps not so unfortunately, I did not partake in this part of the extravagant spread as I don't drink alcohol. There is a reason.

My body has a natural Antabuse-like reaction to liquor that I inherited from my maternal Grandmother Belle. I get nauseous and can even throw up from the smell or just a slight taste of alcohol, so the fine spirits were not a highlight for me. The dinner was not the main event for me either, but the guests and the decor were. The paintings, jewels, and talk at the table from some of the most sophisticated, worldly, have-done-it-all, have-seen-every-thing crowd. Those were the high points that made it so captivating. The people they knew, the places they had been, the conversation about days gone by and their amazing memories were all absolutely enthralling. I am so grateful to this day to have been a part of this remarkable and unique group. They were dazzling, flamboyant and dressed to impress one another. It is one of the most treasured moments I look back on with immense pleasure.

CHAPTER 52

THE DEMANDS OF A POLITICAL LIFE NEVER LET up. Jacques was part of it, so I was part of it. There was a dinner one evening for Valéry Giscard d'Estaing, the President of France, at the Elysée Palace in Paris. The same Palace where the Kings of France and Napoleon himself had reigned. D'Estaing was a Conservative like Jacques. Their mutual archenemy was the socialist leader and later President, Francois Mitterrand. As time and circumstances evolved, Mitterrand became more and more opposed to Jacques and me as an entity, a duo if you will. I was a thorn in the President's side because I was a freedom fighter, opposing any socialist or communistic regime. It was Mitterrand, his associates, and the leftist press who ultimately became responsible for our demise. However, this event was not about Mitterrand, but Giscard d'Estaing, the conservative President.

Jacques, being the Mayor of Nice and National Minister of Tourism at the time, was generally acknowledged as the best and most successful mayor in France. French media deemed us the new power couple. Guests were eagerly anticipating the arrival of the young American First Lady of Nice.

We flew to Paris where a gray official Citroën limousine took us to the Palace, which was impressive as anticipated. The official dinners were in grand style at the Elysée. An army of butlers dressed in white & black guided us inside. The decor was Louis, all the way. Many top officials of the country greeted us and I was seated next to one who started making polite conversation.

He asked me what I thought about the evening and if there was any-thing I wanted to talk about. I quipped, "You know, we're sitting here being very superficial and I think we'd both enjoy the evening more if we just talked about something more interesting. How about sex?"

I thought he was going to fall off his chair. He started to belly laugh, but then caught himself and said he'd love that. As a result, I had the best time at my first formal dinner at the Presidential Palace. Everyone else looked bored and Jacques was curious why we were so animated and smiling all night. I told him later what I had said to my dinner partner and he gasped. He rolled his eyes with a laugh under his breath and said he would surely hear about it the following day.

CHAPTER 53

OUR SECOND TRIP TO DUBAI WAS IN 1981. I couldn't forget the date in October if I tried. Two monumental events occurred on this trip. One was extremely personal for me and the other shook the entire world.

This time, I invited my mother. I wanted her to experience the opulence, mystery and culture. These years of traveling on official business were mind-boggling in every way. I had been living a fairytale life. I wanted to share it and needed a witness that would confirm my experiences. At least I had one person from my side this time to see and understand what and how I was living. I was privileged to grow up in Beverly Hills, but this was definitely another level of existence.

We were back at the fabulous Jebel Ali Hotel. It was wonderful and never ceased to startle and amaze me. It definitely was a dream oasis. Mom was given her own suite and was making friends with the sheiks. One day we were on Ahmed's yacht and dropped anchor far from the shore. Jacques and Ahmed took the launch that was strapped to the side of the yacht to go fishing. Mom and I stayed on the mother ship while she played bridge with three of the sheiks. I was resting which was unusual for me. I'm normally like the Road Runner, the cartoon character who's constantly on the move and gaining ground. I have never been seasick, plane sick or car sick, but I wasn't my usual self. I was tired and feeling nauseous. My mother was very surprised when I told her I felt faint. They radioed Ahmed and Jacques to come back to the yacht. We then returned to shore and I felt great once I was off the ocean. We had a feast of yogurt dipped lamb and chicken skewers with an array of vegetables, humus and, of course, honey-dripping desserts. It had been catered by the hotel staff and was on the dock waiting for us on arrival. A great meal it was. I ate like a horse and couldn't believe my nausea had disappeared.

I wasn't sick for the remainder of the trip, but I was still tired and then it was time to head home. We had planned to stop in Egypt on our way back to Nice. That turned out to be a bad idea since Anwar Sadat, the President of Egypt, had been assassinated October 6, 1981, just a couple of days before our arrival. Of course, it was a major international crisis. Egypt erupted in turmoil as we landed our plane in Cairo for official meetings. We never deplaned. Who would be the new President of Egypt to succeed Sadat? Could this mean a new war between Israel and Egypt? Would the entire Middle East blow up? Would the Egyptians blame the Israelis? Were the killer rebels within Sadat's own government? It all needed to be sorted out.

It finally became clear that the assassins were "radical Islamists"—a term that would become all too familiar to me. They had murdered Sadat because he was too friendly towards Israel and the West. Things were more unsettled in Egypt than we realized. Forget about our official meetings in Cairo. The airport was on highest security alert with all air traffic frozen. We couldn't get off the plane and weren't allowed to fly out either. We were told in the strictest terms not to disembark and the plane had to stay put on the tarmac.

We were there for over twelve hours waiting to take off. I laid down on Jacques' lap and slept like a bear in hibernation for the winter. Finally, word came that we could depart. Upon landing in Nice, Jacques literally had to carry me off the plane because I was so exhausted.

When we got back home he said to me, "You are going to the doctor." He had to fly to Paris the next morning for Parliament. I said I would call him as soon as I finished my appointment. After he left later that morning, I literally fell out of bed and crawled to the bathroom looking for the pregnancy test kit Jackye had bought for me, just in case. I could hardly stand up. Why was I so fatigued? Maybe, because I had an epiphany six months earlier about having a baby. I believed having a child would help make me a better person. It was my most important wish at the Wall.

Jacques wanted to have a child with me and told me so when we first got together. I said it wasn't something I had ever desired, but didn't say no to him because I loved him so much.

I confided this to my best friend, Jackye. I didn't think I could conceive because after all these years without using contraception, I never became pregnant. When Jacques and I were in Los Angeles before our second trip to the Emirates, I visited my Ob/Gyn, Mel Ehrenhalt. He knew my medical history well since he had been taking care of me since I was 19. He gave me a couple of tests to see if I could conceive. The tests came back fine. I was normal and could have a child. He assured me, "I've known you for a long time and can say you have one of the strongest minds of anyone I know and I believe if you want to conceive you will."

I laughed. Then I thought if it happens, it will be a miracle, and it was a miracle. A miracle from the Wailing Wall.

CHAPTER 54

WHEN WE LEFT DUBAI, I KNEW SOMETHING WAS up with my body. I couldn't wait to get home to Nice and get into bed. I must have slept for a day or more. I didn't really think I could be pregnant. I thought throwing up was the main symptom of being pregnant and I wasn't doing that. I was beyond nauseous though, had stomach cramps and was so tired it was debilitating. Losing seven pounds from the time on the yacht until arriving home was not a symptom of pregnancy that I was aware of and literally thought I was dying. I looked at the instructions for the test kit and laid on the bathroom floor till the timer went off. I was so nervous. Time up. I squinted and peeked. There it was, blue! OMG! I was PREGNANT!

I was in such shock I laid frozen in the same spot on the floor for half an hour. My mind was racing a hundred miles a minute, further exhausting me. I managed to crawl back to bed and fell asleep for several hours. Somehow, I got up and dragged myself to my closet to dress for the doctor's appointment. Daniel picked me up and off we went. The doctor confirmed I was with child and Daniel practically had to carry me back to our car.

I got into bed and called Jacques. I used to call him "Bloopie."

He answered and asked, "Baby, what did the doctor say?"

Still in shock, I asked, "Are you sitting down?"

"Yes," he replied.

And I blurted, "I'm pregnant!" There was silence on the other end. "Bloopie, say something!" He was in shock as well.

"Are you sure? Nothing is wrong with you?"

I replied "No, Just pregnant!"

"Thank God!" he said, becoming very emotional and told me, "This is what I prayed for, but didn't know if it would ever happen. I'll come back tonight. I love you."

I said, "I love you too," and fell back into a deep sleep. I never threw up, but just got thinner no matter how much I ate and slept twelve hours a day.

At the same time our dachshund, Selma, got pregnant by a very handsome male short hair smooth doxy. Selma and I were in bed together all the time sleeping. She was my best companion always cuddled by my side. My first trimester was different than what I imagined. I could barely get out of bed and was continuously exhausted. I was only able to make late afternoon events, come back home, eat dinner in bed and pass out again until noon the next day.

Then honestly, at the three-month mark, I started feeling great. I hadn't had much of an appetite since we returned from Dubai and now all I wanted to eat was liver, steak, baked potatoes and spinach with lots of Tabasco sauce. When I saw Jacques eat veal's head for the first time a while back in one of his favorite restaurants, I said to myself, "no way would I ever think of putting that in my mouth." However, I started to crave it and knew something was vastly different. "PREGNANT!"

Selma was due and soon delivered four adorable puppies. Two girls and two boys. The smallest boy was so tiny he wasn't able to get enough milk. He died and poor Selma put him in her mouth, roamed around the house and went into the garden to try to bury him. That night she started convulsing. Jacques rushed her to the vet. She had lost so much calcium nursing the pups that she could have died if he hadn't arrived in time. The condition is called eclampsia. I certainly learned about it the hard way.

We gave one of the pups to Lilou and Marcel Dini, our devoted Niçois couple. Lilou managed everything personal pertaining to me, TK (The Kid) and overseeing the staff and our home. Marcel, her husband, was a municipal policeman who was our bodyguard and driver for TK. What a wonderful family, the Dinis. The other female pup we gave to our cook, Madame Folcheri.

I have to say the Dini family has been my most trusted allies, even to this day. I love them dearly and am indebted to them for the rest of my life and after. They and their three children were family to TK and me. I don't know what I would have done without their loyalty and dedicated work throughout those great years and eventually, the tragic ones.

I was feeling pretty well after the first three months and slowly accepted some important invitations. I saw the doctor regularly in France and at five months had an ultrasound to find out the sex. The doctor didn't want to say the results in front of Jacques because he thought Jacques wanted a boy. So he whispered in my ear, "It's a rose." I was so thrilled because that's what I wished for at The Wall. It works.

Feeling well enough at five months I inaugurated the TGV, France's new high speed bullet train, sending it off on its speedy way. It left Paris, stopped in Nice, and then went on to other larger cities on the southern route. I got to ride with the engineer and helped him navigate ha ha, for a few miles to where Daniel was waiting to pick me up. There were funny press photos of me holding my belly and climbing on the train. The TGV became so popular it was heralded as the train that saved French railways.

CHAPTER 55

WHEN I DISCOVERED WE WERE PREGNANT, Jacques and I decided to deliver our child in Los Angeles because we wanted her born on American soil. This was very important to us because the United States was the best country at the time. It was so important I was able to convince Dr. Mel to come out of retirement to deliver our baby. Doctor Melvin Ehrenhalt became my first personal gynecologist when I was 19 years old. He remained my dear friend and confidant as well as my medical professional until he passed away in his 70's.

So at around three months pregnant I was feeling pretty good to return to L.A. with Jacques to make arrangements with Mel. It was also nearing Christmas 1981, so we were able to spend a nice vacation in Los Angeles, as usual. That was when things began to get a bit...interesting.

My first husband, Bert, had one brother Dennis. They weren't close, but when Bert and I were about to be married I wanted to meet Dennis and his wife Joyce. We drove to their home in the San Fernando Valley and rang the bell. Dennis and Joyce opened the door and from that moment on we became the best of friends.

Since I had time in L.A. waiting for my daughter to be born, I called Dennis. "Let's get together ASAP," he said.

It would be good to see my "DDDD," as I called Dennis. All we had to do was look at one another and we fell into hysterical laughter. Joyce and I were confidantes and the three of us were together all the time. They loved my stories. I used to be a voracious eater. Not kidding. When they knew I was coming over, they'd hide food in their back refrigerator to have something to eat after I left. I didn't know about this at the time, but found out their strategy later. Lol.

Before I was married to Jacques, I started collecting jewelry at the age of 21. I believed it was a better investment than buying clothes—not that I wasn't into clothes also. I was a model and enjoyed different styles of leading fashion designers. My personal style was sportier, but I could get into something elegant for the right occasion.

I was collecting jewelry both for my own pleasure as well as an investment. I'd bring over a fishing tackle box full of my new acquisitions for Joyce to try on. I immersed myself in the study of stones, becoming a virtual gemologist without going to gemology school. I would explain in detail each piece on her wrist, finger or neck. We constantly had fun together looking at the rocks and sharing girlie secrets.

She confided in me and knew our secrets were safe forever. This was all before my return to L.A. to deliver my daughter. My darling Joyce had diabetes from birth and tragically started to decline at an early age. She passed away in 1981 at forty-two years of age, only a year before "the baby" was born. Joyce's passing was a terrible loss for all of us and left a huge void in our lives.

Dennis fell apart following Joyce's death. His whole life and existence changed. I could hardly bear the sadness of losing my best confidante. She and I were so close. Dennis and I had our separate relationship, the three of us had our relationship and even when Bert was with us it was still just the three of us. We were quite a trio. And now she was gone.

Tying the history with my friends combined with my return to L.A. created the following story. Dennis became friendly with Jack Feinberg, a bona fide "wild and crazy guy." Jack was a whirling dervish, but he got Dennis out of the house and kept him from completely going under after losing Joyce.

The plot thickens. Jack Feinberg had a younger brother, Donald. Dennis wanted me to meet Jack and said they were coming over to my home on Benedict Canyon. They happened to show up when Jacques was still at the supermarket. The doorbell rang and I went to open the front door. Jack took a long, lascivious look at me from top to toes and then asked me to show him around the house. The staircase had green carpet with a white stripe going up the middle.

As he followed me up the stairs he made a snorting sound, "I'll follow the coke trail," referring to the white stripe. As I mentioned, Jack was wild and quite knowledgeable regarding drugs. His coke trail comment I thought was kind of clever.

I started to show him the master bedroom. He came up behind me and said, "I want to fuck you." I turned to him and said, "How dare you! I'm madly in love with my husband and I'm going to have his child!" Without missing a beat he said, "If I can't have you I know my brother can." Then he added, "As a matter of fact, he's a model and is leaving at midnight tonight for Paris. I'm calling him now."

I went downstairs fuming. Jack called to tell his brother to get his ass over there to meet the Countess ASAP. If only he hadn't picked up the phone. Donald told him he didn't care who I was and was playing basketball with his best friend. Jack said to him, "Get over here now, no excuses." Donald relented and drove over. I had no make-up on and was wearing a Laura Ashley maternity dress. Not the most alluring presentation, you would think, but it must have been enough. I opened the door and bingo. There he was. OMG.

Donald looked at me and said, "What do I do meeting a Countess? Do I bow or kiss your hand?"

Jack was attractive like James Caan, the actor, but his baby brother was something else. I looked at this gorgeous creature standing in front of me and said, "Anything you want." He was 6'1" with black hair, dark brown eyes, a fantastic body and a handsome face.

Now, I loved my husband beyond. I didn't know that meeting Don would change both of our lives forever. His for the better, but mine not so much.

As we stood in the doorway, Dennis snapped a photo of us. After the photo was developed, we looked like a couple that had always been together although we had just met. Jacques came back from the market and hugged Dennis and shook Jack and Donald's hands. Jack told Jacques that Don was leaving that evening for Paris on a modeling job. So Jacques, always the man with a big gesture, invited him to Nice. He thought Don was gay for some reason, but of course he wasn't. It would have been better for me if he had been.

I knew that it was not a good idea to invite him to our home or for me to see him again. Boy, was I right. However, I couldn't seem to stop the forward motion. Sometimes, things are just meant to be.

We said our goodbyes in L.A. and as soon as Don arrived in Paris, he called me. Jacques and I were getting ready to return to Nice. I wasn't expecting him to call, so when I heard Don's voice on the phone I was surprised. He told me he couldn't stop thinking about me. Unfortunately, I told him I was thinking of him too. When I met Jacques, I only had eyes for him and never ever in my wildest dreams could have imagined being attracted to another male. And yet, here was this feeling.

I knew the phone call was costly, so I called him back. I told him when we were arriving in Nice and would call him to see if he needed anything once we were there. After we got home, I was told there were numerous messages from Don. I admit that made me happy, but of course I knew it was dangerous too.

Once I had settled in, I called him and said; "I told you I'd call you when we were home. Are you alright?" He answered, "Not really." Don and I talked for a while. He told me already he wasn't happy being away from the States and didn't care for Paris, was homesick, and missed me.... and asked, "Could I fly to Nice, the next weekend?" Remember, Don had met me only once for a few hours and, yet, he was missing me. Since Jacques had invited him to come visit anytime if he needed to relax and see the Côte d'Azur, hesitatingly, I said, "yes."

Jacques had one of his secretaries make the arrangements for Don to fly to Nice. It was going against my better judgment allowing this to take place, but knew I needed to see him again.

The next weekend I picked Don up at the airport in my official gray Citroën Limo. When he came off the tarmac, we hugged one another. The attraction could not be denied and both realized our mutual allure could only bring chaos. I was not ready to knowingly put myself in danger and believed my marriage was rock solid. Besides, I was pregnant.

After arriving at "Lou Soubran," the name of our villa on the summit of the street named after J's father, Jean Médecin, I showed Don to his room. It was on the opposite side of the stairway from my bedroom. There were seventeen bedrooms in total, but we had closed the downstairs. So he would be upstairs close, but not too close. I hoped Don's bedroom was far enough away from ours.

It might sound odd, but I thought it was best to keep him away from Nice and Jacques, so I took him on a tour of Cannes, Antibes and Monaco. We then crossed the nearby border to San Remo, Italy. I did a lot of shopping and eating (for two now) as usual when I often came to this adorable sea-side town because it was so conveniently close by. I'm not so sure Don was that interested in the food or the scenery because he was into me and I was, unfortunately, into him.

When I took him to Monaco, I introduced him to my Godmother, Baroness Ety d'Rémusat. She thought he was great, but told me to be very careful. Apparently it was more obvious than I realized. Merde! (French for shit!)

After a second trip with Don to Monaco, he returned to the States and kept calling me. Although our conversations went back and forth about what could and could not be, we were in touch on a daily basis.

When it was time for Jacques, Ernst, our houseman, and me to return to the U.S., I didn't let Don know because I knew it wouldn't be good for me to see him. I was going home to L.A. to have our baby. That was my only priority.

Nevertheless, unannounced and out of the blue, he showed up at our house, which made me really angry. Jacques was surprised by my reaction. He wanted to invite Don for dinner, but I said no. I went upstairs and disappeared into our bedroom.

Don left and Jacques came upstairs to talk with me. He said he knew what it was like to be a young boy in a foreign country and felt the same way when he was in Denmark studying for a year. Apparently, that was the reason Jacques was empathetic towards Don and felt he needed our support and continued to invite him wherever we were. The funny thing was Jacques truly thought Donald was gay. Not!

CHAPTER 56

I WAS SEVEN MONTHS INTO MY PREGNANCY AND time to return to L.A. to begin preparing for the delivery our baby girl on American soil. Dr. Mel had been caring for me for many years and I had total confidence in him. He decided to quit delivering newborns because he wanted to dedicate the rest of his practice to helping women with other medical issues, not to mention he was getting a little older and it started taking a toll on his health. Thankfully, he came out of retirement just for me to deliver our baby.

It was Jacques 54th birthday on May 5th and I gave him a party in a private room at Lawry's because he loved their prime rib. Afterwards, J had to fly home to take care of his city and left me in the care of our butler, Ernst. I was alone with my houseman and in some silly way felt abandoned. On the third night after Jacques' departure, I found myself dialing Don's number. I told him the reason why I was mad at him. He should have never come to the house without calling first. I didn't want him to keep after me because I couldn't deny the connection and knew it wouldn't end well for us. We somehow were connected on a level that really surprised me and I was alarmed.

I kept trying not to think about him, but my mind was drawing me back each time. While Jacques was back in Nice, Don stayed close to me. He drove me to my doctor appointments and did whatever else was necessary to help keep the household going. We would go out to dinner and people would tell us what a handsome couple we made and that our baby would be so beautiful. We fell into a routine that felt normal. Then one day Don came home with a stuffed life-sized cream-colored burlap horse. By its size and appearance it looked like it just came from a carousel, but was stuffed.

Did I say life size? It took up half the wall. Getting it in the bedroom was a challenge, but with Ernst's help they somehow managed.

I couldn't believe it. What was I going to tell Jacques? How would I explain this enormous full size horse in the house? I couldn't say Don had given it to me. That would signify too much about the depth and intensity of our relationship. I couldn't let Jacques know Don had been caring for me all the time I was in LA. I decided to cross that bridge later and attempted to put a lot of things out of my mind those days.

Jacques would call from France every night and we would talk for more than an hour. We'd talk about how much we missed each other and J would say he couldn't wait to come back for the birth. Don would try not to listen to our conversations. I was becoming terribly uncomfortable juggling my conflict with these two. I was so torn between my love for Jacques and the feelings I had for Don. I knew it wasn't a good situation to say the least, but one can't help the way one feels. Jacques was absent physically to take care of me, but Donald was. As anticipated, the day came when Jacques returned to L.A. for the birth of our daughter. Of course, Don went back home. I ended up telling J the horse was for our baby, a grand gift from Don's entire family.

I was so excited to see Jacques and hoped his presence would over-shadow the past two months. We talked and kissed and talked. He went to take a shower as I sat on top of our bed trying to relax. A wave of loneliness swept over me, and my fingers went straight to dial Don's number.

He answered right away and professed, "I miss you!" I was shocked to realize I felt that way too and started to tear up. He was so happy to hear my response and said he'd been in his backyard crying. I was emotionally in a tailspin and knew this was the trouble I was so desperately trying to avoid.

We talked for a moment more and then I heard Jacques returning from the shower and slammed down the phone. I smiled up brightly at Jacques as he approached me on the bed hoping he wouldn't see the tears in my eyes. Oh, my life.

CHAPTER 57

TWO DAYS LATER I WENT INTO LABOR AND called Mom to meet us at Cedars-Sinai Hospital. I was in labor for seventeen-and-a-half hours before finally having an emergency C-section because the cord was wrapped around the baby's neck and I wasn't dilating. It had to be done quickly. There was a real risk to my baby.

Jacques told me what he said to Dr. Mel… "If something is wrong with the baby, don't let her live." He was a tough man who had been through war, conflict, had witnessed mutilations and death on a monumental scale. He believed he was being realistic. I was so scared and prayed and prayed she would be healthy with all her limbs.

When she arrived, I asked Dr. Mel, "Is she OK, and does she have all of her fingers and toes?" He assured me that she was a beautiful, healthy baby girl. I was beyond grateful and told him to put me to sleep at once. I slept for fourteen hours.

I awoke to find many flower arrangements in my room and then they brought me Shawn Joy Erin Ashley Heather Kirsten Magna Médecin. The many names were a tradition from Jacques' ancestors, the Medici of Florence. I chose the first six names and he chose Magna, named after Magna d'Medici. I must say she looked just like Dad sans the mustache and the Montecristo No 1 cigar hanging from her mouth. Most certainly, she was a Médecin. I fell in love at once with this wonderful creation and to this day she is and will always be the best part of me. I have always called her TK (The Kid)—it's much easier than all those other monikers.

After Jacques left the hospital, I felt the urge to call Don. I called and told him everything went well and Shawn was healthy and beautiful. (Shawn is Don's favorite name of her many.) He said he wanted to come over at once. Visiting hours were finished for the night and only family members could come to see me if I felt up to it. I called the nurse and said my brother wasn't able to make it earlier and asked if could he come now. She said it would be OK if he didn't stay too long. Don, being my brother, ha, ha, rushed to the hospital at once. We were so happy to see each other. He went to the window of the nursery to take a peek at Shawn. He'd been with me the last important months of the pregnancy and she was finally here. We were both quite emotional. I hated the conflict of this double life and double feeling. Did I feel guilty? I felt scared more than guilty.

I stayed in the hospital for four days. As Jacques, TK, and I were leaving, the American and international paparazzi were in front of the hospital entrance snapping photos. I wanted to hide and just go home to the house we built off Benedict Canyon. Eventually, we were going to build another home in L.A. for Jacques' retirement. This one was temporary, but extremely comfy and would do for our baby's first home. Jacques told me he'd stay as long as he could, but had to get back to Nice because it was hard ruling from afar for too long. I would be left with Ernst and a baby nurse. When TK was ready to travel, he'd come back to escort us home.

Before Jacques left, we went to get her passport. As they were taking the photo, TK decided to throw up all over me. Oh well, my new American citizen marked her home territory with a bang all over my white sweater.

Jacques and I said our goodbyes. He had been with us for six weeks and had to get back to Nice. With Jacques gone, Don returned. We fell back into the same routine. We were becoming more and more attached. He was fabulous with The Kid and even Ernst had become attached to him. We were happy except for the fact that I would be going home to Nice soon and once again, everything would change. As usual, Jacques and I talked every night on the phone. The double feeling, the double life. It was tearing me apart and kept becoming more and more intense.

TK would be three and a half months old before Jacques returned to L.A. to escort us back to Nice. I wanted her to be born on American soil and made sure it happened. In those days, the U.S. wouldn't accept dual citizenship like they did in France. I felt it was important for her to be an American. France would issue her a passport anyway, but she was an American by birth, period.

CHAPTER 58

THINGS STARTED SHIFTING IN A NEGATIVE WAY after giving birth to our daughter. Jacques seemed to suddenly have a Madonna complex with me now that I was the mother of his child. A woman who was a shrine, an almost holy shrine—that was the Madonna complex, a carryover from his Catholic childhood. There was a certain new respect in his attitude towards me that was not entirely a bad thing, but there was also jealousy and resentment because he wasn't the sole center of my world anymore as he had been. He should have understood my role was different now and I could be both wife and mother. He should have understood and embraced the fact I loved them both with my heart and soul. But he didn't. I know he felt neglected and left out and Jacques Médecin did not like being left out of anything. There would be a price to pay.

I was totally dedicated to "The Kid" during her first year. I wouldn't leave her, not even to go to Paris with Jacques for Parliament meetings. I skipped a lot of official events and functions. My time was committed to my child. We had a tanning bed in our bedroom and I'd place her on a blanket next to me (outside of the bed, of course) when I was tanning, keeping an eye on her every move and making sure she was always comfortable by feeling her mother was right by her side.

I hoped Jacques would realize how important it was for me to be a hands-on mother in the beginning stage of her precious life instead of handing her over to nannies and au pairs.

After her first year, I started traveling with Jacques again fulfilling my official duties and often bringing our baby along. I made sure she was with us as much as possible. I would never forget my baby. But I never forgot Jacques, either.

He never quite got over feeling jealous of my divided attention. Resentment was in his blood and he held grudges forever. I tried to make it up to J by focusing more on him, but everything I did was never enough. He felt that I had abandoned him. Even if he didn't believe that in his conscious mind (he may not have), he felt it in his heart. It was seething in his subconscious and was one of his several insecurities that contributed to the destruction of our bond and love.

It didn't happen immediately or in one moment, but the crack in the marriage was there and would expand. That would still be years away. There were good years, joyous years ahead for the most part, but the snake had slithered its way into our union and would not leave.

CHAPTER 59

ONE NIGHT JACQUES CALLED TO SAY HE'D WRITten me a letter that I would not like. I asked why? He told me, "Wait until you read it and we'll talk." Oh great, I thought. When the letter arrived, it was eight pages. I went into shock. I felt like an earthquake had shaken the security of the walls around me. He told me he knew he was not TK's father, but she had been conceived with Sheik Ahmed Baker during our second trip to Dubai. He wrote how much he loved me and said even though Shawn was not his, he would raise her as his own.

My head was spinning. I called and told him what he said to me was like putting a knife in my stomach. I screamed at him, "You're insane!" Max, his protector (and alleged hitman), had heard a rumor that our daughter was not his and informed Jacques. I told him it was blasphemy and I would never forgive him or Max. He knew I would never have a child with anyone but him. The fact he could even consider writing something so horrible after giving birth to his baby would change my opinion of him forever. (And it did.)

I slammed down the phone. My mind was seething and my insides were screaming in agony from this betrayal. Other than my father and Papa Sam, I'd never trusted a man before.

At that point, I wanted to leave him. However in the beginning of our relationship, he let me know if I ever left him, he would kill me. I thought it was romantic at the time and he was kidding. But now, I knew he wasn't kidding. I had lived with the man long enough to realize what he was capable of.

So I was rightfully scared, and now that we had a child together I realized it was definitely for the long haul. Even though we might stay together, my feelings for him would never be the same from that point on. That was the beginning of the demise of our marriage. Naturally, as hurt and angry as I was, I turned to Don and we became even closer.

I had learned in the early days of our relationship how jealous, suspicious and obsessed Jacques was when other men even glanced at me. In his mind, he would fabricate delusions and accuse me of wanting to be with younger men or thinking I was having an affair. His temper would escalate to a frightening frenzy, like the time in Cannes when we were at dinner with d'Villier and he went crazy about a man who had been across the street—a man I hadn't even noticed.

It didn't happen that often in the first few years, but it worsened as he grew older. His brain consumed with insane jealousy was the reason he imagined the sheik had contributed the sperm that led to our baby. There had to be a doubt in his mind or he probably would have done me in. His Niçois Mafia was capable of murder and would have done it if he so requested. Our life together would never be as it had been.

His insecurity was shocking. He knew how much I loved him, but it wasn't enough. I think the accusation about Ahmed Baker was just a reaction because in the back of his mind Donald was in the picture. That's my opinion.

Jacques' insane jealously eventually caused me to respond in a way that protected my own sanity, and that was to really enjoy what I was being accused of.

Don and I were calling from all over the world wherever I was and seeing one another whenever I was in L.A. He told me if I didn't leave Jacques, he would start seeing one of his co-stars on *Days of Our Lives*. (By this time, Donald had become a successful actor and landed a long-term role on the daytime soap. You may have seen him—his stage name is Don Diamont.) I pondered, could I leave Jacques to be with Don? It actually did not take me long to answer the question in my head. No, I knew I couldn't. It was impossible.

Sadly, Don would be with someone else while I was away from him. He was honest about it and I didn't have the right to say otherwise. Our relationship continued for many years. Although the timing was never right, the feelings were deep and genuine. By the time you read this book, Don and I will have known each other for more than forty years. We both have our respective families now and I'm happy Don found Cindy to share the rest of his journey with. He recently published a book and wrote his version of our relationship. It's always interesting to hear two sides of the same story from different points of view.

CHAPTER 60

BEFORE TK WAS BORN, JACQUES AND I HAD explored the subject of religion together. He had been raised Catholic and I was a religious rebel. As far as I was concerned, organized religion was responsible for wars, discrimination and bloodshed. I thought people should worship who and what they believed in while respecting the choices of others. Unfortunately, that has never been the reality of the world's cultures because in real life that's not how it works. Organized religion has been fighting and persecuting people since the beginning of time which has been the norm throughout history.

Sadly, that's still the way it is today. The Catholic Church would not marry us because we both had been divorced and the priest told me I would have to study for two years to become Catholic if we wanted our daughter to be baptized.

Jacques had quit the Church when he was younger, so the authorities were not very accommodating. I didn't like their attitude regarding him or me. Alternatively, I went to see the reverend at the British Anglican Church in Nice. He was warm, nice and welcoming. I explained it was a tradition in Jacques' family to have their children baptized. He was understanding and said he would be very pleased to help.

He only asked that I have a few sessions with him to talk about my life and personal philosophy. I was glad to oblige and immensely enjoyed our time together. Any time I can experience a positive enlightenment is a gift.

Later, I was baptized in the Anglican Church in a private ceremony with my Godmother in attendance, the Baroness Ety d'Rémusat, who I mentioned earlier. She was a good friend and a wise woman. Eventually, I moved beyond Christianity and all western religions to find my spiritual comfort in India with the Hindu tradition and especially with my special elephant god, Ganesh. I will share more about my relationship with him later.

We had a christening for our child even if the Catholic Church said we couldn't. It was at the British Anglican Church in Nice and was quite lovely, except…

The Church was packed, everyone was there and TK did not stop crying the entire time. Of course everybody thought she was just adorable, even crying. SERIOUSLY? Well, she was adorable, yes, but not so much in the noise department. I was getting used to the accolades because no one would dare say the opposite to me.

I knew the truth. She was a sweet baby, but she made a lot of noise. I was getting a good education with a dual major, in both how to raise a child and the wicked ways of politics.

Coming out on the other side of politics with my life barely intact, I can attest it's the most controlling, hypocritical, soulless, unkind, selfish bullshit business one can experience. You go all in being idealistic, but after dealing with grasping, greedy, demanding humans 24/7, you see how unrealistic your ideals were. I may have said this once before, but I'll repeat myself again, the reality of politics is horrific.

BOOK FOUR

A Slippery Slope

CHAPTER 61

THE PARTY LIFE NEVER CEASED. OUR SOCIAL TIME was consumed by business dealings, political events, and constant diplomacy. Whatever the gathering, it led us to some strange places.

Jacques and I were invited to many dinners with donors who had contributed large amounts of money to his campaigns. They gave and we gratefully accepted. I remember one time in Paris in particular...

We flew to Paris for a fundraising soiree given in our honor. A big limo met us at De Gaulle Airport and we were whisked away to the party. Upon entering the home, we were escorted up to the grand dining room. There were forty-eight guests already seated at a very long formal table. We were a bit late, but they were having cocktails waiting for our arrival to commence the evening. We were guided to our seats by a butler who swept my chair back and pushed me gently towards the table.

The meal was fabulous. It might have come straight off the menu from a 3-star Michelin restaurant. The host and hostess, who must remain nameless for my protection, sat at opposite ends of this enormous table. They got up frequently, gliding around the room to mingle and chat, being the social butterflies and center of attention.

They were impeccably dressed for their moment in the spotlight. The husband wore an Armani tuxedo with a black tie. The wife had on a gorgeous haute couture gown. The dress, cut intriguingly low in the front, was floor length in sapphire blue chiffon with a slit on the right side of the skirt.

We dined sumptuously on seven courses, each one better and more extravagant than the last. I won't bother to describe it because the food was not the final "taste" of the night. The tarte tatin was not the real dessert. There was one more surprise yet to come.

At times during dinner, there was odd laughter between the hosts and a guest as if they were sharing a private joke or laughing at something that couldn't quite be spoken out loud. They would erupt in sudden, crackling laughter and then would consciously quiet down. Some naughty secret had been shared. The host and hostess excused themselves and left the dining room. I didn't think too much about it, but maybe I should have…

We were all quite satiated. Just before dessert was served, a butler appeared and rang a tiny bell. He announced we were to follow him to another reception room after we had finished.

As soon as the waiters cleared the dessert dishes, two butlers appeared and led us down a long hallway to another room where they opened two large double carved wooden doors.

Holy merde! Surprise is not the word; absolutely shocking might be better and we were the guests of honor! There, on a huge bed in the middle of the room, with brass posts reaching towards a black painted ceiling were our two hosts, husband and wife.

The husband was standing on the bed and had handcuffed his wife to the brass bedposts. He was whipping her with a blacksnake whip. They were quite naked. The gorgeous gown had disappeared and the snappy tuxedo had vanished. Underwear and intimate apparel were no longer necessary either.

To my surprise, the other diners were not alarmed. *Hmmmm* sounds and deep grunts began emerging from the crowd. People were swaying on their feet, amazed, mesmerized, and obviously approving. The *hmms* seemed to coincide with each pop of the whip on the wife's hindquarters. There was a kind of rhythm going on and the lady was smiling through clenched teeth. Her hubby, standing behind her was sweating and grinning.

The rest of the crowd started stripping and doing things to each other that were equally kinky and weird. Everyone wanted to participate in the action. They tore off their expensive garments as quickly as possible and everybody was naked and raw except for Jacques and me. People were too busy to notice that Jacques and I were standing there with clothes on observing. Was there fine print on the invitation that we missed?

There were more whips and articles made of leather, glass and metal hanging from the wall. Everyone seemed to know exactly which instrument to use for each purpose. I guess you could say in some strange way, it was rather fascinating to watch people this obsessed and focused. We agreed at that point it was definitely time to leave. Jacques understood what I was feeling, grabbed my hand and angrily muttered, "We're out of here!"

He said he couldn't believe what had just happened and was totally unaware of the private or not so private sexual habits of this couple until now. Unnoticed, we hurriedly left the room, ran out the door and hailed a taxi.

It was a bizarre night, but it wouldn't be our last. I had entered a strange realm, a world sometimes engaging and entertaining, sometimes shocking and appalling, sometimes wonderful, but always over the top.

CHAPTER 62

THE ITALIAN FILM FESTIVAL WAS ONE OF THOSE
"official duties" that was always a pleasure. While the festival was
traditionally held in Italy, the festival board had chosen Nice to sponsor and
host the event for several years.

We also collaborated with the nearby Cannes Film Festival. Due to our
close proximity to Italy, Jacques' view of supporting music and film in both
countries would result in more visitors and revenue for Nice.

There were famous names (mostly foreign actors) attending, who I
was happy to meet. When learning I would be escorting Jeanne Moreau to
the festival, I was especially thrilled and really looking forward to meeting
her. She was one of France's most accomplished actresses and Orson Welles
called her the greatest actress in the world. She was alluring. I first discovered
her in 1976 when she narrated *Lumière*, which had been released in the U.S.
Years later, she starred in *The Lovers*, which was my favorite film she made.
When I told my friends I was to escort her around the festival, they said, "Be
careful." Of course, I asked them why.

Odette, my outspoken buddy said, "Moreau is not fond of women and
may be abrasive with you." After this advice, I decided to welcome her with
flattering words. My driver and I picked her up from the Intercontinental
Carlton. Jeanne was so tiny, being 5'3" to my 5'9." After she stepped into the
limo, I greeted her with flowers and complimented her as the first French
actress I fell in love with. She immediately replied she was thrilled to meet

me and appreciated the great compliment I gave her. Madame Moreau wasn't abrasive at all. She was gracious and charming. There is a secret at the end of this chapter I'm going to share with you that I have never told anyone before. One of those little life-doors that swings open for an instant and then swings shut again before you can decide whether to enter or not. You are then left wondering what might have been.

The following day we arrived at the Negresco Hotel for lunch. Our famous two-star Michelin chef, Jacques Maximin was in charge. He was told to keep a special eye on us. The food was superb.

We had the most interesting conversation about recognition and fame, and how one can become the other. She asked what it was like for me to be the second American woman to hold a position of power on the Riviera. (Princess Grace, who preceded me, was the first and was certainly better known than myself.) We discussed philosophy and shared our positions on some personal issues. I found her warm, intelligent and caring. This was certainly not what I had expected. I really liked this woman.

She lived by her maxims and she shared my favorite quote from Anais Nin: *"Age does not protect you from love. But, love to some extent, protects you from age."*

The awards ceremony was that night. I promptly picked her up and escorted her into the hall with my bodyguard discreetly trailing behind us. The paparazzi were out in droves snapping photos of the fabulous collection of Italian, French and other international stars who were in attendance. We mingled in the foyer with many of the nominees before the awards ceremony began. Everyone wanted to meet Moreau and everyone was deferential to her. She was the queen of the event, but reigned over it in a quiet unassuming way. I was introduced as her friend, Madame Ilene Médecin, First Lady of Nice. We chatted casually with some of the most famous Italian film personalities in the world. I met a dazzling array of film legends—Marcello Mastroianni, Sophia Loren, Claudia Cardinale, Giancarlo Giannini, Vittorio Gassman,

Ugo Tognazzi and others. It was considered to be the greatest gathering of Italian actors and actresses of all time.

Everyone was dressed in sparkling, colorful long gowns and sharp black tuxes. The atmosphere was heavy with the burden of anticipation waiting for the announcements. Outside the entrance of the grand room there were dozens of strings of Tivoli lights and flags representing the actors' home countries. That was the extent of the decorations. The entry and interior of the auditorium were unadorned. It wasn't like the Academy Awards in L.A. The festival planners had decided the stars themselves were the main décor and the visual splendor. They were correct in their judgement and I congratulated the organizers of the festival on their wise taste.

After the ceremonies, Jeanne and I sat in the car and talked. She invited me to visit and stay with her in Paris. I told her I would love to. She took my hand and kissed me gently on the lips. I was taken aback and surprised, but not offended. I wondered how that would play out when I visited her.

Unfortunately, when I was able to travel to Paris, she was out of town. We spoke on the phone a few times and tried to get together, but it never happened. I was just happy to have had the opportunity to connect with her and have a meaningful encounter. One never knows.

CHAPTER 63

IN 1981 WHEN MITTERRAND WAS ELECTED
President, the Socialist Party came to power and took control of the central government. A decree was passed allowing the former palaces of Napoleon to be designated as the official residences of the Regional Presidents in France. Of course, they expected THEIR people would be inhabiting those magnificent structures, although, not in every case...

Jacques was conservative and no friend of the new central government. If the Socialists intended to put the Regional Presidents into Napoleon's old palaces, then Jacques Médecin, Mayor of Nice and President of the Côte d'Azur, would move into the Napoleonic residence in Nice, aka the Préfecture.

We refurbished four floors, which took five months for the design and construction. The Socialists were not pleased because they wanted their own people to occupy these Presidential Palaces. These palaces were summer homes built for Napoleon as his official dwellings when he visited the various regions.

Life became even more interesting. We were in the old city now and the apartments across the street were a stones throw away. My driver, Daniel, would pick me up every morning to start our heavy schedule and escort me into the official limo. Our wonderful Niçois neighbors would wait at their windows for my morning departure, many being curious how I was dressed for the day. They would wave and greet me as I came down the stairs and shout out their compliments.

"Madame Médecin, you look great in lavender."

"We love your Chanel ivory suit."

"You are stunning in your black cocktail dress."

They even clapped at times, giving their sign of approval.

I waved and blew kisses of appreciation because my Niçois neighbors started my day with such adoration and positive support.

Frankly, do you think I ever got a negative comment to my face? I think not. No one was that brave. Ha ha. Even the street people loved me. There was the poor neighborhood bum who would wait down the block telling everyone what good friends we were and pontificating about who I was, what I wore and how nice I was. I would wave to him and smile. I'm glad he thought we were buddies. Everyone votes.

One morning Daniel escorted me out the door and then pushed me in the car rather aggressively. He was trying to shield me, but it was too late. There was a man with balls the size of cantaloupes protruding from his Speedo bathing suit, standing in the street. I was so shocked to see this I couldn't even speak. That was a first! He was strutting his stuff with no embarrassment. Talk about no inhibitions. Vive la France! That had to be some medical condition.

TK was three years old when we moved into the Préfecture. It was on a narrow street with high walls and shuttered windows. Although it was a palace (Napoleon didn't live in any hovels), we were right in the middle of a real Niçois community with our neighbors hanging out of windows from across the street. It was quite unique and I actually liked living in a regal historic abode, and still close to the people…to the working, thriving, throbbing heart of the city.

CHAPTER 64

T K STARTED SCHOOL AT AGE FIVE. MARCEL DINI, Lilou's husband, was our police guard at the Préfecture. His other duty was personal protection for TK and would drive her from school when I was unavailable. I would usually pick her up at least twice a week in between my civic duties.

She was such a good girl I would take her to the local toy store, Contesso, at least once a week after school and let her choose a toy or two. TK would say, "Mommy, you don't have to buy me anything. I don't deserve it." I told her she was such a sweet girl it was my pleasure, but if she really didn't want a gift I would absolutely not force her. I was so touched by her sensitivity.

This little waif of five years old was never affected by her unique surroundings. It never went to her head at all. She's the same today at 40. She amazes me in so many ways. How logical she is, how wise she is regarding very deep issues. My TK is the most real, down to earth, simple, loving, sensitive human being. It's all the more amazing considering everything she's been through. I am so proud to be her mother. TK's goodness always blows me away. My little Vi-Countess. We're definitely a team.

Only she and I know the truth about the dangers and perilous obstacles we faced when we escaped France to live in political exile in Punta del Este, Uruguay. Only the two of us know how terrible the struggle was to be reunited and restore our lives to a place of balance and safety. I will elaborate more later.

Things were not going smoothly on the home front. I had to end the relationship with Don Diamont. It was sad because I told him it was impossible for us to be together since I could never divorce Jacques. All the while, Jacques' insane jealousy was increasing and his behavior was unwarranted.

I decided to escape from a few of my duties and took up skiing. It would be a healthy diversion, which would keep me somewhat composed while mixing in some playtime with my busy work schedule. Ergo, skiing. Little did I know one pleasure would lead to another that would lead to trouble, which seems to be the story of my life. It would begin with innocent fun and then crash into reality.

I started skiing with my girlfriends in France, Italy, Austria and Switzerland. Ety, my Godmother, who had moved to Monaco from Nice, had called to tell me there was an issue with her boyfriend and her husband (she definitely had both). She needed to get away and get her head together. "How about skiing?" I suggested. Of course, it didn't turn out to be just skiing. You will see what I mean.

Her husband knew of the boyfriend and it was a complicated situation. Both "friend" and hubby were much older. Ety's friend had no family or anyone he was close to except her.

He was very wealthy and told Ety he would leave his fortune to her if she would divorce her husband, Roger, and take care of him until he passed. So, that's exactly what she did (with her husband's blessing). French culture is definitely different; especially when it comes to the many rampant affairs in their culture that sometime last as long as their marriages. They are much more liberal in that regard and don't have the same sexual hang-ups as Americans.

There were still details and some fine-tuning of Ety's agreement that had to be negotiated and she just wanted to get away from it all for a while to get a clear perspective. I thought it was a great idea for her to clear head with some fresh mountain air.

Ety always loved her husband and in the end went back to him (after her friend had passed), and she did inherit all of his estate.

I admired her for how she lived her privileged life. Her passion drove her instinct and motivations. We had similar sensitivities and despite the disaster, loss and pain I've experienced, I'm too passionate about life to ever give up. I've learned to live every moment for the moment just like my Godmother.

This was the Baroness Ety, my God Mom. She was 5'6" with curly shoulder length light brown hair and in great physical shape. She always dressed to the nines and had panache. Even though some French women may not have the best physical attributes, they possess an amazing ability to put themselves together with an ultra-attractive flair. Their presentation exudes an air of confidence that is definitely appealing to the opposite sex. She was a handsome woman and as straightforward as they come. She told me I was the daughter she never had and treated me accordingly. One of her three sons, Louis-Charles, was gay and a real entitled snot who wasn't pleased when he found out his mother wanted to leave me a piece of her jewelry when the time came. Unfortunately, she ended up developing dementia and I'm sure he wouldn't remind her of her promise.

As for skiing, we decided to go to a quaint resort in Italy. We drove with my bodyguard Daniel, in and out of France, Italy, France, Italy, France and finally stopped in Italy. It was a winding twisted road and one became quite an international tourist just by driving 50 miles back and forth between countries weaving in and out by crossing the border so many times. I was hoping I'd clear my head as well and just have fun on our short excursion. However, it became one more major, crazy, momentous, life-changing event hitting me in the face like a ton of bricks.

All arrangements for our excursion had been made in advance in Nice. Upon our arrival at the resort, the owner greeted our party and escorted us to a cordoned-off area in the corner of an enormous cafeteria. I was observing people entering the restaurant and whispered to Ety, "What happened to all the handsome Italian men?"

Two minutes later my wish or thought was granted. A tanned man in a one-piece black ski suit, black hair with gray sideburns and sunglasses hanging from one ear, dangling against his cheek was standing at the commissary entrance. It was an odd position for the sunglasses, but somehow attractive and sexy. Just one of his quirky habits I came to know very well.

He drifted across the room. I liked the way he moved…languorously, easily, and smoothly, but with definite charm. Very Italian. He found his friends at a table near the rope dividing our section from the public one and sat down facing my way. He deliberately turned his chair around so he would be facing in my direction.

I said to Ety, "Turn your head and look at that good looking man."

She spun around to view him. I could see the approval on her face. "Oh yes," she said, "He's staring and can't take his eyes off you. Can't you see?"

I laughed at that.

We went on talking, but kept looking at the man out of the corner of our eyes. He ate a quick something, stood up, said goodbye to his friends and left.

I looked at Ety and said, "You must be wrong. He wasn't looking at me because he's gone." We finished eating and the owner asked if I wanted to ride with him in his new snowcat to the top of the mountain. We'd all ski down from there. I said sure, got up and headed for the door. I was surprised to see who was standing there.

The sexy man in black was waiting for me. He started speaking in Italian as we got closer. I shook my head and answered in French. He switched effortlessly to French and said he'd been admiring me from the moment he saw me in the cafeteria. He said his name was Alvio Ferretti and lived in Genoa. I stopped to chat. I would give him that much, but kept it within bounds. I told him my first name only. He asked if I would ski with him. I said I would meet him at the top of the slope because I was being driven up in the snowcat. I added I might not be able to keep up with him as he was most likely a very good skier, and I was a B minus skier. (Maybe, a B, lol.)

It turned out he really was not just a good skier, but a great one who had trained for the Olympics many years before as a young boy.

He looked at me curiously when I mentioned the snowcat, but didn't ask any questions. He said not to worry about keeping up with him and I would be fine.

We got to the top of the mountain and I jumped out looking for Alvio. He was waiting for me below the first run. I caught up and we began winding our way down together.

Daniel and Ety kept their distance behind us. They were giving me space. I skied better than I thought and kept up pretty well. I knew he was being kind by not speeding straight down the mountain. He would stop and wait for me, looking back patiently until I reached him.

Alvio was definitely a champ. It was a pleasure watching him in perfect form, artistically carving his edges through the turns. When we got to the bottom, he smiled, thanked me for skiing with him and said goodbye. I thought that was curious and figured OK. Well, at least I skied better than I thought.

I quickly put Alvio out of my mind and didn't expect to see him again.

CHAPTER 65

THAT EVENING, ETY, DANIEL AND I WENT TO HAVE a drink at a popular bar in the village. My doctor friend was driving from Nice to join us for dinner that night and ski the next day. We ordered drinks ahead of his arrival and I ordered my usual Perrier with ice and lime. We were talking away when Ety leaned close to me and whispered, "He's back."

And there he was. At the bar sat Alvio, with his glasses set at that same odd angle hanging from his ear in that provocative manner. Was it a dare or an assertion? I wasn't quite sure what it was, but nevertheless I liked it. Foolish me, I always favored bold, daring, mysterious men and was definitely attracted to tantalizing gestures.

Again, he was gazing at me from across the room with those piercing dark eyes. They were unrelenting as they bore into mine. His eyes seemed mysterious even for a romantic Italian type. His facial expression did not change or subside, not giving an inch.

I stared back at him before I began to laugh. He kept right on looking at me without flinching. I got up to go to the ladies' room and thought this is too bizarre.

I came back from the loo. We were due at a restaurant up the street and walked towards the exit where Alvio was lounging against the wall. He still hadn't taken his eyes off me. I looked at him and he said, "Buona sera, bellissima," meaning "Good evening, beautiful."

I smiled in return and said good evening in Italian. He stepped back and let me pass. I thought for a moment he might touch me as I went by, but no, it just felt like he had. Some sensation from him, some sense of him had swept over me. I felt his aura and found it intriguing.

We left him behind at the bar. I wondered if I would see him again because he obviously made an impression on me. It was an odd sort of flirtation, momentary and fleeting. Would that be it? Just straining eyeballs across a crowded room?

We left and walked up the street to the restaurant. My friend, Dr. Costa, was waiting for us there. We wanted to ski early, so I intended to get to bed a little sooner than usual. We were going to ski as much as we could the following day, have a leisurely lunch and take off for Nice around 5 PM. We finished our dinner and walked back to the hotel.

I didn't sleep all that well. I remembered Alvios' eyes still boring into mine.

Well, who should be waiting for us on the mountain in the morning? Alvio, of course. He must have gotten up very early to meet me. A determined man. I like that.

He was immediately apologetic. His arrogance seemed to have softened a bit. I think he had an actual scare. Alvio said he had gone to every restaurant on the street looking for me last night but to no avail. He was beginning to despair that he would never find me, and I would escape him in the night with his life ruined forever. Italians love to exaggerate, but I admit liking it when they do. He said he finally reached the restaurant where we had dined only to discover we had departed just ten minutes prior. He then ran into the street looking for me without success. Apparently, he was determined to find me in the morning and that is exactly what Mr. Ferretti did.

He said the owner of the resort had approached him at breakfast to inform him who I was and warned he should stay away from me or there would be trouble. Alvio answered it was between him and me and no one else. It made him even more determined than ever to find me. He had some nerve this man. Jacques was well known on the Côte d'Azur as a man not to cross, so that took some balls and I definitely admire a man with huge cojones.

We all skied together that day. I had gained a little more confidence and it didn't take me as long to catch up with Alvio. Unfortunately, Dr. Costa had to leave early to attend to an emergency in Nice. Alvio asked me if my group would join him at a remote country family restaurant for lunch before we were to leave. I relayed the invitation to Daniel and Ety. Daniel gave me a very stern negative look. "No," he was saying. No!" Of course, Ety was all for it. We stayed on the slopes together until lunch.

As agreed, we met at the out-of-the way cozy restaurant. We walked into the dining room and sat in a corner. There was one couple there, surely not from Nice. Alvio said no one would recognize me. It was a family owned establishment with homemade pastas and generational Italian country recipes. The food was simple and delicious. We had a pleasant lunch chatting and laughing. Alvio was a great storyteller and conversationalist. Daniel kept staring at him as if he might pull a dagger out and stab the man. I ignored him. Then, Alvio took out his wallet and insisted on paying. Just before dessert, he grabbed me off my chair and pulled me onto his lap. Ety looked at us and winced. She said in shock, "You cannot do this here!" The walls have eyes and ears. Daniel scowled and gritted his teeth hard enough to break a tooth. He jumped onto his feet and exclaimed, "What happens if you're recognized?"

But there wasn't anyone here, well hardly anyone. Besides us, there was only one middle-aged couple seated across the room. No one else in the place. Although sometimes, that is enough.

Daniel was whispering desperately in my ear.

"Please take it outside," he was saying. "Now, now!"

Why? There were only two other living souls in a tiny restaurant on the backside of a mountain in Italy.

They were getting up and leaving anyway. See Daniel, nothing to worry about. The only watchful eyes were leaving. But, wait…not quite leaving. They were suddenly heading for our table, smiling.

They strolled up to greet me. The male half of the pair said, "Bonjour Madame Médecin, please give our regards to the Mayor." They left, grinning to themselves. Now, that's a coincidence. Merde! Two Niçois! Two of Jacque's voters in this out of the way country restaurant. Merde, again!

Alvio took my hand and led me outside under an open-air patio engulfed within a rustic wooden structure. The snow was sparkling like diamonds from the afternoon sun. He grabbed me, pulled me close and kissed me and kissed me and kissed me. It was passionate and magical. I hadn't felt that way since Donald.

When he finally realized I was American, we spoke both English and French. He spoke excellent English. We'd kiss and talk, kiss again and talk some more. We should have been freezing but weren't. We would gab in French to English with a little Italian thrown in. I assumed he was married. He had been, but was recently divorced under the new Italian law.

This was not good. Our playing field was not equal. He was single, and I was anything but. His business was in Genoa, owning one of the largest frozen food distributors in northern Italy. He said in the future we should meet in San Remo, which was halfway between Nice and Genoa.

Jacques and I were scheduled to go to South America for an upcoming political trip. I had too many obligations and didn't want to leave TK for three weeks. Plus, I had just met this man. My head was spinning and didn't know what to do. I found out soon enough it was a big mistake not going with Jacques on that specific trip because he would find something in Uruguay that was going to interest him. Jean Oltra, our press secretary, introduced him to a so-called journalist named Marisol Nicoletti and that was the beginning of true treachery. The future events might not have come to pass if I had been there with him. Everything would have been different—maybe, who knows.

CHAPTER 66

OH, I HAVE MADE MY MISTAKES. I'VE BEEN CARE-less, impatient and hasty. I've been naughty and been bad. I've thrown caution to the wind and then experienced the eye of the hurricane. This connection with Alvio was too amazing. I decided not to go with Jacques and made time in between my official duties to meet Alvio in San Remo, only 30 minutes from Nice.

Jacques left for South America without me. My explanation was I had very important appointments I couldn't get out of which seemed to satisfy him for the moment.

I knew I had to see Alvio again even if for nothing else then curiosity's sake. Here I was on the way to meet a man in Sam Remo I barely knew. Daniel was driving me. How many ways could this be unwise?

It had been a pleasant drive, but I was anxious and nervous. I didn't know what

Alvio looked like in civilian clothes. I'd only seen him in ski gear. Would I even recognize him?

We arrived and drove through the narrow streets and winding alleys that make up the old city. When we found the street Alvio had named, I abruptly told Daniel to pull over. I said, "Leave me and pick me up again at 10 PM." I thought his eyes would pop out of his head. I'm sure he imagined Jacques cutting out his tongue for this by leaving me alone with another man. He knew I was very firm and wouldn't budge. As I will explain in detail later, I had expected him to give in and guard my indiscretions since he pledged his unconditional loyalty to me after I told Jacques to get him out of jail.

He gritted his teeth and reluctantly said he would pick me up at 10. He didn't like it, but would do as I asked. Alvio and I would have a few hours to get to know one another better.

As we slowed down, there was Alvio leaning against a lamppost wearing beige trousers, a pale blue-and-white striped shirt, navy blazer, brown loafers with tassels and his famous black-rimmed glasses hanging from his ear. He was so Italian and incredibly chic. I had liked him before, but I liked him even more now. Alvio had been attractive in his ski gear with all that shiny black plastic, but he was more gorgeous now in this elegant, carefully crafted outfit just oozing sophistication, style and charm.

We'd made plans to meet on a back street not far from a little trattoria that Alvio knew. Leaving Daniel behind, Alvio grabbed my hand as we sauntered down the street to the cute little cafe. It was a small space with a dozen intimate tables and the aroma of wonderful homemade cuisine was mouth-watering.

We talked nonstop. Two hours flew by. There were two English women seated near us who were anxious to stop and say hello as they were leaving. One of the ladies said they couldn't take their eyes off such a romantic handsome couple who were so much in love. Alvio and I looked at each other and giggled. I wanted to tell them we'd just met, but didn't want to burst their bubble.

After our seductive meal, Alvio hailed a cab to his hotel room. I knew this was going to happen. I knew I was there to make love, but everything was moving quicker than I thought and couldn't quite wrap my head around it.

Unbeknownst to me, Daniel was supposed to never let me out of his sight. Regrettably, I learned that later. He had specific instructions to keep his prying eyes on me at all times. If I just went into a shop or a restaurant, he was supposed to be by my side. While I was a pampered bird in a gilded cage, I was still a prisoner. But this time, I was going to shake free of him to test my wings for a few hours. Daniel would not be happy with my plan, which I expected.

CHAPTER 67

I**T WAS A TINY BOUTIQUE HOTEL. HIS ROOM HAD** a seating area with a sofa and TV. Alvio pushed me gently onto the couch and started slowly caressing me. He said he wanted to take his time and did just that. He was methodical and after seven hours of steamy "interaction," it was time to leave. Was I a bit exhausted? Yes. Alvio was a superb lover and told me he studied sensual sex in China for two years. I was impressed with what he learned. Actually, it was the art of being completely still, allowing your sexual muscles to react on their own without any other bodily motions. I love being introduced to new experiences and this one was a skill I still enjoy today.

At 10 PM, Alvio safely escorted me to the corner where Daniel was waiting. We had made arrangements for me to return the following day. I met him as many times as I could until Jacques returned from his three-week official trip.

Alvio kept changing it up and getting better. Just when I thought we had reached the heights of ecstasy and delight, he would come up with something new.

Well, I can't tell you everything we did or describe every new invention of lust and desire because that would be a book in itself. I will say this; if there ever is an Italian version of the Kama Sutra published it will have been written by Alvio, with footnotes by Madame Ilene Médecin.

Daniel was worried and told me the situation was becoming too risky. Little did I know he was reporting my moves back to Max, who in turn was reporting to Jacques. I trusted Daniel, foolishly, because he owed me big time, so I believed.

About two years prior, Daniel had asked me if he could take a year off to open his own restaurant. I said that would be fine but I wanted Alain, a police buddy of his, to be his replacement. I liked Alain. He was funny and efficient. He said he would be honored to be my driver. Again, this was an exception to the protocol of selecting personal protection from the official pool.

Daniel opened his restaurant, but it quickly became a sordid murderous affair. It seemed he was "cooking" a lot more than being just a "restaurateur." Questionable events began occurring in and around the property. Two men were shot and killed and drugs were involved. Daniel was arrested and thrown in jail and convicted. He was looking at a lengthy sentence and fell into a deep depression. Although it was his own fault, I felt sorry for Daniel.

I missed Daniel as strange as it may sound. We had started from ground zero together while I was defining myself as First Lady, trying to figure out my duties as the wife of the Mayor and experimenting with my new job. He had to physically protect me on several occasions. I decided to speak to Jacques about getting him out of jail and bringing him back as my driver. Jacques was hesitant, but wanted me to be happy.

Daniel returned as my driver and bodyguard once more. Anyone would believe his redemption would have resulted in his undying loyalty and gratitude. Naturally, I assumed he would be indebted to me, but no. Instead, he chose to betray me at the same time he professed his loyalty. He went back to reporting my unofficial whereabouts and goings-on to Max, who carried the nasty tales on to Jacques. Maybe, Daniel made an arrangement with Jacques before he started up again as my driver. Was that the deal?—Jacques would spring him from jail and re-install him if he would dutifully report my every move to Max? Maybe? That had to have been the deal they made.

I didn't find out about this, the spying and tales told behind my back until years later. Daniel turned out to be a dishonorable, ungrateful bastard and I will never forgive him. He was a manipulative climber who didn't care who he stepped on to reach his goals and who clearly had no sense of loyalty or gratitude. If our paths ever cross again, I'll spit on him.

CHAPTER 68

WHEN JACQUES RETURNED FROM SOUTH America, he seemed different. He was with me again, but not really with me. Of course, it was a woman. As previously mentioned, I had eventually learned Jean Oltra had introduced him to Marisol Nicolletti, an Argentinian living in Uruguay. She was a so-called journalist and married to an architect. She may have been some kind of a writer, but I doubt that she was much of a journalist. She was short and dumpy with black hair and dark eyes. Jacques' usual type was tall, thin, blond and statuesque. She was definitely not that, but was in her early 30's and he coveted youth. Jacques was in his 60's at this time.

If Marisol (the Scammer) had a husband, architect or otherwise, he was easily forgotten. She certainly didn't let that get in her way and went after Jacques like flies on shit. As insecure as J was about getting older, he was vulnerable to a female like that who knew how to cater to his ego. So he started an affair with the harlot from South America and, before long, she recruited another harlot, her friend called "Bitchy." That moniker may have been coined from her behavior as a hard-core prescription drug and ether addict.

Remember, I wrote after the baby was born Jacques accused me of conceiving our daughter with Sheik Ahmed? From that point forward my true love for him was over. Jacques killed my love with his accusations. I didn't drink or do drugs. My only vice was having lustful romantic affairs. If

Jacques hurt me and he had, I would act on my favorite vice and seek personal solace. No apologies.

Am I being hypocritical? I don't think so. I had and was having an affair with Alvio. I was still a dutiful wife and loved Jacques, but not in the same way as before he accused our daughter of being the Sheiks'. I was holding up his reputation as mayor, politician and civic leader. I continued to fulfill all my duties as First Lady of Nice.

CHAPTER 69

ALVIO HAD ASKED ME TO MARRY HIM AND MOVE to Los Angeles to live happily ever after. Of course, this was impossible. It was borderline delusional, but I do admit giving it a moment's thought. What if I could make a deal with Jacques to be in France when he needed me to help with campaigning and then return to L.A. to live with my daughter and Alvio? We could have what is called an open marriage. He could be with whomever he wanted. I could be with Alvio and still maintain our public persona together. Maybe?

No. I knew Jacques would kill me before he'd let me divorce him and he would never agree to an open marriage. J was traditional, but cheating was okay. That was the extent of my moment's thought on the subject.

CHAPTER 70

I WAS ALWAYS BUSY WITH OFFICIAL DUTIES. NICE was very popular with an increasing number of distinguished visitors coming every year, which meant more work for the First Lady. Although I found time to slip away and meet Alvio, I was still performing my civic obligations and Jacques was proud of that.

Alvio and I started playing tennis and gin rummy together. We were pretty much equal at both activities in the beginning, but he became angry when I started beating him. In those days, I was very athletic and a competitive opponent. European men are more sensitive than American men when a female consistently beats them. I discovered that when I started besting Alvio in both categories. He believed as an Italian man he should be better at things than a woman (Italian masculinity and pride).

We were together for a long time. Alvio lived in the same hotel in San Remo for two and a half years. I grew to understand him and loved him very much. He was a proud decent man. Due to high taxes in Italy, he put his company in the name of his brother who lived outside the country. It was a big mistake because his brother stole all his money and I could do nothing to help him. By that time, I was just trying to save myself.

CHAPTER 71

THE TRAIN WRECK WAS APPROACHING AND THE collision occurred at Christmas time 1987.

We had planned to be in Los Angeles for our Christmas vacation as usual and left in early December with Jacques, TK, Lilou, and me. Our first night seemed all right even if a bit tense. Jacques was in a bad mood these days, but I thought the situation was manageable. Boy, was I wrong.

The next morning I was sitting in the breakfast nook having eggs over-medium and bacon. I looked up to see Jacques coming into the room. He was already fully dressed in travel clothes, which was a surprise. There was a satchel in his hand and I knew something was up that couldn't be good.

I slowly set my coffee cup down and looked at him.

He approached and stood next to where I was sitting with his body towering over me. He turned the satchel inside out and emptied the contents on the table. There was cash filled to the brim. He said he was leaving for New York on official business. I was shocked. He told me there was enough to handle the move from our home on Deep Canyon in Beverly Hills, which we had just sold. Following the sale, the plan was to move to the Beverly Hills Hotel where all of us would relax for two weeks and then head back to Nice.

I was, of course, stunned. Erratic and frightening as Jacques could be, I hadn't been expecting this. Lilou was with me to help with the move and all the details. I was flabbergasted he was leaving all the responsibilities up to me. I would have to sign the papers, pack the contents of the house and arrange storage, schedule the move to the hotel and handle all of it without him. Thank goodness Lilou was there. I told our daughter that Daddy had to leave suddenly to take care of official business in New York.

He snapped the satchel shut, spun on his heels and exited the room. I sat there totally stunned.

I was a wreck. Of course, by now I realized Max had been filling his head with surveillance regarding Alvio and that was what this was all about. This was his reaction.

He never called from New York or had any contact with me while we were at the BH Hotel. I received no word of his whereabouts, what he was doing, or crucially, who he was with. I called my stepdaughter, Martine (who I thought I was close with), in Nice and asked if she had heard from him.

Martine knew nothing. I was trying to put up a good front for her. I didn't cry or scream, but she realized something was wrong. While left in the dark, Lilou and I took care of everything regarding the sale of the house, packing it up, and putting belongings in storage units. It all seemed to be coming down on my head at once. I couldn't stop shaking with fear because I didn't know what was waiting for me in Nice, but it was certain to be unpleasant. I kept close to the hotel as I dreaded the trip home.

We spent Christmas and New Year's at the Beverly Hills Hotel without my dear husband. TK and I had a sad dreary holiday and tried to smile and pretend everything was all right. There were lots of presents, but they meant nothing. Christmas was over and New Year's passed and then we were on the plane. I was very apprehensive about what would happen when I stepped off the aircraft.

Daniel was waiting at the airport. I asked him what he knew of the rumors about Jacques and me. He said he wasn't allowed to tell me. I told him that he forgot who saved him and his loyalty should be with me. He bowed his head without saying a word.

I was angry. I told him to take my bags up to the guest room when we got home and went into the bathroom to shower and get ready for bed. But there was something waiting for me. A letter from Jacques was on the vanity. The envelope looked very thick. Jacques always wrote long letters and I opened the envelope with tremendous trepidation. I was shaking because I expected it would be very bad.

It wasn't at all what I anticipated. It was an amazing surprise. I opened it and started to read.

"My Darling Wife, I know you won't forgive me for my actions…"

Jacques then wrote how much he loved me and always would. He asked if I could ever forgive him. He went on and on and said he would be coming home late, but would understand if I was sleeping and we'd talk in the morning.

J said that he was getting old and thought I might be bored with him. He would turn the other cheek and not ask me any questions about my private yearnings. He would accept our present circumstances and one day we would retire in the States. Jacques said we would always be together not just because of TK, but because our deep love was pure and true.

His letter broke my heart. I felt an emptiness, but knew somehow we still loved one another even if he hated me. It was sad to see a man this bold, brave and successful thinking he was getting too old to be a good husband and lover. I knew it had to be an exaggeration. He was the ultimate politician and even though I wanted to believe his words, I didn't. I knew how he manipulated people and always waited for the right moment to strike. Even if it were years later, he would exact his revenge and make sure to annihilate his opponent.

I decided to write a note telling him, of course, I would forgive him. Jacques knew he was the love of my life. Even though we were having challenges in our relationship, I knew we'd be fine and get through this together.

After writing the note, I was so relieved I broke down and sobbed. I had my bags brought downstairs to our bedroom, took a sleeping pill and conked out.

It felt like I was dreaming when Jacques came in and started to hug and kiss me. He was crying and saying I love you, I love you, please don't leave me. I hugged him in my stupor and dozed off again.

CHAPTER 72

I WAS SUPPOSED TO MEET JACQUES THE NEXT DAY at a campaign luncheon for Jacques Chirac. Chirac was head of the Conservative Party and was running for President of France. He was in Nice to solidify support from Jacques since J was the major political muscle on the Riviera. Chirac had to make sure the Mayor of Nice and President of the Côte d'Azur was on his side. They were going to "pound the pavement" and work the crowd for a while, shaking hands and drumming up votes. Of course, I was there to help.

Everyone had heard the rumors, the stories about Jacques and me. They all had heard, from Chirac to the busboys in the kitchen. All eyes would be on us in anticipation of how Jacques would greet me. The entire city had heard we were at odds. Everyone was on edge watching us with fearful, cautious eyes, wondering what would happen now.

Daniel drove me to the restaurant. As we approached, I could see the crowd lined up on the sidewalk shouting words of encouragement and support. Of course, the throng of paparazzi was there as I exited the car. I sucked in my breath, projected myself into my campaign ready mode and walked towards the restaurant. I was wearing a striking but conservative red and white checked Chanel suit and entered the dining room with my confident model strut. My smile was genuine and I was ready for the show.

I thought I was prepared to handle the crowds and the clamor even if my insides were shaking, but it was more than I'd anticipated. There were hordes of people staring at me, trying to press close to see my reaction. I'd just been through some marital challenges with Jacques and we hadn't spoken yet because he left early in the morning before I awoke. Being more fragile than I realized, I relied on my public persona mode to project the happy and smiling face no matter the situation or circumstance.

Cameras were clicking and flashbulbs were popping everywhere. The paparazzi were out in droves.

Jacques saw me and came over at once. He touched my shoulder and grabbed me fiercely, pressing his body against mine. He put his arm around me and bent me back in true romantic style, kissing me long, lavishly and hungrily. It was a kiss of the ages and definitely a crowd pleaser. The paparazzi were in a tizzy and the crowd ate it up. They clapped and shouted, "We love you Madame Médecin, we love you!"

They loved me indeed and I loved them even though I knew it was superficial. I was sorry to delude them, but had to play along with the script. The show must go on and Jacques loved drama. His amorous gesture was a success. The French love romance, especially when it comes out of fire and conflict and when lovers have been quarreling only to fiercely reunite.

It worked for the constituents and it certainly confirmed our united image with the famous photo of us on the front page of the Nice Matin newspaper. The people loved it, the papers loved it, and we got letters of support by the score praising our great love story of the decade. I wanted to believe things would be okay from then on, but I knew Jacques and was right to be suspicious.

J was phenomenally adept at compartmentalizing his thoughts and actions, separating his past and present life. He would bury uncomfortable feelings deep in his heart and soul. Then one day, unexpectedly, his demons would come out. He would dig up old memories and relics from the past at the most appropriate or, should I say, the most inappropriate and harmful moments when he could inflict the most damage.

Out of the blue, he would mention something he might have heard or learned years before to surprise his opponent. He also had an infallible memory and never forgot anything nor ever forgave anything. Typically, he would lull a person into complacency. Then the knives came out and anyone opposing him was cut to shreds. (Speaking metaphorically, of course.) Jacques could and did slice anyone up he disliked or feared when it was useful to him for political advantage. You did not want to stand in his way. In politics, the higher you are, the sharper the knives. Mafia blood and an ancient tradition of Medici murders with a certain French smugness for clever misdeeds created the foundation for Jacques persona. He was an adversarial creature when he wished to be and, in fact, one with a feral and vicious heart. However, on the surface he was the most urbane and sophisticated man in a "diamond in the rough" sort of way.

He was very skilled being quick with words and verbally adept. Jacques could talk his way out of anything and could seduce and persuade anyone woman or man. His serpent-like tongue could destroy any person who was foolish enough to challenge him.

He had a brilliant mind, which I truly admired. Even though I still loved Jacques and was fascinated by him, I was no longer in love with the man. I think he used the best part of his brain to strategize and defeat his opponents, but unfortunately it sometimes meant me, his wife. It all started with his unwarranted accusations and extreme jealousy at the beginning of our marriage. This eventually pushed me away and I sought solace through romantic affairs, which culminated in the demise of our relationship.

Jacques loved to win, but so did I. Tragically at the end, we both lost and our lives would never be the same.

Even when you love and admire your mate, it's challenging to be a politician's spouse as other political wives can attest. When you've come to doubt and fear your spouse, the role becomes unstable and very stressful.

We were very good actors both on stage and privately with one another, but I knew somehow the true love would always be there even if buried under the surface. I will always love Jacques as the incredible man who fell for me hook line and sinker. He was my knight in shining armor and gave me our daughter and a fairytale life I had only dreamt of.

CHAPTER 73

OUR LIFE WAS A RICH AND WILD SCENE, BUT eventually it meant less and less to me.

Mouaffak al Midani, a Syrian billionaire, had a castle in Cannes along with multiple homes around the world. Was he a social friend or a supporter? He was a man who wanted to ingratiate himself with the top leaders of the world by showering them with gifts and money for their campaigns. He wanted to make sure when he needed something they would be there to do his bidding.

We were continually receiving invitations to his home for dinner and Jacques finally insisted we go because Mouaffak had indicated he would become a major donor. I was not particularly interested, but Jacques was insistent. After declining the invitation a few times, I finally accepted.

Arriving at his castle in Cannes, I could see it would be another grand show. The driveway was lined with men in Arabian-style robes wearing classic Arabian headwear (the egal), all armed to the hilt with automatic weapons.

We were welcomed by a properly attired silent butler, leading us into the drawing room. The main house was enormous with many annexes and secret passageways. There were numerous smaller residences on the property to accommodate distinguished guests. Once we were seated, Mouaffak came bounding in with a few packages handing me the largest. He was wearing a black suit and white shirt. His hair had been coiffed like Elizabeth Taylor's, all black and poofy.

He greeted me and said, "Madame Médecin, thank you for accepting my dinner invitation. I hope you'll visit me more often."

I smiled and opened my gift. OH MY…a diamond and gold necklace from Cartier! I grinned because I certainly did the right thing by finally accepting his invitation.

I laughed and said, "My dear man, I'll come for breakfast and lunch too. Tomorrow?"

We all laughed and were led into a completely over-the-top dining room decorated in gold, silver and marble decor. This was certainly the definitive über luxurious dining space.

After the meal Mouaffak asked us to come upstairs to his study, but first he wanted to give us a tour of the house. Every bedroom had its own spa bath and some bedrooms had tubs large enough for six people. There was art from ancient masters, although not rivaling the Gould Collection. Gilt, gilt and more gilt—gold plate as common as shellac. Sinks and tubs and staircases of the finest Carrera marble. It was definitely impressive.

When the tour was done, we sat in his private study. I was enveloped in a large red velvet chair and listened to what the man had to propose. He asked if I would be amenable to host parties in his mansions in Paris and in Cannes. I would become his official hostess with an offer of $1,000,000.00 compensation and also providing me with an unlimited budget to stage the events. "Whatever was needed," he said. I would oversee all the details making sure the parties were grand, exciting, fun and memorable. Jacques was taken aback, but curtly answered, "It's my wife's decision. She calls the shots."

Al Midani also wanted to open an antique shop for me in Monaco. He wanted me close and available to him when he needed me. In return, he'd deposit the million dollars in my American bank account and set me up in the shop as well. I was stunned. I knew Jacques would not be happy if I decided to take Mouaffak up on his offers. Jacques looked at me and again at Mouaffak. "She can do what she wants." We had come for a donation for J's campaigns and a sweet smile from his beautiful wife had helped, but I knew he'd be jealous and angry about my unexpected gifts and business proposals.

Mouaffak had discovered my birthday was coming up and wanted to throw me a huge bash. He said I could invite anyone I wanted and he'd fly them in on his private jet from anywhere in the world.

After Jacques and I returned home, we discussed everything Mouaffak had offered. I told him I wasn't sure about hostessing or the antique store, but I did want him to give me a birthday party. Jacques was not too communicative and again said, "It's up to you." Then he left for the kitchen to get a late-night snack.

I went to lunch a few days later at the castle to help Al Midani with ideas I had for my birthday. I couldn't believe what an event he was planning.

He had a beautiful residence on the lower part of the property that could house four couples. I knew I couldn't invite my mother and her husband to the same gathering with my father and his wife as it would only create problems. The two couples did not get along. Mom visited me in Nice twice a year. Since my father wasn't able to attend Jacques' and my wedding because my mother was in attendance, I decided to invite him and his wife to my birthday bash. My father and I had grown even closer after I became pregnant with TK and wanted him to share this experience with me.

I chose the largest bedroom for them and Mouaffak asked me if I liked the color or would I like to change the color. It was pale blue and ivory with gilded accents. You don't repaint a masterpiece. I told him I thought they would love it. I had also invited Stephanie, my best friend when we were eleven, and her husband Leon. Dayle and Abe, who had been my long time friends, also received an invitation. Mouaffak told his decorator to change the colors in the other bedrooms where my friends would stay and had the living and dining room redecorated as well.

As the party plans progressed, he decided to send first class tickets on Swiss Air instead of one of his jets. During their week stay, Mouaffak would provide a Michelin 3-star chef to prepare their meals while they were on the estate and each couple would have a Rolls Royce and driver to escort them anywhere they desired. I was very excited. My French friends, of course, would be there as well to support me. Jacques also invited a few people and the list was kept at seventy.

Jacques seemed to be getting silently angrier with me and it was really uncomfortable. He liked my father and was happy to see him, but didn't take any meals with us or make an effort to socialize with the group. I was losing weight. When I'm nervous or unhappy I lose weight, and I had a feeling things would come to a head soon. I had already lost six pounds.

Whatever my worries about Jacques, Mouaffak took my mind off them for a day. He gave me an unreal fantastic party, which was an extravaganza and one of the grandest birthday parties of my life. There was a table which had an enormous silver punch bowl filled with the finest beluga caviar (to be eaten by the spoon) flown in that day from the Caspian Sea, as fresh as you could possibly get. I don't like caviar, but I saw Steph diving into the bowl like she was in heaven. Although I'm a meat and potatoes and comfort food girl, I was happy to see Steph enjoying herself. The food was exquisite and we had a lot of fun. Steph was an actress who played JR's whore on the successful TV series, *Dallas*. I kept introducing her as my friend "La Pute de Dallas," which translates to "The Whore from Dallas." People were surprised and perplexed because they failed to immediately make the connection with the TV show, but heartily laughed nonetheless.

"What?" they asked. "She's a whore from Dallas, Texas?"

"No, no, no! I meant she's on the TV series, *Dallas*, and plays J.R's prostitute." Lol.

The entire week was extraordinary and over the top. Everyone had a great time and most of us were in a wonderful mood.

Regarding Jacques, I knew I had to say something. When everyone left, I confronted him and asked, "What specifically is the root of your anger?" He refused to discuss it. Everything had been wrong since "that" letter. He would always love me and we would still move to the U.S., etcetera. I had time to think about what he wrote, but didn't believe one bit of it now, especially the part about us leading separate sexual lives with no questions asked. I thought it was a clever tactic for Jacques to suggest that. I believe it was just a ploy to see if I'd really take him up on it. I sensed danger.

By not discussing it, this meant J was pent up and seething with anger. I knew it was only a matter of time before he exploded. Daniel was still feeding info about my every move to Max, who passed it on to Jacques. All those nasty stories in his head were eating him alive.

CHAPTER 74

I KNEW I HAD TO MAKE THE DECISION TO END THE relationship with Alvio and start anew with Jacques. I realized neither of us would ever trust one another again, but I had to try because of our daughter.

My birthday had been a success. My friends had fun and it was great to see them, but there was smoke in the air. I soon discovered Daniel's continual betrayal and fired him on the spot. I chose my new bodyguard and driver from the official chauffeurs' pool. His name was Jean-Claude Allegretti.

After all the betrayals, I wanted a driver to be totally dedicated and loyal to me. I met with Jean-Claude and asked him if he would be that man and if he could handle the stress. Jacques knew Jean-Claude wouldn't be spying on me as Daniel had and objected to my firing him. In the end, I got my way. JC, as I called Jean-Claude was a rugged, tough-looking man who regularly worked out. He was professional, a great driver and respectful. I liked him very much and over the next two years we shared unbelievable experiences that bonded us on a deeper intimate level.

Because he was my bodyguard, I spent more time with JC than anyone else. It's an interesting relationship when you're depending on a specific person to protect you under any circumstance. He was responsible for getting me safely and on time to back-to-back official events among my other duties. We were always together, even going to Switzerland while spending nights there on business.

On one of my yearly summer trips to Los Angeles, I decided to take JC with me. I showed him around and I drove. He was impressed with my parking abilities and never imagined me driving. Surprise! If you don't drive in L.A., you're cooked. I want to say to you Jean-Claude, if you're out there reading this book, "Hello." I want to say how much I appreciated all the risks you took because of me. We were in it together, weren't we?

He was loyal to the end except for the disappointing moment when I was arrested at the airport in Nice. He was waiting for me in the baggage claim, but when he saw me enter the area accompanied by the gendarmes he took off, not wanting to be implicated. I guess he might have felt that he abandoned me which hurt him somehow, but I understood why he left, not wanting to get into trouble. I forgive you for that JC and will always be grateful for your incredible support and discretion. Fortunately, Lilou and my American friend Joiana were in the baggage claim waiting for me as well.

CHAPTER 75

MY OFFICIAL DUTIES VARIED MORE AND MORE, covering every kind of event, ceremony and public gathering. Some of them were quite exotic, even bizarre.

I was asked to judge a bodybuilding contest. That sounded quite interesting and I agreed to be there as it was something new I hadn't done before. I judged the dog contest every year with Princess Antoinette in Monaco, but that didn't involve men's bodies. I knew this would be fun.

I brought along my American friend, Cathy Dariel, who was Girls' Vice Principal at AIS (The American International School). Cathy and I became buddies through her mother Lynn, who was President of the American Club. As an American and the First Lady of Nice, I was bestowed the title of Honorary President of the American Club. I knew Cathy would enjoy a day off from school.

We were really looking forward to judging this very male contest. We sauntered in with my bodyguards, took our seats and the men came one at a time on stage to be admired. After much scrutiny, they all posed together for one last look. When I presented the trophies, awarding the golden chalices to these wonderfully sculptured bodies, I thought to myself this was one of my official duties that was NOT a duty!

I loved AIS and sought to support the school being an American, so much so I asked Jacques to donate land to build a new AIS facility. I didn't want our daughter attending a French school because, frankly, they're too stressful. AIS was a great alternative with forty different nationalities in attendance. Physical Ed is not as important in French schools as it is in American schools and I believe the curriculum should be well balanced between academics and athletics. AIS did that. I always encouraged my daughter, "Do the best you can in school, that's all I ask." I believed children shouldn't be pressured to achieve. I provided guidance to help TK find her interests and allowed her to rise to her level of ability.

During the Christmas holidays, the international students and their families would set up stands in the cafeteria and serve their country's cuisines. I told Jacques we must make a Niçois specialty. Being the chef he was, J called his men to bring over a wood-burning oven to make "socca." This is a delicious and healthy chickpea pizza made from chickpea flour, olive oil, fresh rosemary and black pepper. In Nice, they sprinkle white pepper on top. I brought my friends to the event and we must have each gained at least five pounds. The other thirty-nine mothers had gone all out serving their homemade favorite dishes.

CHAPTER 76

I T WAS 1988 AND ANOTHER BIRTHDAY YEAR. BUT, not just any birthday year because it marked a significant milestone of decades.

Forty big ones for me and Sixty for Jacques. Oddly, we both arrived at this momentous milestone at the same time, though we were twenty and a half years apart. But, forty, I think is when a woman starts to wonder if she is aging and sixty is when a man first questions his manhood or lack of it. It was a year of significant changes for both of us.

So, we celebrated our birthdays. J's came first.

Jacques' 60th birthday party was planned in the Louis XIV restaurant at the Hotel d' Paris in Monaco and would be very grand indeed. There were 64 guests seated at eight round tables, a full array of pink and white floral center pieces with shiny diamond-like accents in-between the roses, elegant crystal chandeliers, sterling flatware, with a violin trio and a 6-course meal planned by the Michelin Star Chef exclusively for the Mayor.

It seemed to be a busy year for family matters and timely events as well. Martine, Jacques oldest, had been married the year before and Anne-Laure, Jacques' middle daughter, was getting married later that year. While one generation of the family grows older, the other is just beginning to bloom as it usually does. I had hoped the family celebrations would bring back some closeness and togetherness that would somehow return us to friendship and love. I could always hope.

My birthday was six months away in November. Of course, my dear friend Trevor Mound was invited to the party.

Trevor and I had a special connection. He was tall and looked like Ichabod Crane with a very long nose, hollow cheeks that sunk into his face and a protruding Adam's apple. His looks were definitely memorable, but even more remarkable was his BRILLIANCE. He was one of the three most charming men I had ever met in my life. Jacques and Nino Cerruti, the Italian designer, were the other two.

More about Nino later. He was the opposite of Trevor—completely indiscreet and improper. But one was a Brit and the other Italian. Different cultures, different men.

CHAPTER 77

I MENTIONED EARLIER ABOUT JUDGING THE DOG contest in Monaco sponsored by Princess Antoinette, the sister of Prince Rainier. She had sent me a request asking me to be a judge. I was very happy to accept her invitation because I'm a dog person. I loved seeing all the breeds as they strutted their stuff on the red carpet. The Princess and I had such fun together chatting and evaluating the doggies. I knew she also liked cats and asked her what breed she would suggest for my daughter. I wanted TK to be exposed to all types of animals and we already had Dachshunds, fish, a goat and a rabbit. Sadly, my first doxy Selma ate Caresse, our poor bunny. A cat would be our next acquisition. After some discussion, Jacques and Antoinette both suggested a Chartreux, which is a beautiful French gray cat with golden eyes. Antoinette loved the Chartreux and said if we chose a female and named it after her she would buy little Antoinette a jeweled collar. She was a Princess of her word.

We found an adorable female kitten and named her, of course, Antoinette. Soon after, our Antoinette received the promised jeweled collar from the Princess. It was dazzling in lime green leather and semi-precious stones of amethyst, péridot, blue topaz, citrine and pink tourmaline.

Antoine, as we called her, was the sweetest cat ever and was very worthy of the regal adornment.

CHAPTER 78

NINO CERRUTI, THE FAMOUS ITALIAN DESIGNER, wanted to open one of his boutiques in Nice. Jacques gave him permission and when the store was inaugurated we gave him and his staff a congratulatory dinner. At the last minute, Jacques couldn't attend, so it was my responsibility to entertain them and to schmooze Nino. I didn't know of Nino and had no idea what I was in for.

He was a very tall man with a pronounced nose and heavy dark looks. He wasn't good looking, but charm dripped from every pore. As I mentioned, the three most charming men I ever knew in my life were Jacques, Trevor and Nino. They were very suave, each one of them. I mean suave, the very definition of male gentility and charm. Of course, Nino was my dinner partner that night and we talked non-stop throughout the meal. He was intelligent, interesting and, oh, so smooth. The inauguration of his new shop was the following day and he wanted me to choose something from his collection. "Anything you like," he offered. It was a generous gesture.

The following day at the boutique I chose a beautiful off-white silk outfit with a pale coral silk blouse and a long flowing off-white jacket to coordinate with pale coral Palazzo pants (very simple sleek Italian style). I cut the ribbon for the store and gave my "Welcome to Nice" speech. Nino asked me to have a drink with him after the event so he could speak with me privately. I was curious to find out what he wanted to say.

We sat down and he whispered in my ear, "I want to invite you to Paris, my Tigrezia," which means little tiger in Italian.

I looked at him very surprised and said, "I actually am leaving for Paris in a couple of weeks to be outfitted by Chanel for the inauguration of our newly built convention center, the Acropolis."

He said that would be perfect. He wanted to give a dinner party for me at Cassell's, a famous nightclub in Paris like Regine's. I told him that would be very nice and I would be coming with three of my girlfriends and my bodyguard. He said he couldn't wait to see me again and would start planning the party.

Two weeks later, our little entourage arrived in Paris. I had my fittings at Chanel where they offered me sixteen gowns for all the Acropolis' opening events and I was absolutely thrilled. I had started wearing Chanel when Karl Lagerfeld decided to design for them years back.

Lagerfeld wanted to bring in younger women as his clientele and I loved that he had revamped the collections. I was a true fan, so to have Chanel offer to dress me was an honor.

We arrived in the dining room at Cassell's for our anticipated soiree and there stood Nino welcoming us with his usual suave aplomb. He introduced us to his guests and his French wife.

I found it interesting he placed her at the opposite end of the table, quite far away. I was next to Nino surrounded by my friends Jackye, Odette, Helene and, of course Daniel, my bodyguard. We had hors d'oeuvres and ordered dinner. During the entrée, I felt a hand go up my dress and begin caressing my inner thigh. Nino! I was really shocked. I took his hand and removed it from my leg. I looked at him and said, "Are you crazy? I'm surrounded by my people and your wife is at the other end of the table. Just stop it!"

He was getting very drunk and I was getting nervous. After dessert and coffee, we descended downstairs to the disco.

Jackye, my best friend, whispered, "I think he really likes you."

I laughed and said, "What was your first clue?"

"I saw how uncomfortable you were at a certain point and figured something was going on under the table."

"Oh, great," I said. "Did anyone else notice?"

She answered, "Let's hope not."

There were three tables loaded with champagne. I don't drink, but the girls were enjoying it. Nino asked me to dance, so I accepted since he was our host. He drew me in close on the dance floor, bent me backwards and started kissing me.

This was another one of the many bizarre moments I experienced as Madame Médecin. I was pushing him away when a bottle of Dom Perignon flew toward us like a missile! It just missed my head and exploded on the dance floor. Nino's wife had thrown it. She was advancing towards me like an angry fire-breathing dragon. Nino grabbed her to hold her back with Daniel quick to the rescue, dragging me off the floor. Madame Cerruti was quite inebriated and screaming at Nino creating a huge scene.

Like I needed any more upheavals in my life. Nino somehow got her under control and insisted on driving us back to the hotel. Daniel was against it, but seven of us piled into a small car and took off. Nino was definitely drunk. He was passing cars and driving erratically on the sidewalk. His wife was in the car with us, which was not a smart move. She began shouting at him again in the tiny car. We all looked at one another in amazement. It was a surreal scene we were experiencing and it was still unfolding. We were packed in like sardines, seven adults in a compact car. Madame Cerruti, stuffed behind me in the back seat started screaming again. I thought she might shatter our eardrums. Nino was so drunk, grinning like a fool that I wondered if we were going to get to the hotel alive.

I don't know how we arrived at our destination, but we did. Nino called me his Tigrezia again and said he would call me the next day. I rushed inside and said good night to everyone. When I got to bed, I relived the entire bizarre evening as all of it was racing through my head. It takes a lot to surprise me, but this did.

I was curious to see what Nino would come up with next. He called the following morning. "I want to apologize for last night," he said over the phone, very meek and sounding subdued.

I told him the whole scenario was outrageous, but since no one got hurt I had to admit it was rather hilarious.

"I want to see you again while you're still here in Paris," he said, "but my wife has forbidden it even though she knows it wasn't your fault."

"OH REALLY?" I laughed. "What a surprise! You were totally out of line and beyond indiscreet."

"I know," he said, sounding even more contrite.

Nino and his wife had been invited to the main upcoming inaugural night at the Acropolis. He said he would attend without her. I wasn't sure that would be a good idea, but he seemed pretty insistent, so I left it up to him.

My entourage headed back to Nice and my buddies said it was one of the most absurdly entertaining trips they had ever been on. They loved being with me because there was never a dull moment.

Some fragments from the evening were fascinating even to me and some were frightening to say the least, but that was my life. Sometimes very entertaining and sometimes quite unbelievable.

Nino called me a few times before the Acropolis premiere and pleaded that he wanted to see me again without my bodyguards. I still liked him despite everything and said that could be a possibility. He called me right before the big event and said he wanted to attend the opening to be with me. Sternly, his wife forbade him to go to the gala and told him never to see me again. Otherwise, she'd demand a divorce. Believe me, I understood and wished him well with a final goodbye. It was the last time I spoke with Nino. He was a man of such charm even if he was quite out of line incessantly pursuing me. He was just being an Italian male with deep passion and very expressive emotions. I love Italian men.

Nino was married and I shouldn't have been surprised. It may not have even occurred to him to elaborate on that. This was the way it was done on this side of the water. I learned a lot about relationships in Europe, which were very different from America. Varied norms exist in different cultures. When Americans dared to have affairs, they hid them and kept it secret. I find it hypocritical in 2023 many alternative lifestyles are accepted in the U.S., but mistresses and cheating are still taboo.

CHAPTER 79

T HE YEAR JACQUES TURNED SIXTY-ONE, HE TOLD
me that we were going to the famous La Prairie Clinic in Switzerland to
get "youth" shots. They were injections that would keep us young or younger
made from the placentas of baby calves.

Among many celebrities, Ronald and Nancy Reagan had been there
for the treatment consisting of seven injections filled with a unique serum
derived from these baby bovines. I guess Jacques thought it was an endorse-
ment that proved the validity of the procedure. The shots were meant to boost
the immune system and make it better and stronger, resulting in people being
able to stay younger and remain more youthful.

That was the pitch anyway. Forty was the youngest age allowed to
enter the program. This would become the worst threat to my health I had
ever experienced.

After arriving at the clinic, we were ushered into a room consisting
of two hospital beds and not much else except side tables. A doctor and
nurse came in to take our vitals and interviewing us regarding our mental
conditions. They asked what we expected from the treatment and what our
weaknesses were. We had to run on a treadmill to make sure our hearts were
in good condition and then take a respiration test to gauge our lung capacity.

After all the preliminaries were finished, we were served a light meal
and advised to go to sleep early as the shots took a lot out of our bodies and

adjusting to the formula could be difficult. It was a grossly insufficient warning. They understated and I mean understated the pain!

The next morning two nurses entered the room with 14 syringes. Seven for Jacques and seven for me. We didn't have a clue about what we would feel or what the shots would be like and I hadn't given it much thought. Some shots hurt more than others and some not so much. I was too trusting. After the first shot, I knew that giving birth to a baby was a walk in the park compared to this and there were six more to go. It was excruciatingly painful, like liquid fire being shot into my veins and hips. I was writhing on the bed in terrible agony and so was Jacques, who was usually tough as nails. I thought I was going to vomit and pass out after the third shot. How I got through the seventh one, I don't know.

The nurses finally finished and I felt horrible. The shots and accompanying pain had drained every ounce of energy and strength from my body. The only feeling remaining inside of me was a deep unrelenting soreness. It was right in the middle of my body like a red-hot poker searing and coursing through me, taking hours to finally subside. Jacques was in as much agony as I was and this was a man who could go to the dentist for a root canal without being administered any anesthesia. So, for him to admit he was hurting, it had to be really, really, really BAD!

We were there for four days and I couldn't wait to get home. I didn't ever want to go through that again even if it was supposed to make my immune system stronger.

I certainly didn't feel any better after a couple of weeks and came down with a cold. I started to feel a raspiness in my throat and esophagus. My stomach burned which it never had before and my bladder area felt funny and abnormal.

I went to my doctor in Nice who gave me antibiotics for ten days. No improvement. Although I was put on five different sets of strong antibiotics over a period of two months, I was still getting worse. Panic was setting in. What was wrong with me? Jacques was worried as well. I flew to L.A. in desperation and made an appointment with my doctor to take extensive tests. I was told I had a golden staph infection that was eating away at my mucus linings, most likely the result of the "youth" shots given to me at the La Prairie Clinic. The shots were supposed to build up my strength, but instead they infected me and diminished my strength.

My doctor said this was serious which I already knew. He suggested I go to the Mayo Clinic in Rochester, Minnesota to have a complete evaluation. I did just that and flew to Rochester.

Every part of my body was checked. They performed every test possible to find out how to help me.

One doctor at the clinic took me aside and said he had a great doctor friend in Portland, Oregon who could help me. All the doctors so far had concurred this was very serious, but none of them seemed to know what to do about it.

I returned to Nice to discuss going to Portland with Jacques. I had already spoken with the doctor and knew I might be there for a while. He explained that he was going to experiment with the strongest antibiotic available at the time, Vancomycin, which would be introduced intravenously through a catheter in my arm all the way to my heart, pumping the drug 24/7 into my system. I prayed this would work.

I flew to Portland and stayed alone in the hotel. A nurse would come by morning and night to replace the infusion bags. I was given a portable pack in case I wanted to go out and stretch my legs. That went on for three weeks. I existed on McDonald's burgers and vanilla milkshakes. That was the extent of my appetite during the entire ordeal.

After three weeks, I had more tests to make sure the golden staph had been killed (instead of me) and thank goodness the infection had been arrested. But, and it was a huge BUT, it left me with a ravaged mucus lining and ongoing chronic pain. The burning agony was an incessant feeling, like hot fiery coals being dumped into my stomach, esophagus and urinary tract linings. I was desperate!

Back in Nice, the doctors wanted to calm me down, so they put me on a benzodiazepine with a shorter half-life than Valium. They started me on 100 milligrams a day. That's a mega-dose of a powerful drug. Although I still felt the fire in my belly, I was able to function a little better. The doctors may have been trying to help, but their actions and motives weren't entirely pure, either. They were all too familiar with Jacques, his temper and his vengeance. The doctors wanted to keep me drugged and calm, so Jacques wouldn't be angry with them. This enabled me to attend important functions with minimal disturbance.

CHAPTER 80

OF COURSE, THE MUSIC NEVER STOPPED. IT WAS a continual parade of events with celebrities and dignitaries always visiting. Anthony Quinn was arriving in Nice to exhibit his paintings. There would be a private gallery showing with an intimate dinner to follow. My attendance was mandatory and I was looking forward to the meal. I enjoyed him as an actor and had questions to ask him about his artwork.

He brought his wife, Jolanda Addolori, who seemed pleasant enough with the four of us dining. The conversation went well until the two of them started bickering, making it clear they had major issues to work out. Actually, they were amusing. I said to them I thought they were kind of cute going back and forth and, at least, they were communicating. Anthony laughed and said they were at it all the time and shrugged it off. The three of us were gabbing away when I noticed his wife had a sour look on her face and wasn't saying a word. I asked her if something was wrong. She blasted me.

"How dare you talk about our behavior!" she shrieked. Her anger was not making her face pleasant any more.

I was shocked by her vitriolic response and wanted to tell her, then don't air your dirty laundry in public especially when you're our guest. Remember my husband allowed your spouse to exhibit his artwork here and it is not a smart move to insult his wife. I silently said that to myself and thought it better not to say it out loud. I was attempting to bear the continual pain from this insidious staph infection. I meant no harm, and Anthony knew it. He was beyond apologetic and put his arm around me as we walked out. The evening had ended rather abruptly after Madame Quinn's outburst. No way was I going to sit there and listen to her vile crap any more.

Tony whispered in my ear that they had been having problems for many years and not to take it personally. She was offensive, especially with younger pretty women. I was also disturbed and more sensitive than usual because of my condition and got into bed as soon as we returned home. Jacques assured me she was completely out of line and not to give it a second thought.

Interestingly enough, Tony divorced the vile one not much later and married a younger, much nicer woman. But for me, it was a turning point... another spin of the wheel spiraling downward. After that incident, I decided not to attend any more functions. I felt too vulnerable physically, mentally and emotionally to deal with the public. On top of that, I was obsessed with trying to find some way to cure myself. Although I knew 100 mgs of Tranxene a day was keeping me functional on a certain level, I would have to get off it soon. I was very aware of its addictive properties and was becoming dependent. I had an American friend named Joiana, who invited me to attend an AA meeting with her in Monaco. She had a daughter who was a recovering addict. Joiana regularly attended meetings as a support measure to help her cope with her daughter's addiction. I thought it might be a good idea to go with her and check it out. It was an interesting group including one of the Beatles whose name I won't disclose. It was quite an eclectic mix of known personalities.

Joiana thought the meetings would help me understand I was addicted and needed help. I didn't want to admit it and when my turn came to introduce myself I gave my first name and said I'm not an addict or an alcoholic.

However, as time passed, I certainly learned otherwise with the help of St. John's Hospital.

CHAPTER 81

POLITICALLY, THE ATMOSPHERE WAS GETTING
scary. There were rumors the Left was going after Jacques to discredit
him because he and his family had ruled the Côte d'Azur since 1851, and the
Leftists wanted Médecin territory for themselves. Jacques was a capitalist who
believed in free enterprise and individual freedom. The elite Leftists believed
the opposite, desiring all the personal luxury and privilege for themselves
while controlling the masses like herds of cattle.

The Médecin dynasty had an amazingly long run. Italy united in 1851.
All the many princedoms, dukedoms, city-states and little fiefdoms finally
came together to unite under one nation under the great Garibaldi.

Nice was in the middle, between France and newly formed Italy. The
people of Nice were allowed to decide which country they wanted to be part
of. The Niçois voted to join France, and that's why Nice is French today and
not Italian. They chose France because Napoleon was the tough wealthy
leader and thought they'd get a better deal by joining him. The Médecin
family had ruled Nice and the French Riviera since Italy's unification. The
Socialists were hell-bent on bringing the Médecin era to an end.

Jacques' imposing presence in Nice and on the Riviera was that of
a god-like entity. He was and still is today highly respected to the point of
reverence, especially among the Niçois and the most loyal "Médecinists."
Women would cry at his feet and men would bow on the street. "Jacquou"
was truly loved and worshiped. This same admiration produced envy and

animosity among his rivals, especially Raymond Barre, the former Prime Minister of France.

Since Mitterrand, the Socialist leader, became President of France in 1981, political rivalry also became more heated. "King Jacquou" was the absolute ruler on the Riviera and swung conservative votes in every election. Although Mitterrand acknowledged Jacques was the most effective mayor in France, this did not provide any sway in Jacques' favor. He was just out for power and control and viewed him as a threat to his socialist agenda. Mitterand's fear continued to escalate especially after he became President. He wanted to get rid of J... wanted him gone and didn't care how.

We were in danger, but Jacques refused to discuss these issues with me. I was still terribly ill and we were no longer the strong united force we once had been.

CHAPTER 82

BY 1990, JACQUES' POLITICAL ENEMIES WERE IN full force. He had a mole inside the opposing Socialist Party who kept him informed of their strategies to dispose of him. Jacques learned from this spy the Socialists were planning to initiate charges against him, alleging wrongdoings. Clearly, this revelation greatly affected J's mental state. One must understand "Jacquou" was a cherished and beloved leader by the people of the French Riviera even to this day. So the specter of these pending allegations was unsettling to say the least. Jacques' resilient facade began to slowly crumble under the stress of these unfounded accusations. His vulnerability became apparent with his increased paranoia and delusions not knowing who to trust. Jacques told me that we would be escaping France to live in political exile in Uruguay because there was no extradition. I realized later what a coward he had been to deceive and abandon TK and me, only to be used as his cover. We were left completely at risk while he safely fled the country.

While his plans were still in the making, he decided we would go to the U.S. for a vacation. In my mind this was crazy and a terrible time to go away, especially as the plot was beginning to thicken. We had been invited to Deer Valley, Utah to stay with friends for a week. For Jacques, he used this time away to continue receiving reports regarding the Socialists' plot. With this information, he was able to create a strategy for our escape. I was unable to enjoy the visit for obvious reasons. I huddled in the bedroom riddled with fire scorching my mucus lining and fear pulsing through me. My mind was filled with dread.

Then the call came while we were still in Deer Valley. Jacques got word from his man on the inside that the Left was making its move. We were scheduled to go on a cultural exchange trip to Japan after we returned to Nice. Ordinarily I would go with him, but I was still too ill. The informant said Jacques would be arrested and charged with embezzlement and other crimes when he returned from Japan. Handcuffs would be waiting for him.

As we continued to devise plans for our escape, Jacques decided he would complete the mission to Japan without me and then fly to Uruguay where there was no extradition. That was the plan. Was it possible the Leftists would push up the timetable and arrest Jacques before he took off for Japan? What if they thought he had learned of their plot? They might have to act sooner and arrest him as soon as we deplaned. It was going to be a scary flight home.

This was the grand scheme of Raymond Barre, the Prime Minister when Valéry Giscard d'Estaing was President of France. Barre was extremely ambitious and wanted to rule Nice and the French Riviera himself. He wanted Jacques out of the way and with Mitterand's help Barre believed he could take over and be elected.

When we arrived, Jean Oltra asked to speak to me privately. He pled, "Jacques listens to you. I'm begging you to convince him to calm down and attempt to make friends with Mitterrand and Barre. Perhaps it was not too late."

I told Jean I wasn't sure Jacques would listen to me now, but I would give it a try. He said Jacques was being outrageous and making foolish statements about Jews never turning down a gift and it was all over the press. As I said earlier, Jacques was really losing it.

The French press is leftist and they were intentionally misquoting Jacques saying he was a racist. I knew he was not a racist. During WWII, he escaped into the mountains and lived in a cave with 200 Jews who were hiding from the Nazis. They were comrades in arms, fighting side-by-side while risking their lives for the freedom of France. He was not anti-Semitic, but the Left was smearing him to say he was. They were going to use every weapon they had in their arsenal to get rid of him even if it was false. This was no different than what is occurring today, especially in the U.S., with the Leftist media spreading their vermin, determined to destroy America.

Jacques was in a frantic state, but I repeated Jean's message. He listened and I knew he understood Jean was right, but his pride wouldn't let him do it. Ego and pride will take down the most powerful men if they think they can't be touched. The downward spiral was gaining momentum.

I was continuing to freak out about my health. It would have been better if TK and I went with Jacques to Japan and then just fly straight to Uruguay. However, I was still too sick for the trip. We would be separated at our weakest and worst time while I was so ill.

What was going to happen to us?

CHAPTER 83

JACQUES WASN'T ARRESTED WHEN WE RETURNED from Deer Valley to Nice. There was a heart-stopping moment when we got off the plane and saw several gendarme (national police) who seemed to be staring at us, but then nothing happened. We hurried past them out of the airport and home. Jacques left for Japan the next day. Once in Japan, he would escape to Uruguay. So far the plan was working, at least for my husband.

Meanwhile, I was abandoned in the belly of the beast. TK and I were to stay in Nice until Jacques was safe. Then, and only then we were to fly to New York and on to Arizona where Martine, Jacques' eldest daughter, was living and waiting for our arrival.

I was in a horrid state. The golden staph had eaten my mucus lining and the pain was unbearably excruciating. It was hard for me to think straight. All I knew was I had to get my daughter and myself out of France ASAP.

Jacques sent word we were going to be held under house arrest because the Leftists believed he'd return to get us. Wrong again.

I truly believed he wouldn't be coming home for TK and me. At this point, he abandoned us for his own safety and we were being disregarded as pawns.

This was not the man I fell in love with. He had completely gone to the dark side. The pressure was killing him and he had become totally out of his mind. I had to take care of my daughter and myself now.

We were to stay with Martine until I got better, then fly to Uruguay and join Jacques. Lilou and Marcel, our faithful guardians who lived downstairs at the Préfecture, were told to pack as many of our belongings as they could and send them through Italy to storage units in Arizona and Uruguay. Italy was 30 minutes away.

Of course, they had to do this quietly and on the sly. Jacques didn't want to alert the French authorities who would have stopped us in our tracks.

Jacques called me once he was safe in Uruguay. He instructed me to go to one of our vaults in the Préfecture to take out all the cash and 200 of his watches. I put the watches in a suitcase and gave it to one of our trusted men to fly from Nice to Paris and then Uruguay. I kept the cash.

After removing the items out of the vault, I gave the suitcase to Jean-Jacques Robin, who was Jacques' reliable courier. But when he arrived in Paris to connect flights he was stopped at customs and the French police confiscated the suitcase with all its contents. Most of the watches were gifts from dignitaries acquired over many years. All were from top designers and many were personally engraved. The watches were extraordinarily valuable and some were worth tens of thousands of dollars. They were his individual property and definitely not ill-gotten gains.

France has not been alone in the customary tradition of political gift giving. It's worldwide. There's always the typical jealousy, cheating, stealing, lying, etc. in politics and it doesn't matter what political party you identify with or what country you're living in.

CHAPTER 84

WHILE JACQUES WAS EN ROUTE TO URUGUAY, TK and I had been left at the Préfecture to cover for him. We could only do that for so long. By this time, the city officials and police realized Jacques was not returning to Nice from Japan. Presumably, they figured he was on his way to South America. That made TK's and my position untenable.

I received a phone call from Jean Oltra telling me that we were to be placed under house arrest until Jacques returned. We had to move fast because the gendarme would be coming soon. He said to pack a few things, get TK out of school and Jean-Claude would take us to the airport where I could secretly board a Pan Am flight to New York. Jacques previously had made a deal with the President of Pan Am to implement a round trip direct flight from Nice to New York. So, Jean Oltra contacted him and said it was imperative my daughter and I were on that particular flight. This was accomplished covertly. No one was supposed to know we would be on that plane.

I emptied our personal vaults at the Préfecture and Jean-Claude, my loyal driver, whisked me to AIS—the American International School to pick-up TK. My American friend and girl's school principal, Cathy Dariel, was in her office. I walked in as calmly as I could and told her not to ask questions. I said I was there to take TK out of school immediately and not to mention it to anyone. We went to the classroom and Cathy got TK. When she came out of class she was confused, but happy to leave. I hurriedly dragged her into the car. She was eight years old.

I packed our passports two and suitcases for each of us. Our sweet cat, Antoinette, was still wearing the jeweled collar from her namesake, "The Princess." She would be staying with my Hungarian friend, Dora, and her fiancée until she could be sent to us. Our dachshund, Selma, was left with Lilou and Marcel to be sent later as well.

When we arrived at the airport, we were taken to a private room where the Pan Am President and Jean were waiting. I was such a wreck and so racked with pain from the golden staph I didn't know how much longer I was going to be able to maintain a strong front for my daughter. I desperately wanted to be strong for TK and protect her, but I felt like I was on the verge of physical and emotional collapse.

Pan Am was very helpful and lived up to their promise. The president wished me well. We snuck onto the plane at the very last minute and I was praying we'd take off without any more problems. We finally lifted into the air and I was so grateful to have gotten this far.

The flight attendant delivered a lovely Hermès scarf from the in-flight shopping magazine with an unsigned note saying in French, "Hope you will be well and safe." She said it was from a gentleman on the flight. Apparently I was recognized, whoever he was.

During the entire trip, I reflected on what had occurred in just the past few days and was frightened about what the future held. I knew, somehow, I had to get well and eventually fly to Uruguay to join Jacques. When we arrived in New York, I no longer had my diplomatic passport. I was bringing a lot of cash as well as some of my personal jewelry in two brown paper bags stuffed into a large carry-on. If I was searched, this would make me look suspicious and I knew it. We arrived at immigration and the woman officer asked why I was coming to the United States. I stated I was an American citizen living part time in France. I was very ill and would be here for three weeks seeing my doctors. By looking at me, one could tell I was in extremely bad shape. She stared at me for around forty seconds then waved me on.

We retrieved our luggage from baggage claim and passed through customs where they asked if I had anything to declare. I said no. Once we were out of the customs area into the main hall, I went straight to a phone and called Lilou to say we had made it. She was crying and said our departure had been leaked to the French authorities. They had called ahead to U.S. officials to stop us at immigration to be placed in detention and held until we were sent back to France.

That was half an hour after we had arrived and already passed through immigration and customs. We had just squeaked in under the wire.

When I heard this, I literally dropped to my knees, shook and cried. I hunched over with my head in my hands. Poor TK was too young to understand the true gravity of the situation. How could I explain it without scaring her even more? She was already nervous and upset seeing her mother sobbing and it was a horrible moment for both of us.

I said to her, "Baby, we're safe now," and that was the most important thing she needed to know at that time.

I was looking over my shoulder every second we were in the airport. We left on the next plane for Arizona, where Martine would pick us up to stay at one of the houses Jacques had built in Scottsdale. We planned to retire in Pinnacle Peak and had built a large home for the three of us. I went to college during a year in Tempe. It wasn't my favorite place and I wasn't ecstatic about living in Arizona permanently, but first things first. I just wanted to somehow get well and speak to Jacques about our future. At the time, I didn't realize he wouldn't be able to come to the States to join us because he would have been extradited and prosecuted in France.

CHAPTER 85

MARTINE PICKED US UP IN PHOENIX. IT WAS good to see her. She was warm and supportive even though I knew it was just temporary and would not last.

I had to get well before I could go on to Uruguay. That was my priority before anything else. Jacques and I decided TK and I would temporarily stay near my mother in Rancho Mirage while I went through some sort of detox. As I later realized, the inept French doctors had prescribed a daily100 mg dose of Tranxene to mask the pain from the golden staph, but also to keep me calm and quiet for the benefit of the mayor. As I came to learn, the initial dose of Tranxene is 15mg, graduating to 30 mg as a normal daily dose. Obviously, my dosage was a bit unusual to say the least. I had been overprescribed because the doctors, like most people who revered and feared Jacques, wanted to remain in his good graces. Ignoring serious consideration of the long-term effects, the doctors wanted to shut me up to make me somewhat functional in order to please my husband.

When I arrived in Arizona, I called the Betty Ford Clinic to inquire about their program. They said it would be a major detox and I definitely had to be monitored. I rested at Martine's for a couple of weeks and then we went on to Rancho Mirage. I knew Jacques had settled in Punta del Este in Uruguay. We were in contact, still hoping soon to be together. I couldn't imagine what the future would actually hold for us. I rented a small home near the school TK would be attending in Palm Desert. I hired a nice woman to help me around the house. Upon speaking with the Betty Ford Clinic again, I was told I'd have to complete the program and stay for a minimum of six weeks. I knew that would be impossible. I couldn't leave my daughter for that amount of time. TK was already unhappy and understandably frightened. So, I decided to detox by myself while living at home. I worked out a plan. Over the course of a month, week-by-week, I lowered the dosage of Tranxene. I was continually in pain from my damaged mucus lining, but thought the first step was to get the drug out of my system. It would be a monumental effort, but at least I would feel like I was moving forward. Unfortunately, I came down with a cold.

My body was so weak and my mental state even weaker. I was still on fire. I believed I was doing as well as I could, but the cold didn't help. When I finally was down to the lowest dose, I stopped taking the Tranxene not realizing it was too big of a jump.

On the fourth day of complete withdrawal, my body crashed. I thought I was having a heart attack, dropped to the floor and started to convulse. It was the side effect of being off the drug. I had no idea it would be this bad. I had no idea what was happening to me and believed I was going to die. I kept passing out and finding myself on the floor. My head was so foggy, lost in my own mind, I thought the walls of the house were closing in on me. Crawling on the floor into my bedroom, I curled up in the fetal position. This was not the way I wanted to die, especially in front of my daughter.

I loved life, but couldn't go on in this condition. Unable to think clearly, everything was so frightening, dark and awful. I was in agony and at this point believed I couldn't be cured.

I decided to gather up all the Tranxene pills I brought with me from France and leave a letter sending TK to Punta to be with her father. While my daughter was still in school, I told the housekeeper I was going for a drive to clear my head. Then I drove straight to Idlewild in the mountains above Palm Springs where there was snow, which I adored.

It was like I had horse blinders on. I couldn't see on either side, only straight ahead with the thought of ending my life. I wrote an elaborate letter explaining my feelings and how sorry I was not able to raise my TK who I loved her with all my heart and soul. Someday, I hoped she'd understand.

I wrote Jacques to raise her well with love in his heart and to keep her healthy and safe.

My brother had visited me three weeks prior and had brought some vodka for himself that he left in my freezer. I told my lady helper to pick up my daughter from school and not to expect me back too early.

I grabbed the bottle of vodka and the bag of Tranxene. I still had 4300 milligrams left. I put on a glitzy pair of tennis shoes my Mom had bought me and took off. I drove to the mountains, which were an hour and a half away, parked my car, locked the doors, got in the backseat and became hysterical. I knew this was the end and accepted it. I took the 4300 mg of Tranxene. Then I drank as much vodka as I could without throwing up and passed out.

CHAPTER 86

I DON'T KNOW HOW MUCH LATER IT WAS WHEN I found myself outside of my car, coherent for a minute and cognizant enough to realize I was eating the dirt from under the snow.

I said to myself, "Ilene, you don't eat dirt," and passed out again.

I don't know how much time went by before I had a strange vision. I saw a long tunnel permeated with a brilliant light. Out of the tunnel, three men dressed in long black coats and dark sunglasses, like characters from "*The Matrix*," advanced towards me.

It looked so bright and lovely at the other end. I seemed to reach out my arms and said, "Please help me" and passed out again. Then, I found myself awake in a hospital room and later was told I had been missing for five days. They said I had been found outside my car, which had been parked in a private school parking lot in Hemet.

At the time, I was not cognizant of much of anything, much less where I was. It was my great piece of luck to have been rescued in the middle of a foolish act. Someone still wanted me here for a while. It was winter vacation and the janitor of the school was checking to make sure everything was in order for the new semester. There was only one of him coming towards me when I said, "Please help me." In my delirium I saw three men. It was not Neo and two men from *The Matrix* coming to get me. He found me outside the car lying in the snow and somehow I blurted out my mother's phone number. I don't remember how but I must have done it. The janitor was a good man.

Thank goodness for him because he phoned my mother to say he found me almost dead, but I was still alive.

An ambulance arrived and rushed me to the hospital. When I awoke I was screaming. I had tubes coming out of me everywhere and they had cut off my glitzy tennis shoes because I had such bad frostbite. My feet were red, black and blue. The doctor wanted to see if I could walk, but I couldn't. My mother had taken to her bed with grief because I had been missing for five days. My parents were beside themselves and contacted authorities everywhere, even in France, to find out if anyone had seen me. When they received the phone call and learned I had been found, they rushed to Hemet to be by my side. I was high as a kite from all the Tranxene I'd ingested and couldn't believe I was still alive. My dad spoke with our family doctor regarding the best course of treatment for my recovery.

The doctor thought it best for me to be transferred to L.A. and admitted to Cedars-Sinai Hospital psyche unit where I would be watched over and given proper medical care. I thought I would be detoxing. WRONG CHOICE! It wasn't a detox unit.

An ambulance drove me two and a half hours from Hemet to Cedar Sinai Hospital in Los Angeles. My father and I sat in front of the admitting doctor as he evaluated my condition. He said he would admit me if I was able to stand up. It took all my force to stand in front of my wheelchair but I did it. I was admitted and survived two weeks in that horrible unit.

It was a terrible place. Regrettably, I didn't have the clearest mind to object to anything when I was admitted. I failed to understand why I had been placed in a psyche rather than a detox unit, which is where I really needed to be. I shouldn't have been there and was pretty much out of it the entire time because of the Klonopin, which had been prescribed for me.

My new roommate was a sweet black woman who was schizophrenic. She saw how helpless I was and took care of my needs. She made my bed, got me tea, rolled me around in my chair and we ate together. If I needed a snack, she'd bring me a plate of everything she could pile on because she was kind enough to offer me choices. There was a daily meeting with all the patients in a large room to review the progress we were making. My first meeting was a disaster. There was this crazy woman, ha ha, who decided I was getting preferential treatment because I was in a wheelchair. She said she was tired of hearing about my feet. In my mental fog I was slow to realize I was being attacked. However, upon having a moment of semi-clarity, I realized the affront and immediately returned to my room.

My assigned doctor had prescribed the Klonopin to treat seizures, panic disorder and anxiety. This was not much different from Tranxene. Side effects included paranoia, suicidal tendencies, impaired memory, hampered judgement and loss of coordination. Everything I already had been going through while detoxing from the Tranxene. From the frying pan to the fire. This was not helping me. In addition, my roommate told me she was being released and I started to panic. Oh no, what would I do without her?

CHAPTER 87

THE NEXT DAY I WAS FEELING REALLY LOW AND rolled myself to the TV room. A young Mexican man sat next to me on the couch and asked why I was in the unit.

I told him a little of my story and said I still was unable to walk on my feet. They were overly tender, but a lighter shade of black, green and blue from the frostbite. He listened intently and said he wanted to help me. He took over where my former roommate left off. He wheeled me around and we talked non-stop. When his large family came to visit, they invited me into the back dining room to share a delicious home cooked family feast. Tortillas, carnitas, chili verde, enchiladas, refried beans, salsa, guacamole, chips, sour cream and flan filled the table. At least I remembered the food. My new friend told me he loved me and wanted to be with me after the hospital. I'll never forget his incredible kindness and the wonderful sweetness of my dear schizophrenic roommate. They helped get me through the ordeal. I don't know how I would have fared without them.

My head was clearing and I finally realized where I was. I became furious now that I could think again. What the hell was I doing in this mental ward! I demanded to speak to the doctor assigned to me at once. When I entered his office, I told him I was going to check out immediately. I said I should be in a special detox unit to help me get off the Tranxene and I should not have been prescribed Klonopin.

I told him about being cruelly attacked by a woman in the group meeting and I didn't belong there even in my disoriented state. I called Dad to come get me. I told him I was coherent enough to find a solution to my own problems. We went back to his home and I started making phone calls to some friends who had been through drug treatment programs.

Everyone I spoke with said St. John's Hospital in Santa Monica was the place to go. I also called the burn center in the San Fernando Valley headed by Dr. Richard Grossman. I learned frostbite can be as bad as a fire burn, only cold.

My parents' doctor came to check on me and look at my feet while I was still at Cedars. His bedside manner had never been warm or cozy. I asked him point blank if I was going to lose my feet. He said it was a good possibility and I would need to get my head together to be strong whatever the outcome. Well, I went into shock. That was the cruelest thing he could have said. Even if it's true, a doctor shouldn't blurt out words like that, especially with a patient as fragile as me. He could see I was vulnerable and weak, yet he hit me with a hammer blow. With his complete lack of sensitivity or understanding, I told my parents I never wanted him to contact me again.

I asked Dr. Grossman at the burn center the same question when he was evaluating me. He smiled, hugged me and said no way was that going to happen. I would not lose my feet, but it would take time and rehab for a sound recovery. From the moment he spoke those words, my attitude became more positive and I knew I was ready to fight for my life and feet. I also called two doctor friends who referred me to a fabulous physician named Dr. Fred Kuyt. He was experimenting with a combination of medications that could be funneled into my body via a tube to destroy the old ravaged mucus lining. This would enable the virgin mucus lining to regenerate. It would be my first opportunity to be able to take care of my physical and emotional needs at the same time. Finally, I was able to see a flicker of light at the end of the tunnel giving me hope I was on the right road to recovery.

CHAPTER 88

THERE WERE WEEKS OF REHAB FOR MY FEET AND I knew I had to deal with the Tranxene problem. I told my parents I was checking myself into an appropriate facility and finally contacted St. John's. I knew at this point the only safe way to completely get the Tranxene out of my system was to have professional help. I made an appointment to see the chief physician of the detox unit with my father. He said he wanted to see me right away. St. John's hospital in Santa Monica was 15 minutes from Dad's home so we rushed right over. We sat down and I started to discuss my history and circumstances up to that point. I explained I never drank or was into drugs except marijuana and hash for around six months when I was nineteen years old. I never smoked cigarettes because I couldn't stand any kind of smoke in my lungs, but I knew I was addicted to tranquilizers as a result of faulty guidance by the French doctors. The doctor wanted me to check in right away. I told him I'd check in the following day. He knew a little bit about my background and started asking me all types of questions regarding Nice and France. Here I was coming off Tranxene and the doctor was a total Francophile who wouldn't stop talking to me as I'm bouncing off the walls. It was surreal, but not as surreal as going through the unit would be, as I soon found out. We went home, packed a suitcase and the following morning I checked in.

I was taken to my room. My roommate was an alcoholic. She welcomed me with a huge hello and an enormous friendly smile. Plastered all over her walls and above the bed were photos of loved ones. She had already detoxed and was a bit too cheery for me, especially the next morning at 6 AM, when she threw back the drapes and turned to me and said, "Isn't it a beautiful morning?"

I looked at her and said, "NO, it is not a beautiful morning for me! Please cheer down."

I was allowed to stay in the room for two days before I was summoned to go to meetings. I would learn so much about drugs and detoxing in the weeks to come. It was shocking to discover how naive I had been about addiction, withdrawal and the effects of prescription drugs. The first large group meeting I had to attend had mostly detoxed alcoholics. There were only two pill users beside myself. These were my people who understood how difficult it was to come off of pills. I made friends with one pill popper, a man from the streets. He would walk the halls with me late at night because we both were anxious and couldn't sleep. He was also detoxing from heroin in addition to benzodiazepines. He explained to me prescription drugs and heroin were the two most difficult substances to detox from although heroin was even more difficult because you craved it mentally and physically even after it was out of your system.

When one is detoxing from pills, the medication would hide in your fat cells and could pop out anytime creating anxiety, paranoia, blackouts and very bad panic attacks. It could take up to two years to fully eliminate the drugs from your body, but afterwards there were no mental or physical cravings. If needed, there were antidepressants to help minimize the side effects.

After my first week, many of the alcoholics finished their stay and left. Then, the new group arrived with an assortment of heroin, speed, coke and pain pill addicts. I was happy to have some kindred spirits going through similar detox symptoms. I have to mention one older man who we called "Godfather." He was so funny and had an alcoholic buddy named Bill. The two of them would quadruple my food order behind my back after I had filled out my meal card. Food would be served on individual trays and when

I would get mine the two men would be hysterical, laughing in a corner. I'd see my tray piled high to the sky with five dessert puddings and three entrees. I'd shake my head and sit at the table while they watched me devour everything. I had lost so much weight, around 18 pounds, during my ordeal. What fun it was putting it back on during the next two years. I even put on an extra 5 pounds.

I went through rehab at St. John's in 26 long days fighting the withdrawals. They were bad. Paranoia, anxiety, convulsing, but I did it.

I actually enjoyed my stay at the unit in a bizarre way even as challenging as it was. It was frightening to find myself in that type of environment with other addicts, but I made some fantastic acquaintances who helped me through. We were all messed up in one way or another, yet together we laughed until our sides split. A speaker named Dorothy Hansen came to lecture one night at the hospital. She was a top AA therapist. I was so impressed by her speech she became my personal therapist for over a year. Dorothy helped me tremendously through the hardships of my continuing recovery following St. John's. I thank her for her loyal support. She also became Lee Rich's therapist, who was my fourth husband. I will explain in detail later. Lee Rich was a trip, but being with him was more Hollywood craziness I did not need. Why do I always seem to attract these constant over-the-top scenarios?

During the time I spent at St. John's, I was given permission to leave the facility once a week to begin treatment with Dr. Kuyt for my mucus lining. After six weeks of the painful procedure, all the ravaged mucus lining from the golden staph was destroyed enabling my body to begin regenerating virgin lining. At this point with my damaged insides on the mend, I was anxious and excited to reunite with my daughter in Uruguay. Honestly, I was scared to see Jacques after everything both he and I had been through. I knew his frame of mind was worse than ever. How could he have ignored the numerous warnings? This chaotic exodus was all because of him and he couldn't or wouldn't admit it to anyone. However in a rare moment, quite contrary to his character, he admitted to me it was his entire fault. Normally, his ego and pride would never allow him to acknowledge failure. Failure in anything for Jacques was never an option. Again, one must understand he was "King Jacquou."

CHAPTER 89

THEN, THERE WAS THE PROBLEM OF THE JOURNAL. I had kept my personal writings about what had transpired leading up to our escape. It described my distress about my golden staph condition, my deteriorating relationship with Jacques and my deep concerns about our daughter. This was my very personal journal and wasn't meant for anyone's eyes but mine because the ink was gushing out of the pen in my criticism of Jacques. It was a manner of self-therapy. I wrote it as I lived it. I hid the journal in a drawer in the Palm Desert home, but Jacques had accidentally gotten hold of it and the shit hit the fan.

How did that happen? TK was packed up and sent to her father in Uruguay soon after my near death experience. By mistake, the journal got packed into her suitcase. Of course, Jacques read it. During my time in rehab I was completely incommunicado, so Jacques' response was to send a long letter to my father. On the day I finished my treatment, Dad picked me up and summarized the contents as we drove home. Yes, Jacques had read my journal and said he was quite shocked at the way I felt. Since I had revealed such horrible things about him, I was actually stunned by his fake sincerity when he expressed his love for me in his letter and said everything was going to be okay. He just wanted me to come to Uruguay to be with him and our daughter. I didn't trust Jacques or his judgment at that point. I knew his vengeance and manipulation would be fired up to get back at me after he read my true thoughts. Deep down, truth being I would always be connected to him because of our daughter.

I had been through so much all I cared about was reuniting with her. The extended time she had been with her father greatly concerned me since I was fearful of his further declining mental state. I knew she must be even more afraid of Jacques because of his horrible, insane temper. He had always attempted to control everything around him and could not tolerate when he wasn't or couldn't be in control. It drove me crazy to think of them being alone together and me not being there to protect her.

Anne Laure, Jacques' second daughter, had relayed to me that her father had been verbally and physically abusive with her when she stayed with him in Punta del Este. I later found out to my horror and regret he was equally abusive to TK as well when I wasn't there.

Jacques, no longer the man I fell in love with and married, had become so angry and vile that it was agonizing being in his presence. His unpredictable moods were frightening. He wouldn't talk about anything relevant to our lives, our relationship or our circumstances. He wouldn't discuss the events leading up to our escape. In his mind, everything was just fine and normal as if nothing happened. Any discussion of the reality would be an admission of his failure. If I had remained in Uruguay with Jacques, I would have fragmented because of his irrational and erratic behavior.

I soon discovered one more reason he had chosen to live in Punta. This was something other than his belief of not being extradited from Uruguay. It was Marisol, the Argentine bimbo. He had been having an affair with her ever since Jean Oltra introduced them on that first trip to South America when I didn't accompany him. They had become close and she was deeply entangled in his affairs. She was draining Jacques financially and talking him into phony investment schemes.

I found that out in a strange way. In Punta, there was a small river near the house. One day I decided to walk there with Selma, my wiener dog. The "casero" in Spanish, told me he wanted to accompany me to make sure

I would be safe. He was the husband of the new domestic couple Jacques hired to take care of the house. I was speaking to him in my broken Spanish as we were walking along. He started telling me how much he and his wife liked me and wished I could be there all the time. I wondered why he might say that and decided to ask him a question of late that had been looming in my mind. I asked, "Is my husband having an affair with Marisol Nicoletti?"

He stopped and turned to me and said, "Senora, I am sorry to say, but you are the only person in Uruguay who doesn't know it."

At last all the domino pieces came tumbling down and the puzzle became clear. I now realized what had been going on over the last year and a half before we left France. Marisol had been in Nice several times to supposedly "interview" Jacques. Jean Oltra had set up the interview. Marisol was getting her nasty hooks into Jacques. She was no journalist. This woman was so evil she managed to convince him that she loved him and then set him up to take as much money from him as she could. She was still married and her husband was either an accomplice in the scheme or just looked the other way. I guess he figured there was enough money in it he could stand another man screwing his wife. She thought she had found the golden goose with Jacques.

She had convinced J to hire her hubby as a supposed architect/builder for our new home in Punta. It was a dreadful design and a totally impractical house. He continually talked Jacques into spending more and more money. He designed a shallow bathtub in a room off the master bathroom the size of a small swimming pool. It was enormous and there was no reason for it to be so large. It took hours to fill the tub and by the time it was full the water was cold.

The shower wasn't any better. I would take a shower at 5 PM every night and be all lathered up when the water would suddenly stop flowing. Why? Because the electricity went out. The town couldn't provide enough electricity even for the 3,000 people who lived there. They lacked the infrastructure with a laughable electrical grid. Electricity came and went and you never knew when it would be on or off. There was never enough.

The first time it happened I screamed. Of course, no one was around so I stood in the shower for probably 15 minutes until the back-up generator turned itself on.

That was the way it was every day. Standing in the shower, getting cold after the electrical grid had failed and waiting for the generator to kick in. When I took a shower, there was a chance I would have to stop half-done, semi-washed, and still covered in soapsuds. Of course, our generator couldn't power all our needs and it wasn't fun.

During the summer it was different, only worse. Due to the high tourist season, December through February (south of the equator), thousands of wealthy South Americans (mostly Argentinians) would invade the town to "wash" their money and build elaborate homes. There was one section called Beverly Hills where the required minimum size house was 10,000 square feet and there were a few at 50,000 square feet. As a result, this created a greater demand for electricity and electrical outages were even more frequent.

These were the days before other foreigners came in and built hotels and casinos. There wasn't much to do during my time there. My choices were to go to the market, go to one of the three open restaurants or take a walk on the beach. I haven't been back in a while, but I heard things have become a lot more interesting. At least, I hope they have more electricity.

Marisol had more conspirators than just her weak-willed husband. She also had introduced Jacques to a friend of hers, an awful woman with the nickname of "Bitchy," an appropriate name if ever there was one. She was a triple prescription pain pill and ether addict. They were partners in crime and I mean that literally. She and Marisol were scamming Jacques to rake as much of his money and property as they could.

Jacques' affair with Marisol was becoming more and more obvious. One day J and I went to pick up TK from her tennis lesson. I waited in the car while he went to get her. Marisol was picking up her son as well and approached J in front of our car. They looked like they were arguing about something and were standing so close, faces almost touching. It looked like two lovers having a quarrel. The casero told me and warned me. So I already knew and this confirmed it.

Staring at them I wondered why Jacques had chosen her because she was completely not the type of female he would normally be attracted to. She was dumpy, homely, and very unattractive, but she was thirty-one and Jacques was desperately chasing his youth. She was his obvious lover standing there in front of TK and me.

CHAPTER 90

ANOTHER TRIP, ANOTHER TORTUOUS TURN OF the wheel. Uruguay was a continuous revolving door with nothing getting better or resolved. I was going back and forth from L.A. to Punta, but actually getting nowhere.

Jacques was living a life now that was totally inappropriate and very much a departure from his original philosophy, which he shared with me upon our first meeting. He didn't want to cheat like he had with Claude and wanted to only be with me, living in love and happiness for the rest of our lives. Yet, he was exposing our daughter to his debauchery and lying to me about what really was happening. He had lost it and in his mind he was still ruling Nice and the Côte d'Azur, all from his desk in Punta. He was juggling me and Marisol.

Spontaneously, Jacques decided he was taking TK and me to Buenos Aires for a few days. I couldn't put it off any longer. At the hotel, I confronted him with everything I'd heard and seen first-hand.

"Listen," I said. "We both have been indiscreet, but I never did anything in front of you and I've always treated you with respect and love. I can't do this anymore. This is too hurtful and at this point it's obvious your malicious behavior is just to get back at me."

I took a deep breath and continued on.

"I almost died from the golden staph and we've lost just about everything we owned in France. You've been doing your best to poison TK against me by telling her I'm an alcoholic, a drug addict, and a whore. Is it any wonder why her behavior is so adverse against me since she's been with you? So, what's the point of pretending anymore? If you're saying things to our daughter against me, at least make them credible."

"You know I don't like the taste of alcohol and never drank. I've never been into drugs except smoking grass when I was a teen. But, you had the gall to tell our daughter I'm a whore? Her mother is a whore! You're revolting! Just be honest and truthful for once in your life and stop playing these sick games. Try to be fair. You're using our daughter as a pawn when you are angry with me. Don't use TK to hurt me because you're only destroying her."

I delivered my speech. Of course, Jacques couldn't handle the truth. He stood in front of me and told me how much he loved and adored me and that we'd always be together. He didn't even attempt to respond to anything I had carefully verbalized. It was as if I hadn't said anything at all.

Great, I thought. So being forced into action, I decided after this not so stellar conversation I would have to handle his insanity by myself. It became crystal clear it would be up to me to save myself and my daughter and the drama continued, as usual.

CHAPTER 91

BACK IN L.A., I DECIDED TO ACCEPT BEING INTRO-
duced to a couple of men that friends wanted me to meet. Jacques and
I were no longer in the same country and as far as I was concerned, we were
separated. It was time to consider another life, another path. I had been with
Jacques for sixteen years. A lot had happened during those incredible years,
bad times as well as amazing and miraculous experiences. It was almost more
than one could imagine happening in that span of time. Sadly, at this point
the bad times had surpassed the great and amazing ones. It was over for me
and it was time to think about a healthier future.

I was introduced to a lovely man from Vancouver who was much older.
His name was Abe Grey. Maybe a bell was ringing in my head.

Remember I said earlier when I was two and a half we moved to British
Columbia, where my father was responsible for investing money for my
Uncle Jack. He established an insurance company that was eventually sold
to Penn Life.

Well, this was a case of life repeating itself and it's a small world. My
parents had many friends when we were in BC, and one of them happened
to be Abe. We discovered the connection on our first date.

I told him I'd lived in Canada when I was a little girl. He had been
introduced to me as Ilene Médecin, not knowing my maiden name. So, at
dinner, we talked about Canada. He finally asked me my maiden name, and
I told him it was Graham.

He looked at me strangely and said, "Is your father's name Jack?"

I said, "Yes." I thought he was going to fall out of his chair. Then, he told me he'd known my parents and had bounced me on his knee when I was a three-year old child. I couldn't believe it. We laughed and laughed and Abe said to me, "You sure have changed."

We enjoyed each other's company and saw a lot of one another. He had a circle of friends in L.A. that we socialized with regularly when he wasn't taking care of business in Canada.

I felt I was getting serious about Abe or I could be serious in the future. I was eager for him to come back from Canada. Then fate intervened, as it so often does in my life, and the storyline continued being wild and strange.

One of the ladies from Abe's group named Virginia ("Ginny") called me after Abe had left for Canada on business. She knew a woman in New York who had a male friend who was getting divorced. He had described to her what he was looking for in a woman. Did she know of anyone in L.A. who fit the bill?

Apparently, Ginny thought I did. She explained everything and asked if this woman could just phone me. I said that Abe and I had talked about getting engaged and were planning a two-month trip to solidify our union and plan our future together.

Ginny said it wouldn't hurt to talk to this woman, would it? I relented and soon after, my phone rang. Her name was Joyce and I told her what I explained to Ginny. She asked, "Do you have a ring on your finger yet?"

I said "No."

"Then, why don't you at least have dinner with my friend? Just think it over and let me know."

Abe was going to be gone for two weeks or more. I thought, why not? It's just a dinner. Famous last words.

Foolish me, again thinking that something "casual" wouldn't be serious or fateful. Everything is serious. The teensiest thing can lead to the biggest most fateful outcome, as it did here. However, the truth is there has never been anything "teensy" about my life.

I got Joyce on the phone and told her to set it up. I thought she told me her friend's name was Rich Lee. I thought he might be Chinese. So when he called me, I wasn't sure who it was.

He laughed and said his name was Lee Rich, not Rich Lee. We were having fun on the phone and made a dinner date for the upcoming Friday.

I had been speaking to Abe every day. He told me he would be gone for more than two weeks but would get on a plane as soon as he finished his business. I was disappointed. Abe reminded me a little of Jacques' good qualities. He also was a Taurus and had that familiar earthiness about him. I'm sure that's why I felt so comfortable and somewhat at peace in his company.

Lee Rich rang my buzzer and I told him to come up to the 2nd floor. I opened the door and he handed me a beautiful bouquet of pastel roses. He stared at me and started giving me compliments, not only about how I looked and what I was wearing, but how enchanted he was with my decorating and what a fantastic job I did with my condo. He seemed so sweet and cheerful. As I learned, Lee was a major Hollywood producer, one of the biggest and best. His name hadn't been familiar to me, but his productions were very well known.

I was still wounded, still healing from all that had happened and missing my TK so much. I was vulnerable and thought of Abe, comparing the two men.

CHAPTER 92

LEE ESCORTED ME TO A POPULAR ITALIAN RESTAU-
rant on Beverly Boulevard called Madeo. We sat at a booth in the corner
and he began to tell me about his feelings, including his past marriages, his
last horrendous pending divorce, and how depressed he had been. I felt
compassion for him while he sincerely poured his heart out.

I put my hand on his arm and listened intently. He also told me about
Lorimar, a production/distribution company he co-founded in 1969 with his
partner Merv Adelson, who was once married to Barbara Walters. Lorimar
Studios went on to become wildly successful with numerous hit TV shows
and awards.

Lee and Lorimar studios produced *The Waltons*, a hugely popular
series made for CBS, which aired for 9 seasons. The show garnered numerous Emmy Awards during its long tenure. Lee's biggest hit with Lorimar was
Dallas, the primetime soap that aired on CBS for thirteen seasons. Lorimar
was on a roll and at one point produced three of the top ten TV shows. After
Lorimar's merger with Telepictures, Lee eventually sold his shares worth over
$200 million. Following Lee's departure from Lorimar-Telepictures, the era
came to an end as they merged with Warner Bros in 1989. He always enjoyed
working and was hired by Kirk Kerkorian (who also owned the MGM Grand
in Vegas and knew my Uncle Jack). Lee became Chairman and CEO of MGM/
UA studio for a few years.

Lee went on and on emptying his soul. I kept trying to soothe him by saying that better things were ahead and not to lose hope. I shared with him the fact I had been through some major life events that at the time seemed impossible to overcome, but somehow I survived and here we were. We had a lovely evening together. I liked him. He was very interesting and a total gentleman.

After dinner, we went back to my place and had chamomile tea, which is always soothing for the weary soul. We talked some more and Lee ended up asking me out for the rest of my life.

I thought that was a sweet thing to say and a nice way of putting it. I said I'd have dinner again with him in a couple of days. He sent me bouquets of flowers and wanted to buy me presents. I told him about Abe and explained I wouldn't accept anything unless we were in an exclusive relationship. That's when he asked me to marry him.

Another dilemma. I am still legally married to Jacques, getting engaged to Abe, and dating Lee who has proposed to me. It looks like my personal lawyer, Ken Warner, will be busy as usual. One of the reasons I find myself in complicated circumstances is I like leaving my options open before making a final decision. Maybe I attract difficult scenarios because I'm so multi-faceted, easily bored and need the excitement. I guess it's just my destiny.

It reminded me of when my first husband Bert came to Nice and asked my help in purchasing a boat in Monaco he was considering. Always gallant, Jacques invited him to a gala we were attending with Jean-Claude chauffeuring. My husband, Jacques, was in the front seat. Bert, my ex-husband, and I were in the back and my lover JC was at the wheel. I'll explain my relationship with Jean-Claude in more detail later. This wasn't just your typical three-way triangle. I thought it was hilarious. I do seem to get myself in trouble juggling men at times. At least, I've learned lessons and applied them in an attempt to avoid too much drama in the future.

I called Abe in Canada and immediately told him I had met someone in his absence. He was quite upset when I said Lee had asked me to marry him. He said, "What about our road trip and our relationship? What are you going to do?"

From our previous conversations, he knew how much I'd been through and I only wanted to be happy with a less convoluted life. Abe said he would cut his business trip short and immediately come see me. I wasn't feeling sure about my decision, so I told him to finish his trip and we'd see each other afterwards.

CHAPTER 93

I CONTINUED TO GO OUT WITH LEE. WE WERE HAV-
ing so much fun. Being a Sagittarius like me, he was up for anything I
wanted to do. I reflected on Abe, who was a Taurus like Jacques. Did I want
to go with a man that reminded me of J or go with unpredictable Lee?

There were such different dynamics between the two men and after
deep reflection I believed I would be happier marrying Lee. So, it came to be
and we married in February 1994. He was easy to be with since our lifestyles
were compatible and he really loved me. Lee also promised to help get my
daughter back.

I needed to get my daughter away from Jacques in Uruguay. He was
not stable enough to raise a child. TK was so afraid of him, which regrettably
I didn't find out until after the fact. I still shudder to think about it now. This
abuse was hidden from me while she was with him.

If I had known at the time, I would have kidnapped her and made sure
he would never see her again. He really damaged our daughter, who today
lives with PTSD and depression. I also suffer from PTSD as a result of the total
experience with Jacques. What had occurred was unconscionable. It was the
end of an era as Jacques' unconstrained ego not only destroyed the Médecin
legacy, but he also abandoned his friends and loyal followers. Jacques even
turned his back on his life-long protector and right-hand man, Max, who had
been dedicated to him and his father Jean throughout their political careers.

I called Abe and told him I decided to marry Lee. I was truly sorry, but I had to follow my gut feeling. I wanted to find a better solution for my future than moving to Canada with a man who reminded me of my former husband. I didn't want to live anticipating the emergence of the dark side of that character type.

Lee gave me a book about himself and his accomplishments in the entertainment industry. He was highly respected. We attended an opening of an art exhibit one evening with many of his cohorts. Michael Crichton, the creator of the prime time drama series *ER* and the smash film *Jurassic Park*, joined us and praised Lee as his mentor and wished someday he could make as much money as him.

He wouldn't have said that if he had known Lee's real financial status. Little did I know at the time Lee was almost broke. A dear friend told me the truth about him and warned me before the marriage. He said Lee had lied to get me. I didn't want to believe my friend because I didn't care if Lee had lost money as long as he was working and could support us. I should have listened to my buddy.

After he left Warner Brothers, Lee went to Sony and then Paramount Studios. I was pretty happy with him and felt he must be doing well. I thanked my friend for the warning and said I'd be fine. I wasn't. Lee had managed to ruin both his personal and business life as quite often happens in Hollywood. One collapse leads to another. I just didn't know the true history, but would soon learn it.

Lee had been married to Pippa Scott, an actress who was never a leading lady, but had roles in a few good films and other television credits. They had two daughters together.

Following his divorce from Pippa, Lee got fixed up with Angela, an alleged hooker who worked at Saks 5th Avenue in Las Vegas and ran with the Mob. This is where his troubles really began. It was a set-up. She had smart people behind her who instructed her how to bleed Lee dry and she certainly did that. They acquired five homes while married. I was told by a woman who worked at Neiman Marcus in Beverly Hills this scammer would order a complete line of designer clothing in multiples of five to have them sent to each house because she didn't like to pack. There's a phrase for that kind of disgusting behavior, but I won't mention it.

I was introduced to Angela's two offspring. She manipulated Lee to adopt and support them on top of all the other monies she swindled out of him. The daughter was a total bitch to me for no reason. At least, the son was pleasant. I'm used to having stepchildren and know having step kids can be challenging, but everyone has to give a little. This scenario had special problems even for a "blended" family. It was not a good situation and Lee hardly ever saw them except when they wanted more money.

When Angela divorced him, Lee's lawyers advised he was being much too generous and didn't have to give away the farm. She had threatened to blackmail him by exposing his hidden past family life with wife and children he had abandoned in New York many years prior. Since Lee was amenable to this grossly unfair settlement, his lawyers were adamant he sign a document to acknowledge he was proceeding against their advice. They didn't want to be sued for malpractice or face any repercussions later.

Angela was finally gone, but with all his money.

Lee, at least, had a fairly decent relationship with Pippa and their two girls, or so I thought. I had lunch with Pippa and we seemed to get along well. Jessica, the older daughter, was okay with me and Miranda, the younger one, was civil. Little did I realize I was walking into a hornet's nest.

Lee had lied to me from the beginning and his family was not aware of it nor was I. They had no knowledge about me until Miranda was getting married. Lee and I were introduced to her new in-laws who coincidentally had met me in Nice as First Lady. They started to reminisce about Nice and the French Riviera and how honored they were to be having dinner with Madame Médecin. They asked questions about Jacques and said they were upset the two of us were no longer ruling the South of France. Everyone at the table was stunned because they had never bothered to learn anything about me and now, suddenly, they were dining with the former First Lady of Nice and the French Riviera. They were shocked and didn't know what to say. It was awkward actually because the Rich family hadn't been very gracious with me to say the least. I will say though that Pippa and her kids never looked at me the same way again. They obviously didn't care what I was bringing to Lee's and my relationship. They only cared about what money he had left. That was my small victory and only a momentary halt in the downward slide.

The shit hit the fan on New Year's Eve 1995. Lee and I had invited my father and his wife to the original Palm Restaurant in West Hollywood. Lee went to pay the check and after trying five credit cards that all failed, he kept mumbling some excuse about "computer error." Dad finally said to hell with it and paid for dinner. I was embarrassed and fuming. When we got home, I jumped on Lee and screamed, "What the hell is going on?"

Lee said he'd take care of it, but failed to explain anything to me at that time.

Prior to our marriage when Lee and I were getting to know each other, he bought me an exclusive phone just for us. In retrospect, I realized he wanted to keep tabs on me because he was so paranoid I would discover his lies. It was like being spied on and followed by Jacques or Daniel all over again.

I was with a friend walking down Rodeo Drive in Beverly Hills and she counted ten phone calls from him as we were going in and out of stores. He had to know who I was talking to, meeting, and seeing every moment. He was afraid I might encounter someone who would give him away.

It should have been apparent sooner, but I was still wounded from all the events that had previously occurred. These events affected me in ways that would be difficult for anyone to understand. Having already gone through maximum shit in France and Uruguay, I didn't want any more of it, so I did a little digging. Of course, what I discovered was disgusting. I found out Lee had been borrowing money from Pippa and friends and had acquired multiple credit cards that he would charge to the max and then apply for more. I knew nothing about this and had been duped from the beginning. Consequently, his un-charming family blamed me for his overspending and this was the reason they treated me so horribly. I didn't learn about that until later.

Lee had neglected to tell me certain crucial facts about his life. He failed to tell me he had a previous wife and two children he abandoned in New York prior to Pippa. At that time, he had been a senior executive with a large advertising company. He didn't want anyone to know about his past secret family because it would identify his real age.

Even though he kept telling me age was a huge factor in Hollywood, I never quite understood why. When we met, he volunteered how old he was.

Naive me, instead of questioning what he volunteered, I said "You look pretty shitty for your age. I want you to work out with my trainer and you're going to eat healthier food."

CHAPTER 94

TALK ABOUT GULLIBLE. I SURPRISED HIM WITH A 60th Birthday celebration, which actually surprised everyone but me. Even though he looked so much older, I wanted to believe him.

His age was kept a secret along with his finances after he and Angela divorced. After their divorce was final, he wanted to meet my parents. We scheduled two separate dinners since my parents were not together. Both dinners were at The Grille in Beverly Hills where Lee was an original shareholder. He assured my father he was extremely capable of taking care of me in the lifestyle to which I was accustomed. He stated his net worth was $200 million and had encouraged Dad to verify. My father had the resources to confirm his finances. Lee said everything would go to me if anything were to happen to him and requested my lawyer, Ken, to write a contract to that effect. What was discovered after the fact was he had transferred everything to Angela. Following the New Year's Eve debacle, he finally told me everything had been given to her because she was blackmailing him about his previous life. Like I said, it made no sense. Although he was a pathological liar, it was true he once was a legendary TV producer and movie mogul. Unfortunately, through his own stupidity, he had given all his money away.

In spite of the lies and his true financial condition, Lee was extremely generous. He was sweet, kind, fun, and told me I was the love of his life. This part was true because he constantly demonstrated it. Even with everything Lee had put me through, the bounced checks, the creditors at the door, his excuses and promises that he would change, his whole spider web of lies, and the IRS attempting to seize our house, I still smile to this day when I think of him. He really was fabulous to me, and we had so much fun together.

Thankfully, he paid for the lawyers to assist me in Uruguay when I went back to fight for my daughter. It was his promise and he found the money for that. I am forever grateful for his support in the attempt to reunite me with my TK.

CHAPTER 95

WITH DIVORCE PAPERS IN HAND, I RETURNED to Uruguay to deliver them to Jacques. It gave me primary custody of our daughter. Although knowing they were only valid in the U.S. and not in France, he grudgingly signed the papers. France doesn't recognize marriages outside of their country, so when Lee and I got married, I was still legally married to Jacques in France. Of course, there had to be a big story about Lee and me getting married on the front page of Nice-Matin, the leading newspaper on the Côte d'Azur. That shocked everyone and drove Jacques even more insane. It was just one more reason for him to hate me and to lie in wait for his revenge. He was in total denial and insisted we were still married and would always be married. J was so angry with me in Punta when I gave him the papers to sign, he threw the pages at me when he finished. Even though he signed, I knew he would never follow through with any of it. I just wanted to have something in writing.

It was a scary time for TK and me. We went on long walks just to be away from Jacques and clung to one another for solace, especially since I was aware my daughter would not be returning with me on this trip.

I told Jacques I was leaving to go back to the States and would return for TK. He drove me to the airport, but it was a wild and frightening ride. An angry maniac was driving that I didn't recognize, swerving left and right, almost going off the road a few times.

I hugged TK at the terminal and told her I would be coming back to get her. We had tears in our eyes.

Jacques hugged me goodbye. Little did I know this would be the last time I would ever see him again face to face.

CHAPTER 96

S ADLY, I HAD TO LEAVE TK IN URUGUAY FOR NOW. I couldn't get her out. Even though J signed the papers, he had no intention of giving my daughter back or complying with any of the terms of the agreement. I went home to Lee who was by my side and supported me. Even though he took advantage of my fragile condition by lying to me about his past, I'll never forget his good intentions. He always accommodated all my needs in a caring manner. For that reason, I am very appreciative and thankful. I had become unsure about many discrepancies that surfaced during our marriage. I wasn't sure who Lee really was because there were so many inconsistencies about everything he told me. On top of all those deceptions, he even lied about his age. He was thirty years older than me and not sixteen. For the most part, I've been with older men and age has never been an issue. So, for Lee to lie about his age with me was undeniably ludicrous. In fact, I was impressed with the energy he mustered to continue working as he did considering his actual age.

Lee had bought me a house on Mandeville Canyon off Sunset Boulevard in Brentwood. He gave me carte blanche to decorate it. I loved that particular home from the time I watched it being built when I was in my early twenty's. I actually dreamed that someday I would like to own it. Who'd a thunk it? I cried when we closed escrow because he made that dream come true.

I made Mandeville into a jewel box. We adored our home. I designed our theater room in the vintage style, like theaters I'd visited in London. It had three main tiers accommodating eighteen people. Each tier had three custom double theater seats with ottomans where two people could lounge very comfortably. There was additional seating with even enough room for my two wiener dogs, Selma and Sophie. I had to have a genuine concession counter complete with soda fountain, popcorn machine and hot dog maker. It was just like in the big cinemas, only a smaller version.

The furniture was forest green with leopard fabric. There was a theater-size screen and a professional projection booth. Since Lee was a producer, we enjoyed pre-release original movie reels and only had to pay the projectionists. These were not videos.

The runners who brought the reels for the weekend said it was the best screening room they'd ever seen. That was quite a compliment since they had been inside many other celebrity homes while making their drop-offs. Our theater comfortably sat 24, with more room on the tiers where additional guests could lounge on huge comfy pillows.

Lee would regularly receive a list of the new releases and we would choose what interested us. I would send our selection to family and friends at the beginning of the week. Friday and Saturday were double features of the latest films in the theaters. Most times we had them even before they were released to the public. On Sunday, there was just one movie. We entertained friends and family every weekend unless we had an important engagement to attend. I especially enjoyed being able to share this with Dad and his wife who had their own special seats. They were always with us and we loved having dinner with them before everyone arrived. I had a great cook, Svetlana, from Serbia who would whip up the most scrumptious comfort food. We always had a full house and everyone was in heaven going to the movies chez nous.

I redid the swimming pool to look like a black-bottom lagoon. We had a great tennis court and a wonderful fruit and vegetable garden where I grew the largest zucchini I'd ever seen. It was so heavy I needed help carrying it into the kitchen.

I put my heart and soul into that home, but we almost lost it. Fortunately, I was able to save it just in time. Lee got into trouble with the IRS. They were talking about seizing the house as part of his assets, but it had been quit claimed to me the year before, so they couldn't touch it. They were ready to attach anything else they thought he owned because he had foolishly left himself so vulnerable. He managed to screw up his finances big time. The IRS was the last straw and I finally had to admit to myself the truth of what I had been observing since the beginning of our marriage. Lee was almost broke and couldn't handle money responsibly.

Once again, the circumstances were all too familiar when things just seemed to unravel. Lee had deceived me and that was another blow. I was still separated from my daughter and prayed she was surviving with her abusive father and his evil mistress. It was too much to absorb again. I started to fragment. I was hoping for a stable, honest marriage. I was trying to get TK back and live a more quiet and peaceful life. It became very apparent that was not in the cards with Lee. Once again, I was dragged into someone else's drama and not of my own doing.

I always admit when I'm to blame for something. I take full responsibility for my actions and try to rectify the situation. I was honest and straightforward with Lee and put all my efforts into making the marriage work. This was not my fault.

With Jacques, I have to admit, we were both at fault. He just went too far with his relentless revenge. J allowed his emotions to run his life and ruin our marriage. His insane anger and jealousy almost destroyed me and did destroy us.

CHAPTER 97

MEANWHILE, JACQUES HAD BEEN ARRESTED IN Uruguay by surprise. He thought he had a safe haven as a political refugee. As it turned out, he was not protected under political asylum because France had unexpectedly brought criminal charges with a request for extradition. He had grossly underestimated his relationship with his Uruguayan government contacts. The onslaught of publicity about his predicament also became a huge factor. After being pressured by the French government, Uruguayan authorities had decided Jacques didn't deserve "political exile" status. The French claimed Jacques was not living as a political exile, the criminal charges were real, and he should be extradited back to France. J would do anything possible to avoid returning to France, so he initiated legal motions to be detained in Uruguay. Initially, they kept him under house arrest for a few months wearing an ankle bracelet. Then he was transported to Maldonado, a slightly larger city than Punta, to be imprisoned for a year. Following that, with all of his legal motions exhausted, he was extradited back to France only to spend another year in Grenoble Prison.

Once I had been informed of Jacques' new situation, I flew to Punta to remove my daughter from this mess. This certainly wasn't for Jacques, but for TK. He left her with his lover as I mentioned. She was one of the worst women I ever met, the wicked witch, Marisol Nicoletti. Poor TK was being starved. She was fed thick watery spaghetti with ketchup as a sauce.

I never saw Jacques again in person. We communicated through his lawyers and letters dropped off by TK when she went to visit him in jail. He was able to continue manipulating our daughter, even from behind bars, because she was so frightened of him from his terrible abuse. Supposedly, he had left all his legal documents in a bank vault that would ensure TK would inherit the property he owned in Punta. Martine's husband, Jean, was in Uruguay and had offered to help me with any loose ends. I knew it was going to be an ordeal. I needed help and was on the phone constantly with Lee who was incredibly supportive. I respected him for that.

I have to mention Dorothy Hansen again, the therapist I met while in rehab who helped me through the detox and kept me from falling apart. I burned up the phone wires between Punta and Santa Monica talking constantly with Dorothy. My anxiety was going through the roof fighting for my daughter. Jacques was unrecognizable with his vengeance. He had bribed the local magistrate to rule against me, preventing TK to return to the States. Dorothy talked me down every night as things became more and more complicated.

Jacques was in jail in Maldonado which was close by, but I couldn't bring myself to see him. Each time I thought I might go visit, I would start to shake and felt like vomiting. I knew I would completely fall apart in his presence. Jacques was an expert at finding someone's weaknesses and exploiting them. He was certainly an expert at finding MY weak spots. As a seasoned politician, he was an extraordinary puppet master. I knew he was waiting for the right moment to punish me more. Time was not of the essence. Jacques would lure someone into complacency and patiently wait to strike at their most vulnerable moment. He would typically annihilate the unsuspecting opponent. I had seen this played out many times with anyone who had dared cross him, so I knew he would play me at the most inopportune time. Being very familiar with his tactics, I refused to submit to him and wouldn't expose myself to his horrid toxicity anymore.

Since Jacques had already read my journal, I wrote him a letter saying there was nothing left to say and nothing left to hide. The truth was something he didn't want to hear, but he had set the rules and now had to accept the painful results. Without a conscience, he abandoned our daughter to live with that piece of dung Marisol, the mistress who was not happy to have the responsibility and didn't give a rat's ass about TK or what she fed her. Again, TK told me Marisol would feed her limp spaghetti with ketchup instead of pasta sauce and that was dinner. TK had been alone and terrified. I wasn't made aware of her abusive treatment until much later when she finally returned to me in the States.

CHAPTER 98

I FINALLY OBTAINED A COURT ORDER TO OPEN Jacques' bank vault in Punta. Jean and I went with my Uruguayan lawyer to the bank to recover the contents of the safe deposit box. When we raised the lid and looked inside, there was nothing in it. Empty.

Jacques had lied once again and left our daughter nothing. Oh, Jacques, what happened to the man I once loved?

Jean, Martine's husband, had turned into a major creep. He came on to me and I had to push him away telling him I wanted none of it. Does everyone go crazy when they go to South America? I couldn't wait to go home and wait for my daughter to return to me. We would be happy together once again, mother and daughter, as it should be. Jacques promised he would send her back to me when he was out of jail. Of course, that never happened. Like so many things, it was another one of his ploys to deceive and hurt me.

After I had returned to the states, I learned most of our cherished personal property was stolen from our house in Punta. Since it seemed obvious Jacques was not getting out of prison anytime soon and I was in the U.S., the thieves and leeches came out of the woodwork. As none of the others would have known their value, I assume Jean took the Scottish dirks. Marisol and Bitchy hastily helped themselves to our possessions. The first casero (caretaker) couple who Jacques had previously fired also decided to clean the house of our belongings. This casero is not to be confused with the second casero who had informed me of J's affair with Marisol and was sympathetic.

There was a wonderful portrait of me that hung on Gucci's wall in Beverly Hills while I was their staff model in the late 60's. I found it hanging on the wall of the first casero couple's abode along with my Lalique pieces, obviously stolen by them as well. They couldn't deny it was my portrait. Obviously it was me, but I still couldn't get the painting back because this was Uruguay. There were other personal mementos of mine that were missing. To this day, everything is still in dispute and none of the stolen goods have been recovered.

It was especially hurtful when Jean, who I trusted, betrayed me. He joined forces with the evil Marisol and conspired to rob me. Martine, who was dear to me and who I hoped I could still trust, wasn't aware of her husband's devious nature, so I thought.

Jean had gone over to the dark side and, shortly thereafter, she became aware of this and they divorced. Of course, it was contentious. Suddenly, he was very prosperous. In a nanosecond he moves to a third world country, marries a new woman and opens a business with an abundance of money. (Must have been those valuable Scottish dirks he stole from Jacques and me.) How obvious can one be? I knew where Jean's money came from, but it was just par for the course with all the scamming, covetous personalities involved. The sharks had been swarming around Jacques and once he was out of the way in prison, they devoured the contents of the house. Continuing to make matters worse, Jacques had paid off the local magistrate regarding TK's custody.

I had gone to the local judge with papers from my lawyers in the U.S., stating I was the mother of TK and had full custody. Well, it didn't do me any good, certainly not in Punta. My Uruguayan lawyer said he knew this magistrate took a payoff from Jacques to give custody of our daughter to his mistress. Of course, he turned down my request for sole custody and there wasn't anything I could do about it.

Again, I couldn't get her out of Uruguay to take her home. I would have to leave her there with the horrible Marisol and the bitch Bitchy. I had no control and the crooked court was against me. I cried hysterically.

This was a foreshadowing of things to come. There would be other crooked courts against me, but of course, I didn't know that yet.

Uruguay is known as the Switzerland of South America. They were very happy to hide money for expats who were dodging taxes in their own countries. It seemed like a never-ending saga, and it was.

CHAPTER 99

EVEN IN JAIL, JACQUES COULD DRIVE ME CRAZY.
As mentioned, he unjustly put my TK in Marisol's custody while he was
incarcerated. I was furious. Her place was with me. I am and will always be
her mother, period. Very sadly, Jacques was using our daughter to get back at
me. The collateral damage she would incur from this experience never concerned him. He lied and continually attempted to turn her against me with
his brainwashing, saying again and again I was a dope addict, an alcoholic
and a whore. Lies and more lies.

Anyone who knows me can attest I never drink because alcohol makes
me ill. I get nauseous even if I smell it. So, Jacques, if you're going to lie
about me make it credible. I was never a dope addict, except if you count
the Tranxene, which was not my fault. I was in horrendous pain with the
golden staph and the French doctors overprescribed excessive amounts of
this tranquilizer to keep me calm for Jacques' benefit. It was their fault and
I got hooked. Thank goodness I had the guts, courage and determination
to recover.

Whore? That was an unhealthy thing to tell our daughter. Shame on
you Jacques!

I had always hoped someday I would be able to return to France. I
love France and miss the Côte d'Azur. Now that will never be. I can't set foot
on French soil even today or I'll be detained. I was convicted in absentia for
being the wife of Jacques Médecin. Under Napoleonic Law, the spouse is

considered to be complicit in the charges whether they were involved or not. There is no "presumed innocence" in France. You are not innocent. You're guilty and must prove your innocence unlike America. In France, you go straight to jail when accused.

I learned this the hard way as I shared in the beginning of this story. I was visiting my dear friend Trevor Mound in Bath, England. During my stay, I thought why not fly to France after. Jacques had been released from Grenoble and had returned to Uruguay. He was no longer in a French jail. I assumed there shouldn't be a problem with me returning to France and visiting my friends. I was under the impression I could safely enter. WRONG.

I had divorced Lee and there was an addendum on the last page of my passport noting my name change back to my maiden name of Graham. That would be my undoing. When I arrived in Nice, the customs man looked at the back page and, even though he let me proceed to the baggage claim, he immediately alerted the gendarme. I WAS ARRESTED!

I truly was in shock. Believe me, I wouldn't have entered France under any circumstance if I had known I was in legal jeopardy. Unbeknownst to me prior to my fateful trip, the saga continued as Jacques was supposed to stand trial again in Grenoble. He was told to stay in Nice while awaiting the date. Not Jacques. He sneaked out through Italy and caught a plane back to Uruguay. Again, I was blindsided. I didn't know and wasn't told until it was too late. I was arrested, tortured and mistreated in the Nice jail. I was scared out of my wits while waiting to hear what the judge would say to me the next morning. It was a horrific ordeal.

CHAPTER 100

I HAD SPENT ONE NIGHT IN THE AIRPORT CELL AND four nights in the women's jail.

Three gendarmes were assigned to drive me to Grenoble for my court date. I say "gendarme" because these were national police not municipal, the distinction being I had a great relationship with the local municipal police. Gendarmes are armed and uniformed with national jurisdiction.

They escorted me in handcuffs to the police car from the Nice Prison, my three gendarmes. Two of them were very stone-faced and wouldn't even look me in the eye. I was still anxiety ridden from the horrible treatment I received at the airport detention and Nice jail. Even though I was handcuffed to one of the men in the backseat, I almost turned into a semi-fetal position. The drive would be four hours and I hadn't eaten a thing. I was suffering from dehydration and adrenaline loss. My body was shaking on and off as I stared out the window unable to take in the rural landscape. My mind was racing not knowing what would happen to me next. Were they about to send me directly to Grenoble where Jacques had spent a year? I knew I would completely fall apart if that were the case.

Halfway to Grenoble, I needed to go to the ladies room. I said to the gendarme we have to exit at the nearest rest stop. Grudgingly, they stopped ahead. I was still handcuffed and the two of us walked to the ladies room.

I looked at him and said in French, "Would you un-cuff me now, please?" He was hesitant. I looked at him and teared up. "What the hell do you think I'm going to do in there? Go through the window and escape? I'm not a criminal and you are not entering this bathroom with me." He took them off and I went in.

When I came out, I asked him if it was necessary to handcuff me for the rest of the journey. I'm not going anywhere. He was the only policeman who spoke with me and seemed a little more understanding of my predicament. He was kind enough to un-cuff me while in the car. The other two in the front seat didn't even look at me.

Of course when we arrived at the courthouse at noon, they broke for a two and a half hour lunch break, which was so typical of the French. In an attempt to avoid the throngs of paparazzi, we entered the building from a side alley access. The kind gendarme cuffed me again before exiting the car. The stalking paparazzi took a horrible photo of me in handcuffs hiding my face (photo at the beginning of the book). That image lingered in the press for too many days.

The three officers and I were waiting in the foyer when I began to convulse and sob hysterically. I couldn't hold back anymore and dropped to my knees. The one officer I had been handcuffed to came over to my disheveled frame and helped me to a chair after my tears had subsided. He disappeared and returned with a sandwich and a cup of hot chocolate and laid them on my lap. I smiled at him and said merci, merci, and started to cry again thankful for his kindness. The other two men still didn't even glance my way.

Finally, after the lunch break, I was summoned to the Judge. There was a court reporter, two Grenoble police standing at the door, the district attorney, and me.

My lawyers were on their way and arrived 15 minutes later. Lilou, who was at the airport when I landed from England, had notified them. I was extremely relieved to see my legal support because in France you're not even allowed a phone call. I was praying someone would contact anyone who could help me.

The courtroom had a high coffered wood ceiling that I kept staring at until my lawyers finally arrived to present my case. I didn't feel comfortable looking around the room and just kept staring up.

The reality of what was happening to me was so overwhelming that I didn't want to see or acknowledge my surroundings. I was numb and yes, it was happening.

I was asked many questions about shared bank accounts with Jacques, properties we owned in L.A. and in France. I never shared a bank account with Jacques anywhere. Whatever properties Jacques owned in France or any accounts, I was not a part of.

Jacques told me when we were first together that he never wanted me to sign my residential status card for France and I should never open a bank account. Whatever property I had in the States was solely my own. There were no financial connections between us. He was attempting to protect me against the leftist leaning government that became totally socialist in 1981, five years after Jacques and I were together.

During the proceedings, I didn't feel anyone in the court including the judge had a biased opinion about Jacques or me. The Court was surprised the case had escalated so far in view of the fact there was no hard evidence.

One of the first things I said when my lawyer arrived was, "Call Chirac." He left the courtroom and called my dear friend Jacques Chirac, the President of France, who had been elected two years before my present difficulties.

Thank goodness he came back and handed the phone to the judge. After they hung up, the judge addressed me and said, "You are free to go with the understanding you will return to France and stand trial after we have completed our inquiries."

That was it. No more questions. I was so relieved and said yes, thank you and goodbye. I was then led out of the courtroom to a rear entrance because the paparazzi were clamoring at the front of the courthouse to take my photo. I was flanked by my two lawyers and literally shoved into their car as the press came around the corner in hot pursuit. I was free.

Curiously, my lawyers told me never to set foot on French soil again… and they were French. They said I would be immediately thrown in jail again upon my return. No thanks. I didn't need to be reminded of the quirky Napoleonic Law regarding the spouse.

After the hearing had finished, I stayed at an American friend's apartment in Nice to rest until I was to fly back to London and then back home to the States. For my first meal we drove to nearby San Remo, Italy and I gorged on Parmesan chicken with pasta. Having lost eight pounds in five days I really needed some substantial food to be able to continue. On my overnight trip through London, I ordered room service and wolfed down fries with an enormous cheeseburger, a chef's salad, and an omelet with cheese, ham, and tomatoes with a side of bacon.

CHAPTER 101

ONCE I RETURNED TO L.A., I TRIED TO PULL MY life back together. A person doesn't recover from something as traumatic and painful as that overnight. I had TK to think about who was still in Uruguay. I was picking up the pieces and moving forward, so I thought. Jacques sent TK to live with the awful scamming Marisol and I had to get her out of there. My marriage to Lee had dissolved with my life once again in turmoil.

Then came the next great shock and another life-altering event.

Jacques had solved one problem. He died November 17, 1998. I know it sounds cruel, but it was the only way for TK to ever return home. The terrible part was that my daughter had already suffered the damage of the abuse while witnessing her father's own mental and physical collapse.

His end was as miserable and sad as the rest of his life had become. It was the fault of Bitchy, the triplicate pill popper ether addict and friend of Marisol. Marisol had introduced her to Jacques and together the two women conspired to scam him for most of his money. Bitchy and Jacques were arguing and fighting downstairs one night. My daughter was on the upstairs landing witnessing it. (TK, I am so sorry.) Bitchy physically attacked him. Jacques tried to strangle her, they struggled and he suddenly dropped to the floor. My poor child had to endure seeing the horror of all this as she cowered upstairs.

This sick female was unmoved by his limp frame. Her actions were totally calculated after she realized he was unconscious. After all, Jacques was worth more to her dead than alive. She waited four long hours before calling an ambulance to rush him to the hospital. Ha, Ha. At the hospital, it was discovered his aortic aneurysm had ruptured in his abdomen and he was put on life support.

My paternal grandmother was put on life support when she was 90 and all of a sudden woke up seven months later from her coma and was just fine. Jacques didn't get a chance to recover. I think he might have if there wasn't an intentional delay to transport him to the hospital. He was insanely tough because there are no other words to describe his physical strength and stamina. Also inexplicable are the suspicious circumstances surrounding the disconnection of his life support after the doctors and nurses had left the room. I know who it was. Was it murder? Yes, of course it was. The body was shipped back to Nice for the funeral. I would have attended, but my preference was to avoid arrest and jail by not going to Nice. Remember that absurd French law where the spouse is responsible for what the partner did and is guilty even if he or she had nothing to do with it? Otherwise, I would have been there. Even dead, I was still angry with Jacques, but I would have given him a final farewell and that measure of respect if I was able to attend.

CHAPTER 102

WITH JACQUES' PASSING, I NOW HAD TO GET my daughter to safety out of Uruguay and away from the evil Marisol and Bitchy. That was my main concern. She was only fifteen, ever so vulnerable and to have been subjected to such undeserved abuse was tragic. Even with my stressful visits to Uruguay, our separation had been long enough during those six excruciating years. I was ready to fly back to Uruguay when I got a call from TK. She was calling from the French consulate in Montevideo and said my permission was necessary for her to travel to Argentina. I was admittedly surprised. I told her I was coming to take her home. She said that she was invited to Bariloche, a ski resort in Argentina, to be with friends and would call as soon as she got back.

I was at a loss for words momentarily, forgetting my daughter hated skiing even after all the lessons I gave her in the French Alps. Although it sounded odd, I didn't want to press her because of the entire trauma she'd been through. So I said as soon as she got back I'd come get her. We agreed and I started preparing my home and decorating her bedroom. I waited and waited for the phone call that never came. I started to panic.

I contacted the American as well as the French Consulate in Uruguay, looking for her. They both told me they didn't know where she was. I begged the American consul to help me, but he was advised not to get involved because they didn't want to rock the boat. I was fuming! This was the second time America let me down. Again, the consul said it was too high profile of a case. I had represented America on the French Riviera, my daughter was an American citizen, thanks to my insistence she was born on American soil, and now NO ONE WOULD HELP ME!!!!!! Shame on your political lying bullshit when my daughter's life was at stake.

I will never forget or forgive the United States government and to this day I know first-hand how corrupt it all was and is.

When Jacques and I held the power, there wasn't anything we couldn't get done and no one would ever refuse to help us. Now, it was too uncomfortable to get involved. It was a repugnant lesson that I will never forget. My daughter was my life, and I was hell-bent on finding her and saving her against all odds.

I then called Martine and asked if she knew where my daughter was. She told me TK was at Jacques' sister, Genevieve's home in Nice. Genevieve was living at the Médecin family residence where they grew up.

I called Genevieve's house and demanded to speak to my daughter. TK got on the phone and I said, "So, when were you going to tell me you were in Nice?!?!! I was so hurt and angry.

"You lied to me about skiing which I thought was rather fishy, but I wanted to trust you. Why did you lie to me? I'm your mother and your place is with me until you're 18. After you finish high school it will be your choice what you want to do with your life and where you would like to live, but until then you're coming home."

TK said, "Mommy, don't be mad, I can stay here with Genevieve, but she wants you to send money for my education and food."

I was stunned. I told her the facts of the matter. "Absolutely not! Your aunt inherited the family home and all the money from her parents' estate. I won't send her a franc! You are not living with her. When you come to your senses, call me," and I hung up.

The next morning TK called and said she had thought about it. She asked if I would give her money to return to Uruguay, so she could live with a family she was friendly with who had three boys. She'd finish high school there and then visit me.

I lost it. I'm the most understanding person in the world, but I won't be disrespected or knowingly taken advantage of. What I wasn't aware of at this time was how damaged she had become. She had been used and brainwashed with the insanely horrible lies her father told about me. At the time not knowing the cause of her lying, all I knew was to apply tough love.

I said to her, "Listen, kid, and listen well. I will never give anyone else a penny to raise you, ever! With your attitude and what you're asking of me, I don't care if you become a prostitute living on the street. Your charming aunt won't support you and your friends in Uruguay want money, so who do you think really loves and cares about you? Me! I'm the only one and you know it. Do not contact me again until you're ready to come home. Goodbye!"

I actually felt better after I made it clear to her and gave my fears up to Ganesh. (Ganesh, my half boy half elephant divine guide from the Hindu philosophy.)

Two days later I got a surprise phone call from Duchess Laetitia D'Arenberg, who was living in Uruguay. She and Jacques were platonic friends and said she wanted to speak with me about TK. Laetitia when on to explain how TK was able to get back to Nice in the first place.

TK had contacted her because Genevieve wouldn't pay for plane fare from Uruguay to Nice. Laetitia gave her the money for the ticket, but wasn't happy about TK's decision. She had heard from her French contacts and friends in Punta that I was a wonderful woman. Laetitia knew Jacques had lied about me being an alcoholic and drug addict. She was also aware of Marisol and Bitchy being cheap money grabbers who had set him up. After almost two hours on the phone, she said she was going to call TK and tell her to stop this nonsense and fly back to L.A to be with her mother. I said how grateful I would be if she could convince her, but after everything that had happened I was skeptical.

Two days went by, so I called Laetitia. She was happy to hear from me because she finally had a long conversation with The Kid and was about to call me. Shawn Joy said yes, she would be with me. I started to cry and profusely thanked Laetitia. I immediately called TK and told her how happy I was and couldn't wait to send her a ticket. She asked me if she could come after Easter, which was three weeks away. I was disappointed, but said yes.

CHAPTER 103

I WAS SO EXCITED WITH THE ANTICIPATION OF MY daughter finally returning home to me. Wherever I had a home, I decorated a special bedroom for my daughter. So that task was already done. I knew her size and went to Robinsons/May, which was a classic department store on the corner of Wilshire and Santa Monica Boulevard in Beverly Hills. My mother and grandmother used to take me to their tearoom for lunch and shopping when I was younger. They still had a great teen department so of course; I went wild buying a whole closetful of hip new clothes for The Kid.

I missed the days when my mother and Nana would dress me up. We'd watch the models showing off their designer clothes as they elegantly sauntered around the large room interacting with the women's lunch group. They served an assortment of delicate tea sandwiches with lovely tea cookies and I was in heaven.

I sent the plane ticket and spoke over the phone with my daughter as many times as I could to make sure she was really on her way. The night of her arrival finally came. I was so excited, giddy and full of pure love that I wasn't prepared for her attitude. I rushed towards her laughing, crying, and hugged her. Her response was very cool and the hug I received in return was not sincere. Her first words to me were, "I'll finish high school here with you, but then I'm going back to Punta."

Not exactly what I wanted to hear right off the bat. I responded as calmly as I could, "Alright, I understand if that's your decision, but while you are here, you might have forgotten that I run a happy home, and you will be happy!"

Her appearance was disheveled. She wore a one-piece jean overall with a ratty looking shirt and big brown worn-out shoes. My poor girl. What had they done to her? From that moment, I knew I had my work cut out for me. I would do anything for her, but I didn't know the depths we both would have to descend before we could start rising back up to some sort of sanity. We would have to go very deep, very far down and struggle to come back to the surface. My daughter was severely abused and traumatized by Jacques and his two mistresses. For the damage they inflicted upon my daughter, I have no reservations about exposing them as I write the facts. Although those two horrible women stole money from me, stole my furniture, jewelry and art objects, I went ballistic when I discovered the cruel and inhumane treatment TK received from them. The term is not excessive. Child services should have arrested them. I didn't care about Jacques choosing these two demented witches as his playmates and making a fool of himself. What is unforgivable was the abuse he inflicted upon our daughter and allowing those sick women to abuse her as well. If I had known any of this while it was occurring, I most likely would be writing my memoirs from a jail cell. Murder…justifiable homicide would be my crime.

CHAPTER 104

WHEN WE FINALLY ARRIVED HOME I WASN'T sure if TK liked the house or her bedroom. I had her room decorated in pastel yellows, pinks, pale greens and sky blues. There were special touches for her bedding like cream-colored flowers with stripes coordinated with lacy pillows, shams and a down comforter. She had a closet full of new clothes. I had high hopes for a lovely new beginning and homecoming. I prayed she would share those feelings too. Oddly, as I gazed at her waiting for a reaction, she seemed completely void of any emotion. TK certainly didn't express any bubbling enthusiasm or appreciation of my efforts.

She was quiet after I showed her the room and closet. She looked at me and said she didn't like any of the clothes I had chosen for her because they were not her style. Considering her tattered appearance coming off the plane and scanning the frayed mess of used goods in her suitcase when we got home, it was very apparent she had not been taken care of properly. Jacques had spent and lost most of his money and couldn't even afford to provide decent attire for our daughter. I told her we'd gather up everything I purchased and return it to Robinsons, so she could choose her own wardrobe. That appeased her. After a good night's sleep, we returned the 50 pieces of clothing the next day. She tried on a few things, but only chose a pair of jeans and two tops.

That was all she wanted. I figured we'd fill her closet as time went on.

CHAPTER 105

I CONTACTED MARYMOUNT, A PRIVATE CATHOLIC girls school, because she had been attending a Catholic school in Punta. I wrote a letter explaining our circumstances and asked if they would view this as a special case to enroll her mid-term. We set up a meeting where I spoke with a seemingly understanding admissions counselor. I was crying, emphasizing my daughter's frightening plight to finally make it home to me and the tragic death of her father. I wanted her to be in a safe environment and hoped they would help her.

I left the meeting feeling positive. Boy, was I wrong. I received a letter telling me that they were not going to admit my daughter. I was furious. Again, the Catholics had shown themselves to be insensitive and hypocritical. They had no concern for anything other than their pocketbooks and sexual secrets. This was becoming an all too familiar experience.

The Catholic Church wouldn't marry Jacques and me in Nice because we were both divorcees. Although this was typical Catholic policy, they were willing to make a special exception provided Jacques made a huge personal donation. Jacques told me he would get back at them and his response was "Fuck You." He said their greed was typical, hypocritical and shameful. As it so happened, we had a very happy civil ceremony at Nice City Hall.

Following TK's birth in the Médecin tradition, we sought to arrange her baptism at the Catholic Church. The priest informed me the baptism could not take place unless I made a vow to study the Catechism for two years, become a devout Catholic and that our daughter would attend Catholic school. Oh and, of course, another huge personal donation from Jacques. Thank goodness, that's when I found my wonderful reverend from the British Anglican Church.

When I attended Arizona State University, my Catholic girlfriends enlightened me with their horror stories about the priests' and nuns' sexual hypocrisy. That was 1966 and 1967 before all the lurid tales of their perversion started coming out. So much for Catholic schools. To hell with them.

I still needed to enroll TK in an appropriate school considering her circumstances. All of a sudden it dawned on me. There was the French Lycée in Los Angeles that Jacques had inaugurated many years before. It was founded and owned by Raymond and Esther Kabbaz, who were from Nice. They were true "Médecinists," as loyal Médecin followers liked to call themselves. I contacted them and their response was they couldn't wait to see my daughter and me.

When I met with Esther, she had already heard about our escape from France and our time in Uruguay. She was so sensitive, caring and reassuring. I knew they would take good care of TK. I can't ever thank them enough for being there for us and providing her with a well-rounded international education.

My girl had to take a few entry tests. Unfortunately, the results showed she was behind due to her tumultuous past life and educational background. She was definitely behind in math and science and could have been put back two grades, but the Kabbazs' only put her back one. She excelled in languages. That came easily to her, which was not surprising considering the years she spent bouncing from French/English to Spanish and now to English/French. Her ease with languages would become very important to her later. It was really a gift from her father who spoke nine languages.

I became close to the headmaster Alain Anselme, who later became a wonderful confidante and companion. The executive staff was very hands on in guiding TK how to catch up with her studies. All the positive support helped make her school experience more pleasant, which made it easier on my nervous stomach. It was such a monumental relief being able to trust and confide in the Kabbazs' to have my daughter's best interests at heart.

TK had to take a summer math course to bring her level up to her correct age grade. I told her after she finished, if she wanted, I would send her back to Punta to be with her girlfriends.

CHAPTER 106

S HE WAS REALLY SHOCKED BY MY OFFER. HER reaction was a result of the brainwashing and lies from her father's poison against me. Jacques had told her he was afraid if she came to the states to visit I would keep her and never let her go back to Punta. All the lies from his anger and resentment had been deeply ingrained in TK, but now the truth was being exposed. This was a mentally disturbed man who thrived on revenge and used our innocent daughter against me.

I only began to understand the depth of Jacques abuse of our daughter from her behavior once she returned home. Unfortunately Jacques had been using our daughter, as I mentioned, as his pawn to wound me.

As I reflected on my time in Punta, the complexity of his deceit became obvious. After a lengthy delay due to my health issues, I finally arrived in Punta to be reunited with Jacques and her. My relationship with him was strained as a result of his inability to communicate and not address true issues. We were able to communicate, I thought, regarding TK. Following our escape from France and my delayed arrival in Punta, it was decided I would also have a residence in L.A. to be closer to my mother and father during those challenging times. Jacques had agreed when I was in L.A. our daughter would be with me except during her school year. Jacques obviously could not travel to the states for fear of extradition. Anyway, we would be spending most of our time together in Uruguay. I was in Punta initially for three months and then had to return to L.A. a couple of times to take care of my new real estate purchase and furnishings. As I was very busy during this time and TK was in school, Jacques was supposed to fly her to L.A. when both of our schedules permitted. All of this seemed reasonable at the time.

I was always very fair in negotiations with Jacques regarding her because she was my priority.

Once again, Jacques was lying and the agreement was not honored as planned. At the beginning of our arrangement between L.A. and Punta, I mentioned I was in the process of acquiring a new residence in Beverly Hills. Jacques was supposed to send TK to me in L.A. after everything was completed and furnished. However, since TK had enjoyed a wonderful happy time with me during her first two trips, he refused to send her again. Jacques once assured me because of his experience with his first wife, Claude, who had turned his second daughter Anne-Laure against him, he would never again let a child go back and forth between the parents. He was very emphatic saying it wasn't playing fair and was hurtful to the child. What a hypocritical statement that came from his mouth. I wanted to get TK out of there and back to the states with me. I still had hopes of us living together soon, not knowing it wouldn't be until she was almost sixteen. Altogether, the ordeal lasted six long years!

Jacques wanted sole custody of her to control her mental and physical movements, which was his manipulative way of controlling me. He lied to our child about me, filling her head with toxic lies to poison her attitude towards her own mother. He was so cruel and sadistic to use poor TK in this way, especially to prevent her from traveling to see or be with me. In order to see her, I had to travel from Los Angeles to Punta. I did this regularly, staying for three to four months at a time. I knew it was going to be a fight to get my daughter out of there.

Jacques wanted to alienate TK from me out of jealousy and spite to drive a huge wedge between us. He resorted to saying horrible things behind my back to my baby, things that were pathetic lies without one ounce of truth. It's called deflecting the facts from oneself.

You (Jacques) do something bad, and then you accuse someone else (me) of doing the things that you were doing so you can shift the blame onto them and make them the responsible party. You accuse your opponent of the thing you are guilty of. Sounds like the Democrats today. Deflect, deflect, deflect.

I learned the political tactic well because Jacques schooled me in it.

No wonder when "The Kid" got off the plane she was standoffish and cool. She was afraid of me. Her father had brainwashed her into believing her mother was a monster.

CHAPTER 107

I MADE GOOD ON MY OFFER FOR TK TO VISIT HER friends in Punta for summer vacation. So, off she went for a month. When my daughter returned home she was a bit sullen and asked to see a psychiatrist. I asked my doctor friends for competent referrals. I made an appointment saying it was somewhat urgent. Luckily, the doctor was able to meet her the next day. We held hands while walking down the hall and I told her I'd be in the waiting room when they finished. I was nervous because I wanted everything to be as smooth a transition as possible. Maybe, she could get things off her chest and be prescribed some helpful meds for her anxiety. The psychiatrist walked her out after the session and introduced himself. I smiled and said I hoped it went well and asked when would he like to see her again.

He looked at me oddly as TK took my hand to leave. What was said in the session might not have been as positive as I imagined. She saw him a few more times and then asked if I could find her a female therapist instead of a male. Little did I know until years later the reason why the doctor looked at me so strangely.

Joy, one of her middle names that she goes by now, had been telling the doctor the things her father said about me. As a result, he was expecting to see a drugged out alcoholic. Nice, huh?

This same mischaracterization occurred when I went back to Punta to fight for the inheritance promised by Jacques for TK. Martine's husband,

Jean, was supposed to help arrange our stay at an apartment owned by Serge, a friend of Jacques. He and Jean were there to pick me up at the airport. Serge complimented me how healthy and beautiful I looked as I exited the plane, but in a curious manner. I thought it was a bit odd the way he said that to me right off the bat since we had just met. When we got back to his apartment he kept offering me drinks at dinner, which of course I politely declined. The third night he asked me if I was on the wagon. I looked at him and responded, "Why in the world would you think that?" He said Jacques had told him I was an alcoholic and a dope addict. I laughed and shook my head making it very clear I hated the taste of alcohol and never drank. Drugs, I was never into unless you consider smoking marijuana and hash during 6 months of my life when I was in my early twenties (in the 60's). I don't consider my addiction to the French prescription pain meds as a result of my La Prairie nightmare in the same context as the picture that Jacques had painted for many people.

That was when Serge became aware of Jacques' jealousy and anger towards me realizing the stories he had been fed were total lies. Serge said he couldn't believe Jacques had chosen to surround himself with those witches whose only objective was to drain his bank account. He wondered, "Why couldn't Jacques see it?

All I could say was, how right you are. Unfortunately, Jacques' ego was so captivated by their youth and feigned attention. He believed their lies, chasing his own youth as they deceived him into investing in fraudulent financial schemes. They not only took hefty commissions, but also stole personal property belonging to Jacques and me from our home in Punta. This included my own very personal belongings I acquired before our marriage, which I dearly treasured. He left our daughter absolutely nothing. I know I'm reiterating again and again about certain things regarding the escape, the stolen goods, and the injustices because I definitely wanted to get my point across. While these occurrences are outlandish and sound so unreal, it is factual and the truth is astounding to the average person. Living in the United States protects one from the outside world and it can be a very naive outlook. American tourists typically go to see museums, shop, eat, and take in the scenery. They think they know a country from just visiting and taking in the typical attractions.

Well, not necessarily. If you really want to understand a foreign culture, live there for a year and then have a discussion with me. All I'm trying to say is how grateful I am for traditional American freedom and values that should be honored everyday.

CHAPTER 108

THE LYCÉE SCHOOL YEAR BEGAN AND JOY AND I went to the initiation meeting. Mr. Alain Anselme gave the welcoming speech and explained the upcoming curriculum. TK had not been in a great mood since she returned from Punta. I had hoped she would benefit after seeing the new (female) therapist. However, she was morose and sullen and I wasn't sure why. I thought she might just be missing her friends. I was trying as always to be upbeat and positive. But there is a limit. I won't be disrespected. Mr. Anselme and I were speaking French when Joy said to me, "Why don't you speak English to him? You're just showing off that you speak French."

I took her aside and said, "Listen, you're out of line by saying that in front of Mr. Anselme. Don't ever try to embarrass me in public again. Say it to me in private if you must. I'm giving you everything you need plus more because I'm a responsible mother and it's my pleasure to take care of you. Since you returned from Punta, your behavior is unacceptable. You will not continue like this. I suggest if you're not happy with me or what I have to offer, please go back to wherever or whomever you think you'd like to be with and see who really cares. See if there is anyone else who wants to financially sponsor you or love you as much as I."

And, I added, "If you decide to stay here with your mother, then I suggest you make sure you respect me even if you have to fake it until you realize I'm all you've got. I am the only one that has your best interests at heart."

I was so pissed! I thought that covered the basics. Things did get a little better after our conversation. School started and then all too quickly Christmas vacation was upon us. I thought it would be good for TK to go back to Nice and stay with her aunt for the holiday. She said she missed Nice, so I bought her a plane ticket. The look on The Kid's face was again filled with complete shock and again she reiterated that her father said I would never let her travel or let her out of my sight. Jacques' lies were evaporating one after the next. When would she realize it?

TK was a victim of Jacques' deceit. His method was to continually deflect, meaning he would accuse the other party of the same wrongdoing he was guilty of. That was Jacques' method, not mine. So, off she went. I said, "I hope you enjoy yourself and call me as soon as you arrive."

TK called to say she arrived safely. Day one, day two and day three went by. Her third night, my morning, she called quite upset. I asked her what was happening and boy did I get an earful. Things had begun to shift or had they? Her mind had slowly been defogging and she finally was becoming aware of the facts.

"My aunt is treating me like Cinderella!" I could tell she was on the edge of tears. "All she makes me do is clean the house which is 25,000 square feet, go to the market, set the table for at least seven people, eat and then clean up. Genevieve won't even buy me toiletries and said I had to pay for them myself."

Then, the biggest surprise came when she said in a pleading voice, "Mommy, can I please come home now?"

I was not expecting that! I told her, "No, you cannot come home now. You will stay the entire time and then hopefully, you'll appreciate what you have with me and realize I'm the only one who loves you and who will always take care of you."

TK was so disappointed to hear she couldn't immediately come home, but tough love usually makes a deeper impression than just acquiescing.

All I can say is when she returned and got off the plane she ran into my arms telling me how much she loved me, missed me and she had had an epiphany which made her finally see the truth. It sure was different from the last time she got off the plane at LAX! She apologized for her behavior and admitted she had been brainwashed by her father. She finally realized everything he told her about me was a lie. She understood he was the one responsible for restricting her activities by not allowing her to travel, date or have fun. He only wanted to keep her around to take care of him when he got much older. TK said she did not want to see Genevieve again or her snotty offspring.

Following her revelation, TK started to heal with help from other professionals and our love for one another flourished once again.

CHAPTER 109

F ROM THAT POINT ON MY DAUGHTER AND I WERE
communicating and working things out together. She had been severely
damaged by all those events. As a result, we went through some rough times
going to counselors and psychiatrists sorting out her anxieties, fears and
insecurities. At one point in a joint therapy session she revealed how she felt
about instances where I had hurt her when we were in Nice. I wasn't aware
at the time I was being selfish, but after hearing her version my stomach
cramped. She was sitting on the couch. I stood in front of her, dropped on
my knees and got hysterical, begging her to forgive me.

I said, "I can't feel any lower or apologize more profusely. I just want
you to understand that I wasn't aware at the time I was hurting you. I was
wrapped up trying to keep myself as balanced as I could sorting out my
own problems. I tried to keep you close to me as much as possible, but there
were times I wasn't able to handle the political climate. I was at my wit's end.
We were being attacked. Your father was having major problems with the
Socialists who were doing everything they could to destroy us. I was trying
to protect you the best way I could under the circumstances."

That all came out in the session and I was distraught for a while feeling
guilt and remorse. The few years preceding our flight from France were very
challenging. I would leave TK in the care of my trusted Lilou and Marcel
and disappear for a few days trying to clear my head. I'd chosen Jean-Claude
Allegretti as my bodyguard when I finally got rid of Daniel. We'd go to Italy

and Switzerland on business trips and shopping. I really needed to try and put worrisome thoughts out of my head and trusted Jean-Claude because we genuinely cared about one another. I needed to rely on him because he was one of the few allies on my side.

But, back to the session. Once TK saw how her father's deviant influence affected her perceptions and devastated me, she began to understand my feelings and forgave me. Soon after, my TK began to blossom and to this day we are each other's biggest allies. We are the only ones remaining who know the truth about what really happened in Uruguay. We're the only two who know the details about the escape from France, and who remember the gruesome atmosphere in the house in Punta. However, we were not the only witnesses to Jacques mental decline. It was a frightening time and I'm amazed we survived. Since the sessions, with TK's ability to slowly share shocking facts, I became aware of Jacques horrible treatment of her during the time I was in L.A. and unable to protect her in Punta. His temper was completely out of control and his behavior erratic. Indelible scars remain on both of us from his abuse.

We both live with PTSD, but thanks to Ganesh my guide, my prayers to reunite my daughter and me were answered.

I fell in love with Ganesh when I went to India during my first visit. He's a favorite Hindu Deity, half boy-half elephant. He removes obstacles in your path to success, peace and fulfillment.

If you don't get what you asked for, it's because it wasn't right for you. He then will place a better opportunity at the right time to assure your goal. He blesses new endeavors and protects his followers.

I love the Hindu philosophy. It's colorful, playful, fun and fascinating. I've traveled to India 12 times. Italy has my heart, but India has my soul. I related to the movie *"Eat Pray Love,"* with Julia Roberts, because her travels and interests paralleled mine, except my third country would be Thailand, instead of Indonesia. I'm drawn to Italy, India and Thailand. I go to India as often as I can for my inner fulfillment, cleansing and happiness, and of course the food.

CHAPTER 110

MY DAUGHTER BEGAN OPENING UP ABOUT HER experiences in Uruguay during the time I wasn't there. These were horrid revelations as I mentioned earlier. As everything had been concealed from me, I was completely unaware.

It became clearer with each conversation TK had been living with fear on a daily basis. I knew Jacques was not in his right mind, but I had no idea until then of the depths of his vile anger. TK described how he would take his rage out not only on her, but also on his middle daughter Anne-Laure. It was physical as well as mental abuse. If I had only known.

We began the healing process, which is a never-ending journey. People who have experienced it know this. There's tremendous trauma to attempt to overcome. The pain and sorrow to get through those times and then having to deal with recurrent bad memories needing to be resolved in your mind. Shocking events change people's lives and you have to learn to comprehend reality on a different level.

TK finished her junior and senior year at the Lycée Francais in Los Angeles. Following graduation she wanted to try her independence and asked if she could move to her own apartment. I told her if that's what she wanted I would help her find one and we did. There was an apartment building close to the school where she wanted to be. It was a studio, which worked out best for her needs at the time.

After a couple of years, she left L.A. for Boston to continue her education. She got her degree working in a court of law translating from Spanish to English. She could instantaneously translate the words in Spanish and convert them into English simultaneously listening to the Spanish words that kept firing at rapid speed. TK could have worked at the UN. (She is that good with languages.)

CHAPTER 111

AFTER BOSTON, TK DECIDED TO MOVE TO Chicago and worked there for a couple of years before returning to L.A. While she was gone, I'd been trying to figure out what would be best regarding my future. I received a telephone call from a friend who had met a socialite from San Francisco. My friend spoke with this woman who had heard of me and wanted to introduce me to some very eligible, quality men. I thought why not. She called and we spoke. All of a sudden I was leaving the next weekend to head up north meeting back-to-back dates. I arrived Friday morning in San Francisco and had lunch with a very religious Jewish man who was lovely. The only problem was he was Orthodox and committed to living a totally devout life. I liked him a lot, but had to decline. That is not the lifestyle for me. There was no way in hell I was going to shave my head and eat kosher for the rest of my days.

I had dinner that night with another nice but boring man. He had a nephew working as an artist at Disney Studios. When I returned to L.A. I contacted him and we became good buddies. He was so talented and together we created beautiful art projects. His name is Patrick Ferrand, and I still communicate with him today. He's a fantastic portrait painter and painted a few mural scenes on my bedroom walls. I have many of his exquisite works.

Saturday, the following day still in San Fran, I had breakfast with Man A, lunch with Man B, and dinner with Man C. They were nice, but not my type.

Although, there was another man I thought might be a candidate. He was much older than me by 28 years. However, being accustomed to relationships with older men, I was comfortable with him. His name was Richard Goldman. He had inherited two billion dollars from his late wife Rhoda Haas, an heiress from the Levi-Strauss family. Richard and Rhoda had four children, but the oldest son had died of cancer.

CHAPTER 112

I MUST SAY THAT NEVER IN MY LIFE HAVE I MET A more greedy, selfish, pretentious or cheap man especially considering the resources at his disposal. His three remaining offspring were like their father only worse. They were beyond pretentious, classless and mean. They spent lavishly, excessively and wastefully on their own personal luxuries but were always at odds with their father. I found that out soon enough.

It was necessary to meet them if there was going to be anything between Richard and me. Richard had asked me when we first met to go to Hawaii and meet his two sons, their wives and his grandchildren. His daughter wouldn't come. Although I was looking forward to meeting his family, Richard was compelled to share lurid details with me about his unworthy offspring, especially his son Doug. We stayed at the Four Seasons on the Big Island in Hawaii. After I was settled and unpacked, Richard and I went to the pool. Doug, the youngest son, was lying face down on a lounge chair.

Richard introduced us and I said, "Hello nice to meet you," and extended my arm to shake his hand. He lifted his head up and turned to me and then turned back to his prone position completely ignoring me. How absolutely rude. I learned no one had anything good to say about him. The other son was more polite, but he too already had begun to plot against me before arriving to Hawaii.

Richard pursued me hot and heavy from the moment we met. I wasn't quite sure about him after our first date, but I was going to give him a chance.

He called me when I got back to L.A. and started to make all these plans for our future over the phone. He had some very elaborate ones about what we would do, where we would live and what our lives would be like. He didn't waste any time and then proceeded to ask me if I knew who he really was.

I replied, "You're Richard and that's all I know."

"Well, "i" (for Ilene)," he proudly said, "I'm worth two billion dollars, so there won't be a problem regarding money."

He went on to tell me I was the only other woman he had ever loved besides his late wife Rhoda, because I made him happy. (If that was possible, ha ha!) I had only known him for a few days. This was moving rather fast.

When we arrived in Hawaii, I booked a massage at the hotel spa. I sauntered over anticipating a relaxing hour. I was on the table waiting for my massage therapist who was a bit late when she burst through the door looking very upset.

She said she needed a few more moments to get over what had just occurred with her previous client. However, she was shaking and started to cry. I asked if she was all right and she began to tell me what had allegedly just taken place. Being aware I was with the Goldman party, she said I should look out. Her client was Douglas Goldman, but she wasn't sure who I was with, him or the father. She said she started massaging him when he got a hard-on, threw off his towel, and demanded she relieve him. After throwing a towel back over him, she ran to find her supervisor to have the man kicked out. I started to laugh. Now, these were her words, not mine.

Gee, what a surprise. I told her I was with the father. Richard had already bragged to me about hiring hookers for himself when his wife Rhoda was ill. So, why would I be surprised by similar antics in young Doug? His alleged behavior was very indiscreet and disrespectful considering his wife and children were nearby at the pool. With pleasure, I shared my new found information with Richard. He became very upset and went to chastise the "black sheep" as he referred to Doug from time to time. I had been raised to keep my mouth shut because of my family background and knew how to keep secrets. But, I didn't want to keep this secret under wraps. I couldn't wait to tell Richard about Douglas. What an entitled, hypocritical, mean, angry, cheating loser. My massage lady who was visibly shaken relayed all of this alleged behavior first hand to me. (We all know what "alleged" means to protect oneself. Lol.)

At the poolside I was reading a book Mom gave me about a Saudi princess. Lisa, Doug's wife, saw me reading it and asked if she could borrow it after I finished. I said, "Yes, but you must return it because it belongs to my mother, it's her only copy, and it's out of print."

Of course, she took it and never sent it back. I waited and decided to call to give her a piece of my mind even after I broke up with Richard. I told her "Thank you Lisa, for not keeping your word. You definitely are one of them even after telling me how miserable you were in your marriage to Doug and would have loved to divorce him."

We returned from Hawaii and I stayed with Richard for a while, though now I wonder why. He had a large house on Nob Hill in San Francisco. The decor was plain, tasteless and totally bland. The only piece of remote interest was an original Chagall hanging above the living room fireplace, which his conniving children coerced him into buying. They'll be ripping each other's throats out to see who gets it.

Also, I would get a mouthful from anyone working for Richard about what a bastard he was, and believe me all this was unsolicited. They were eager to tell me stories about him being such a huge prick. His newest driver told me Richard would berate him if he stopped at a stop sign. He was told not to stop and just plow through, so as not to waste time. Richard would yell at him while I was in the car. One day when we were alone, the driver told me he knew he would be fired and couldn't get away from Goldman quick enough. Of course, he was fired. He kept in touch with me for a while just to make sure I was OK and to see if I was still hanging in there. That was nice of him. There are a few good people in the world, but definitely not in the Goldman family.

Richard fired everyone who came to work for him except his late wife's secretary. There was also a sweet older woman who helped out with the cooking on the rare occasions we were home. I lived with Richard on long weekends for seven months, flying from L.A. on Thursdays to San Fran and flying back home on Sundays or Mondays.

Even those two women who hadn't been fired yet, talked about him with disrespect and disdain.

Rhoda's secretary continued working at the house after she had passed and filled me in on more dirt about him and his "rotten kids." She had a lot to dish out.

I witnessed him regularly mistreating the help. He didn't treat people like they were human. This useless man was SO cheap it was embarrassing. One evening Richard told me that we were hosting a small political cocktail party. He said he had told the housekeeper what hors d'oeuvres to serve. The guests arrived. We all sat in the cramped living room that was surprisingly small, on small couches next to a small coffee table in this small room. The non-abundant cocktail plates of tiny hot dogs wrapped in dough that had been frozen were the main event. There were a few celery and carrot sticks, some crackers and a few slices of cheese (not imported). Now, I've been invited to the homes of people who were not wealthy where they served a scrumptious spread that honored their guests. Not here and not Richard. I was appalled when I saw what miserable, stingy portions were being served to the invitees. They felt it too. Nobody looked happy munching on their carrots and half-frozen mini hot dogs with their knees scrunched up against the coffee table. We were sitting on tiny couches in the tiny room. What a lousy, selfish host.

I've never met anybody to this day worth two billion dollars, more or less, who was so stingy, so lacking in decorum, who treated people with such pretentiousness and who was so embarrassingly cheap. I always believed anyone who was stingy was stingy of heart and Richard was the proof of that for sure. If you have an open loving heart you can be generous with family and friends. Even Richard's so-called friends couldn't tolerate him and would joke about his cheap, controlling behavior. Of course, they opened up to me because they knew what he was all about and were curious why I was with him. I have to admit I was asking myself the same question. Please note, I have used the word "cheap" repeatedly to emphasize this horrible classless person.

At one point I relayed all this to Richard. He could have cared less. If things weren't completely his way he'd expunge you from his life or have one of his children boot you out the door.

Richard had his lawyer prepare a prenup, which would give me a certain amount of money each year in the event of his death. He knew if he left me anything in his will, his children would make my life miserable.

I started out caring for Richard the first time around and wanted to be with him. He falsely presented himself to me as kind and generous. I left him when I found out the truth. He was nasty, condescending, a mean bully and weak.

He didn't forget me, though. He contacted me five years later and said he'd gone out with a lot of women during our time apart, but realized I was the one he wanted to be with and marry. He begged me to return to him and said he had changed and wouldn't allow his family to interfere in our relationship. I should have listened to my father during my first go around with Goldman. When Dad met him the first time around, he told me he definitely did not like him. His first impression, in his words, was that he was a cheap classless bastard. Luv Dad.

I told Richard if he let his family intrude in our lives or if they tried to force him to leave me as they did the last time, I would walk away at once. He gave me his word that nothing like that would happen again and that's when he presented his deal.

He offered me a lot of money to be with him and said he would put the designated amount in a separate account to make sure his children wouldn't be able to contest it when he passed. I thought about it and decided, why not? That's what I should have told his friends when they asked why I was with him the second time around. If he had changed and wanted to leave me money, why not? Let's be practical.

Of course, Richard lied again.

I had to legally change my name because of the French government. Actually, twice because I was on a political list with charges still hanging over me from France. My lawyers advised me it would be a wise move. The name I picked numerically, Taylor Heart, added up to the number 8 in numerology, which is success, wealth and prosperity. A good number.

But here I went again. I had accepted Richard's proposal, but then out-of-the-blue Richard's lawyer called my lawyer and told him I would have to prove I wasn't this major porn star. "Taylor Heart" happened to be the moniker of a famous "adult" actress.

Well, I am not a porn star and it should be obvious to anyone. I'm on the Internet as Madame Médecin. That should have been enough proof and frankly, how low and disgusting can anyone get to accuse me of something so off the wall? Nevertheless, I needed to address the matter and had to sign all these papers denying I was the porn queen. What a joke.

As I feared, his kids again had unduly influenced Richard. The porn star scenario, much like previous false insinuations the kids had cooked up against me had been brewing since the minute we got back together.

I finally had enough of this toxic family and how disrespectfully they treated their so-called friends and hired help and people in general. This time it was over for good. His wife had been the source of the family's wealth and from what I heard about her, she was a very dignified woman. When she died, Richard and those spoiled pretentious brats inherited a part of the Levi-Strauss fortune. No one liked him or his children and everyone especially disliked Doug, the third son. I've been with some incredibly fascinating men in my life, but Richard was by far at the end of the opposite scale. He was one of the most vapid males I had ever known. Those are the Goldmans: tasteless, classless, greedy, entitled, horribly penurious and shameful. (And I'm being very polite.) Did I get my point across?!!!!!!!! Goodbye and good riddance. Don't FUCK with the Countess!

CHAPTER 113

URING THE GOLDMAN ERA #2, TK WAS NO LON-
ger living with me, so I bought a wonderful condo at The Granville
Towers, an historical building in West Hollywood. It was a legendary French
Normandy style landmark at the intersection of Sunset Blvd. and Crescent
Heights that housed many famous celebrities throughout the years. In ear-
lier times, old-time movie stars like Clark Gable and Carole Lombard were
regulars. Lombard had a pied-à-terre there where they would meet because
Clark was still married. It was their romantic getaway pad.

It was eventually converted into condominiums. A retired ballerina
bought one of them on the second floor for a very low price. It was not expensive at the time because it required a complete renovation.

The lady went to work on her place and made it a marvel. She was a per-
fectionist and had the taste of a European aristocrat. I think she paid around
$200,000 for it and put in a minimum of $800,000 for hand-cut designer
marble and semi-precious stone floors with all the accouterments. There were
carved moldings everywhere, designer fabrics in ivory lace for the window
treatments and then, the entryway! Orange carnelian and onyx lined the floor
segueing into the living room, dining room, kitchen and bathrooms. Beige,
ivory and white artisan cut marble designs defined each space in several
patterns. There was a beautiful crystal chandelier in the dining room. It was
the finest décor I had ever witnessed in a property I wanted to purchase. I
was sure I would keep it forever as my safe haven. I loved living there. It was

a great location and the neighbors, an eclectic group, were a hoot. An old flame of mine Dan Melnick, the producer of That's Entertainment, All that Jazz, Straw Dogs and many more films moved into one of the penthouses. This enabled us to easily visit and commiserate about the good old days that held great fun memories.

One of the best cake and pie bakers in L.A. lived in the building. At the time she only had one shop on Melrose Avenue called Sweet Lady Jane. I frequented her special dessert haven all the time. To this day I still crave her white signature cake with berries, and her rhubarb and strawberry pie with a scrumptious buttery crumble crust.

There was an indoor pool in the building decorated like an old movie set with tropical murals and décor from the 50s. I was given a perfect parking spot next to the entrance door. The foyer was old world charm with the nicest men working at the front desk.

There was a wonderfully large lit fountain at the outside entry and the residents kept the fountain and common areas in excellent condition. I loved living there. I could travel, close up my place, tell the concierge to hold my mail and take off for as short or as long a time as I wanted.

During this period I was living between The Granville in West Hollywood and Goldman's on Nob Hill in San Francisco. During one of my stays in S.F., I got a phone call from Shirley, my Dad's wife. It was not good news as she said my father was dying. He hadn't been well for several years, being troubled with various health issues. Of course, I took the next flight out to be with him. Dad passed away in my arms at the hospital on January 22, 2005. It was a tremendous loss for me. I lost my father and friend who shared movies, walks, lots of good eating and special secrets. He was a pillar in my life and is always in my heart.

CHAPTER 114

ONE DAY AN ACQUAINTANCE OF MINE WHO WAS a real estate agent called to ask if she could talk to me in person. I was surprised at the urgency, but was curious. She arrived in no time and we sat down with soothing chamomile tea. Boy, was I taken aback when Denise told me a new buyer had come to her office and said he was looking for a condo and described mine to a "T!" She asked if they could have a showing since it wasn't on the market, but I had no intention of selling which had been discussed before.

"Oh, all right," I relented. Let's set a time when he can come over. He wanted to see it the following day. Around 4 PM my buzzer rang and they came up. We were introduced and I showed him around. He was a small Middle Eastern man who was a dermatologist/plastic surgeon and was moving to L.A. from San Diego. It didn't take him long to tell me my condo was exactly what he had envisioned and asked how much I would let it go for. I told him this was supposed to be a decorative showing and not for sale. He didn't skip a beat and offered me double what I had paid two years earlier. I was surprised and told him I would think about it. Since my motto in the past was to unintentionally buy high and sell low, I realized I better make the right decision and not regret it either way.

CHAPTER 115

WHEN MY FATHER WAS ALIVE, I WANTED TO build a wing onto his home to use as my pied-à-terre because I traveled so much and would always be able to come back to a safe haven. My father and I grew very close after I became pregnant and I wanted to be near him as he aged. He thought it was a great idea. I would be able to cook his favorite dishes, which made us both very happy. Unfortunately, Dad passed before I was able to build the wing. His wife was nicer to me while he was alive. After his passing I thought the wing could still work, so I called Shirley telling her of the offer on my condo. I asked if she would still be open to me building onto the house. I would make some money and save a lot as well because I wouldn't have to purchase another abode for a while. I would be able to enjoy traveling knowing my things would be safe and secure. Shirley said OK and I started to get excited. This would be the first time I made a profit on a piece of property, ever!

I called my agent immediately and told her it was a deal.

I moved into Dad's office in the back of his home for four months during construction. The room was large with an enormous desk that had belonged to my Uncle Jack. It had been in the office he and my father had shared together in Westwood. The desk had history behind it, family memories and good vibes. I slept on a trundle bed that wasn't too uncomfortable.

I designed a fabulous suite across the backyard patio, gutting the second bedroom and creating my own personal space. It would have a stone fireplace in the sitting area, an enormous walk-in closet to hold my wardrobe with a light salmon marbled and mirrored bathroom. There was a special area for my bed and a double-sided blackout curtain dividing my sleeping space from the sitting room.

My life had taken another unexpected turn. I was now responsible to do the marketing, cooking and baking for Shirley on a daily basis. She wasn't easy to live with and wasn't keen on my traveling so much, wanting me at her beck and call. When I was getting ready to depart for the day, she would sit on a chair in the den watching sports on TV with a grimace in an attempt to make me feel guilty. I didn't.

Most mornings she would criticize my outfit by telling me, "Are you really going to wear that? You look like a clown!" Or she would say something nasty about me not enjoying my day or ask why did I have to go out all the time? Lucky for me I had a solid core and a good sense of who I was, so I'd shake my head, roll my eyes and just get out of there as soon as possible.

When the construction was finished, I loved how it came out and happily moved in from the office. Life went on with me ignoring her constant barbs.

Shirley was not well. She had COPD, a bad back and migraines. My housekeeper, Anna, came to clean four days a week, but Shirley wanted her to be there more and take care of her when I was traveling or just out.

CHAPTER 116

DURING THIS TIME, I WAS STILL WITH MY COM-panion, Alain, who I had met at the Lycée School. He would spend weekends with me. Alain, like me, was a traveler and had studied in depth the different countries he wanted us to discover together. He would plan wonderful trips for us around the world that were on a completely different scale than when I traveled with Jacques. He would plan all the sightseeing from an educator's perspective so I learned much more on a grassroots level, closer to the culture and within reach of the local people. I enjoyed interacting with them and exploring off-the-beaten path local eateries. We were even invited for dinner with people we had just met who were fascinated with these other friendly, cultured creatures…us.

We were in Nepal and hired a guide to take us not to the usual tourist attractions, but into the countryside to mingle with the residents. He told us he would take us to his home village and we would see real Nepalese life. As we entered the village he said it was the first time he'd ever brought an outsider there. We walked down a narrow path where I saw a young woman with an old-fashioned washboard doing her laundry in a little creek. There were absolutely no modern appliances yet the clothes were scrubbed, cleaned and hung on a long cord to dry. All the tiny shack homes had a small front yard where they kept their livestock consisting of cows, chickens and goats. As we continued down the narrow path I saw five women sitting on their front porch drinking tea. There was a gate I decided to enter to speak with these women. Alain was worried about me disturbing them, but our guide followed me and explained to them who we were. They welcomed us in. The house had six tiny rooms with small beds, an outside toilet and a washbasin where they could wash their faces, hands and brush their teeth. I saw one toothbrush and a hand towel. They were all smiles and called for one of the daughters who spoke English to come and translate alongside our guide. The women loved my outfit and kept touching me and the fabric. They stared, laughed and couldn't get enough information about where we came from and what it was like living in America.

I had the best time with our cultural exchange and wanted to stay longer, but our guide was taking us to his home to meet his family and taste his mother's cooking. We said our goodbyes and some of the women had tears in their eyes knowing that most likely our paths would not cross again. I was sad as well, but knew I would carry those incredible moments with me forever. Certainly, it was more interesting having tea with them than going to Spago in Beverly Hills and listening to everyone talk about their purchases of the day.

We walked up a narrow grassy path and up a winding wooden staircase to the main room of our guide's home. His sister had delivered her baby in the room a few days earlier and was lounging on a huge pillow. His mother and two brothers were helping their grandmother in a cubbyhole preparing food. Everyone sat on floor cushions chatting away with dogs and cats running around. This was a multi-generational family living together with practically no amenities and they seemed happy and joyful. There was no indoor plumbing except for a tiny sink in the cubbyhole for cooking and cleaning the dishes. They served us Dal-bhat-tarkari, a spicy lentil soup served over boiled rice or different grains, and sometimes mixed with vegetable curry. There were spicy fermented pickles and a flatbread to soak up the broth.

For dessert there was Napali Peda, a candy made from sweetened condensed milk, with pistachios on top. Everyone sat on the floor and ate with a large wooden spoon and fingers. I was thrilled and fascinated how they all lived together and looked out for one another. I learned about their eating habits, sleeping arrangements, how they spent their leisure time and weekday routines. It was a rudimentary village that was closely knit. People seemed relatively happy living together and helping each other unselfishly. To this day I can clearly picture the lovely ladies sitting on their long porch sipping tea and me enjoying every moment spent among them.

CHAPTER 117

A LAIN WANTED TO GO TO THAILAND AND INDIA. I hadn't been to either country. I was supposed to go several times to India with Jacques on a cultural exchange between Indian cities and Nice, but priorities arose every time and our trips got canceled.

I told Alain, "You plan it and I'm there."

He took off for Delhi a few days before I was able to leave, but I told him he didn't have to meet me at the airport because our guide, Selvan, would pick me up and escort me to the hotel.

As I stepped off the plane I saw hundreds and hundreds of bodies packed together like sardines. Wall to wall people. I was fascinated seeing all these Indians crammed together with the biggest smiles on their faces. I suddenly felt my spirit lift and felt calm and lighter. Wow, what a sensation! Sel, as I came to call our personal coordinator, was standing in front of me holding a sign with my name on it. His smile was so big it was infectious.

The traffic was horrible on the drive to the hotel, even worse than in L.A. Sel introduced me to our driver, Ram, who I have to say was an incredible asset to our journey. He drove us from city to city while navigating through the worst traffic and the craziest drivers I'd ever experienced. I had been exposed to slums all over the world and seen poverty and squalor before, but what I was seeing through the car window was unbelievable. Ram would always retort, "You need three things to drive in India; good brakes, good horn and good luck."

I learned over the years traveling with Jacques that poverty is different in every country because of the attitudes of the people. I have been to India 12 times now with the services of my same local crew. Poverty there is different from what I had seen throughout my travels around the world. No matter how many public houses were built, the people from the streets would last maybe up to four months in the projects before they were back living in their original habitats. That's where they were the most comfortable. They may have been poor, but they seemed to handle it without anger. They were smiling and the feedback I heard from the street people I spoke with was surprising. I heard it with my own ears. They liked where they lived and were not unhappy.

One day I left my hotel on foot to go to the end of the block where there was a large mall. I saw this man with spindly legs and arms and a short torso with a huge head sitting on a large skateboard. I stopped to give him some cash. He smiled at me and laughed. "Thank you, thank you," he gushed. I looked at him and asked, "Are you OK?" He seemed so kind and had a beautiful aura about him. I couldn't help but ask if he was happy. He beamed at me and exclaimed, "How can I not be happy when I meet someone so lovely with such a heart? You make my day!"

I couldn't believe it. On my way back to the hotel I stopped again and gave him a little more cash. His acknowledgement and the beautiful words coming from this poor crippled man were an inspiration I will never forget. There are moments in life that open your mind and change your perspective by teaching you what's really important. It gives you a new outlook on the human spirit. This was one of those moments.

Wherever I traveled in India, from the south to way north, I had experiences with the culture that blew my mind. After 14 trips I can say with all my heart that India evokes my mystical soul. It changed my life for the better. My guides and friends, Lakhsmir from Udaipur, Selvan from Delhi, and Ram from way up north near Dharamshala where the Dalai Lama has his home away from Tibet, took me under their wings and helped me discover parts of their country that average tourists would normally never experience. These men have been my buddies since my first visit to their country. They take great care of me whether I'm traveling by myself or with a partner. I want to acknowledge them and say THANK YOU for being such positive influences in my life. Namaste.

CHAPTER 118

J ACQUES WAS MINISTER OF TOURISM FOR FRANCE
from the beginning of 1976 to the end of 1977. Nice was a sister city with
22 cities around the world, so we traveled. I believe everyone should have the
opportunity to experience what has gone on and is occurring in the world.
I've learned when one travels and sees countries very different from America,
you can then form a valid opinion of the USA before spouting off negative
comments you've acquired from the fake media. Having been involved in
politics, I'm certainly aware how the media can use biased opinions to skew
the facts. My husband and I were victims, experiencing it first hand.

That's why my mind has always been open to learning about new
countries and cultures yet very protective of my roots and my own country,
The United States of America. I did my best at the time when I was First Lady
of Nice and the Riviera, by representing the U.S. and to promote a positive
opinion of Americans to France and the world.

Reflecting back, I wish I had done more. I still want to establish a
homeless shelter for abused women. Not just a place to live, but also a complete healing center with a psychiatrist and counselors, plus teachers who
could train them in their individual areas of interest and prepare them to
earn a living on their own. It would be a home and a shelter that would give
women self-esteem and teach them to be self-supporting. One day I still hope
to realize that dream.

India changed my life by giving me a slow-flowing awareness of pure truth and love. I don't want to sound saccharin, but I was able to practice this awakening and to bring that new awareness into the next phase of my life. This was something I had never thought I was capable of. I couldn't get enough of India and traveled throughout the country every year for at least a month on each trip. I studied the Hindu philosophy enough to fall in love with Ganesh, the half-boy-half-elephant god. Ganesh is the remover of obstacles, but he also puts up obstacles when you pray for something and it's not good for you. Ganesh will always guide you on your best path and bless your endeavor as I mentioned before.

On one of my solo trips to India, I decided to do a pilgrimage to as many Ganesh Temples as I could reach. I started in the South of India in Mumbai. Then on to the middle of the country in the Rajasthan region where Jaipur and Udaipur were located. At each stop I bought a Ganesh statuette in lots of different materials made from wood, resin, glass, and silver. Some were gold-plated or covered with semi-precious stones or bedazzled with rhinestones. I now keep Ganesh with me in my car, in every room in my home, and have a Ganesh charm I wear around my waist. The moment I started to love him and understand what he stood for I became a true fan. I ask him to help me in all aspects of life and he's answered my prayers 100%. If I wanted something badly and it didn't come to fruition, of course I was extremely disappointed. The normal response would be how could you desert me, but I knew better and knew he was just waiting to give me the right sign at the right time. Then all of a sudden out of the clear blue sky something would fall into my lap that was much better for me than my first desire. That's how he works, protecting you from your challenging wishes, and granting you your best ones.

CHAPTER 119

O VER THE MANY YEARS OF EXPERIENCING INDIA, I've found a relative calm and peace. The gentleness of spirit in the majority of the Indians is heartwarming. The vibrant colors and aromas of India are a constant reminder of celebrations and fun events to look forward to. They're always having a festival or preparing for one. They celebrate their favorite deities, all birthdays, weddings, births, deaths and anything else they can think of. My favorite is the Festival of Lights held from October to November. It's called Diwali. The festival is associated with Lakshmi, the Goddess of Prosperity, and marks the beginning of the fiscal year. The word Deepavali means rows of lights so all Indian homes and shops are lit up with small, cup-shaped oil lamps made from baked clay. It's a lovely, inspiring sight.

I've written quite a bit about India because it became such an unexpected gift of love, knowledge and enlightenment for me. The best was yet to come.

I had come to the conclusion I would never fall in love again. Jacques was the love of my life, and I couldn't imagine a man who would be able to fill his shoes. It made me sad that at this point with all the knowledge and wisdom about love I had gained over the years that I would never really be in love again. I believed I finally knew what to do to have a healthy relationship and also, with my near-death experience I became more empathetic and compassionate. After having learned so much it didn't seem like I would be able to experience what I finally understood about being a more mature loving partner.

I wasn't unhappy. I suppose you could say I was resigned to just having male friendships, with love being out of the question. I had my daughter who was the most important person in my life. Again, I had broken up with Alain six months prior, but after dating too many men in the months that followed and finding no one who excited me, I was tired of trying to find someone who would knock my socks off. I didn't think it would or could happen. I didn't even want it to happen or so I told myself.

In August 2006, my mother and her husband went to visit his cousin and wife who had left San Francisco to move to Bozeman, Montana. The next year they rented a nice house and Mom invited me to join her. I had never been to Montana, so I was curious to see what the draw was. I was only going to be there for a week.

When I landed in Bozeman, there were hardly any people inside the airport. It was quaint and homey. Mom picked me up and we went straight to the house. It was a beautiful location with a fantastic view of rocky peaks rising up from evergreen forests. I don't drink coffee in the mornings anymore, but I found myself sitting on the couch, sipping decaf and relishing the beautiful scenery. It had been such a long time since I was so relaxed.

CHAPTER 120

WHILE IN BOZEMAN, I CONTACTED A REAL estate agency as I usually do when I'm visiting a new city I'm attracted to. Elaine, my designated agent, returned my call and came to pick me up that afternoon to show me around. E, as I called her, wanted to point out areas where she thought I should be looking to buy if I ever decided to make the move. I told her I was planning to rent the house my mother was in for the month. It would be August, starting the next year, which I did for the following three years. Elaine became my buddy and we spent every August viewing homes that could be rented or someday purchased. We looked forward each summer to laughing and giggling as she toured me around.

We scoped out the area and saw some great homes for sale. The prices were amazing; sometimes jaw dropping, especially for someone coming from California. A house in Bozeman was two-thirds less than it would have been in L.A. and that was with an acre of land!

Alain was with me the first two weeks of August. The following summer he had to return to Los Angeles for work. I invited friends to come stay during the last two weeks. The weather was beautiful and dry with occasional mountain rain. Everyone loved the simple, healthy, clean way of life…especially me.

Bozeman wasn't sophisticated or pretentious like other cities.

I had never been to a Target store before, so I decided to give it a try and buy some assorted items. I looked forward to having this new experience.

There was a list of five things to purchase. I entered the sliding door and a young blond woman around 30 approached me. "Good afternoon, can I be of assistance?" she asked. Well, I was floored that anyone would come up to me in a big box store being so helpful and friendly. This was definitely not Los Angeles!

I said hello and told her this was my first time in Target and if she could just point me in the right direction I'd be grateful. She answered, "Hand me your list and I'll take you there." I was astonished because she did, all the way to the other end of the store cruising down three different aisles. She then walked me to the checkout counter and got on the PA system announcing, "We have a first-time lovely customer visiting Target, please give her a round of applause!"

I was so surprised when all the checkers started to clap and cheer. Who'd a thunk it? I had an incredible day at Target!

I was still getting to know Bozeman, and even with my lousy sense of direction I found my way around town without too much difficulty. This was my third summer in Montana, August 2008.

CHAPTER 121

I WENT BACK TO L.A., WHICH WAS STILL HOME
although it was feeling less and less like it. Still, September had started,
the summer heat had lifted and I was feeling good. Sunny weather I hoped
led to sunny outcomes. I made the decision to stop dating and decided not
to be with type A+ personality older men. Jacques, Abe, Lee, Richard (excuse
me while I gag) and even my first husband Bert were much older than me.
They were all hard working driven men with huge egos.

Alain was not like that. He was definitely masculine and very male,
but in a gentler, kinder way. He was an astute academic, a man who loved
thoughts and thinking. He had a zest for traveling and planned incredible
trips. Alain was an ideal companion. Al calmed me, was very low key, knew
my background and understood I would never marry or fall in love again.
Jacques was the love of my life and no one in my mind could ever affect me
the way he did. "Quel dommage" (What a pity), but that was the way it was.
He was the father of my child and our life together had been, well, bigger
than life. Even in the worst moments it was grand in an awful way, but when
it was good, it was magnificent. We built castles in the sky. It was history,
sometimes violent and dangerous, sometimes heartbreaking and tragic,
but always big and grand with great moments painted on a huge world
canvas. Our residence in Nice was a wonder, a magical palace, like a fairy-
land. Reiterating, the Préfecture had been one of the summer residences of
Napoleon, his personal palace. The governor of the region, appointed by the

central government was given the privilege of residing there during a two-year term. Jacques, being President of the Côte d'Azur, was able to live there as long as he held the position.

The building rocked, danced, and dazzled with the parties I hosted. Our home was the perfect venue for entertaining, meeting the public and putting on a colorful display of life on the Côte d'Azur. There were huge ballrooms where I could hold a variety of events like luncheons for the wives of government officials, American Thanksgiving dinners, Christmas celebrations, charity fundraising galas and a birthday party for my daughter. One year we invited TK's entire school for her sixth birthday celebration.

I had great event planners. There was a wonderful man who was a designer and virtual ringmaster. I would tell him what I wanted and no matter how over the top my ideas were he'd find a way to get them done.

We produced spectacular themed displays for any event, but he outdid himself for TK's birthday. I gave him suggestions and told him I wanted the celebration to be spectacular. We hired magicians, a balloon maker, live llamas, and jugglers. We had a bouncing miniature house, a stage full of lively actors, and food stands featuring a variety of international cuisines.

For me to be able to do this for my baby girl and see all the fun the kids were having was an incredible feeling. Jacques gave me free-reign to express my artistic self with these events. He admitted they were the best parties that Nice and the Préfecture had ever experienced and everyone who attended was in agreement.

CHAPTER 122

I TOLD ALAIN I WOULD STOP GOING OUT WITH other men and would spend the remaining years we had left together traveling and enjoying the simpler things in life.

But times are always changing, aren't they? If your eyes are open, one experience prepares you for the next. Alain did that for me. If I hadn't had the exposure of Al's kind, low-key personality, I wouldn't have been able to fully appreciate or understand the next series of events that once again would change my life. Thanks to him I was ready for this new and deeply meaningful chapter.

I was happy about my decision to lead a calmer existence and see the world with Al in a way that was totally opposite from the way I saw the world with Jacques. He made me promise not to leave him again and told me it would kill him if I did. I said, "I'm very pleased to spend my twilight years with you because I know you understand me. You understand my relationship with Jacques has permanently damaged me and I will always live with some type of PTSD."

He said yes, he understood. And so, we were together again.

That was the last August we would spend together in Bozeman.

I knew in my heart that I would never find anyone to love after Jacques. As I mentioned earlier it made me sad, but I was becoming ok with it. With all the awakenings and new awarenesses I had finally achieved, I thought I knew how to compromise and put out the effort it would take to have that kind of loving coupling. I was positive it wasn't going to happen again for me. But life (or Ganesh) always springs unexpected surprises.

CHAPTER 123

O CTOBER 1ST, 2008 WAS JUST A NORMAL WEDNES-
day morning. I was having my standing weekly manicure at 11:30
with Rose. She had recently changed locations and was now on Brighton Way
between Camden and Bedford in Beverly Hills. I met Jacques in the same
area at the Brighton Cafe, on the corner of Brighton and Camden. This was
32 years prior.

Rose, my long-time manicurist, and I were chatting away when a man
walked past us and stood in front of the occupied cloakroom waiting to put a
smock on. I hadn't seen his face, but I noticed he was dressed differently than
the usual Bev Hills businessman. Most men in BH wore suits, sport jackets,
or casual slacks with a nice button-down shirt. This man was wearing fitted
jeans, a black T-shirt and black sandals. When the cloakroom was empty he
entered and then exited with his back towards me, stretching both arms above
his head and sliding his fingers through his thick pitch-black hair. He was
so hot from behind I wasn't sure what ethnicity he was. He could have been
Italian, Greek or Latin. When he turned towards me I saw he was Asian. He
wore Oliver Peoples round tortoise shell glasses and smiled at me with the
most alluring smile that lit his face up and the room. Now, I've always had
a type. Perfect height, 5'10" to 6'0," black hair (not frizzy), dark bedroom
eyes and of course, sexy. Being the rebel I am I like a no-nonsense funny
personality, an intelligent, honest, caring, sensual and loving male who is a

risk taker. Of course, there's a lot more to like and hope for, but I thought I'd play it by ear if I ever met "that" person.

So, I smiled at him too. He was standing close and I just spoke up. What came out of my mouth was, "Hello, you look familiar. Have we ever seen each other before?"

He replied, "You look familiar also. Maybe we saw one another at an event or a gala?"

He was having his hair trimmed by a French woman named Jeanne. Rose had introduced us because of my French background and she knew who I was. He sat down in Jeanne's chair. I was trying not to look over and said to Rose, "Do you know who he is?" She only knew he was a client of Jeanne's.

I looked at Rose and told her, "All I wanted to do when I saw him from behind was approach him from the back, put my arms around his waist and hug him."

Surprised, she stared at me with eyes wide and said, "I've never heard you talk like that!"

And, she was right. This was not normal for me. My grandmother taught me very young that it was important for the man to pursue you and never make the first move or be the first to say I love you. I had lived by those words until now or should I say then?

After he finished his haircut he came over and said it was nice talking to me and to have a wonderful day. I said the same. Then he left. I couldn't help staring at that hunky body go out the door.

CHAPTER 124

WHEN ROSE WAS DONE, I TOLD HER THAT I WAS going to ask Jeanne a few questions. I wrote my name, email and phone number on a piece of paper. I asked Jeanne who he was and if he was married or involved in a relationship. She said he was a great guy and was divorced from one of her closest friends. He'd been living with a German woman for four years, but not content.

Now, if she had said he was happy in his relationship or was an A-hole, I would have walked away. But, she did say he wasn't happy. So, for the first time in my life, I made the initial move. I gave her the scrap of paper with my coordinates and asked when she spoke with him if could she please convey my message. If he isn't interested that's fine, understood and Merci. This was three months after I pledged to Alain I was with him for the duration. I felt horrible, but couldn't help it.

The only other times I had a reaction I couldn't control were with Howard, my first lust in high school, Jacques with the "*coup de foudre*" (love at first sight), Donald, when I opened the front door, and Alvio, my Italian... and now this. However, this was very different because these other men had approached me first.

I was so attracted to him and curious as to what he was all about. I had never been with an Asian, but I sure wanted to learn about this one who (Jeanne had told me) was 100% Japanese. His name was Duane.

That night he emailed to ask if I wanted to have lunch the following day. I figured Jeanne had called him and gave him my contact info. I hadn't written anything else on the note.

I had a tight schedule the next day and emailed him that I wished I could meet him but there was an important meeting I couldn't cancel. He emailed back. What about Friday? I had a few things to do, but said yes, I would really like to have lunch and proceeded to cancel those Friday plans.

He asked if I had a preference for Italian, French or Japanese. I said Japanese, of course, and he suggested a Japanese restaurant on San Vicente in Brentwood close to my dad's house. I had dressed very differently for our lunch that day from what I had been wearing when we met each other at the salon. Then, I was wearing a bright colored, long gypsy style skirt purchased in India, a sleeveless turquoise lace top and colorful gold sandals with Indian ethnic ankle bracelets. My hair was in a topknot.

But, for our first lunch I was going to pull out the stops. I explained to him that my mother, who embraced the culture from an early age, raised me eating sushi. I was seven years old when I tasted my first tuna roll. You bet I wanted Japanese food and to experience it with this man. I wore my hair down, donned Versace deep purple silk jeans, slipped on a yellow and purple long-sleeved blouse with purple flats to match, and added a touch of mascara, red lip liner and loads of perfume.

He was in the corner of the restaurant as I sauntered in. He looked at me and was surprised how different I appeared from the salon two days before. He stood up to greet me, pulled out my chair, and we immediately started talking non-stop.

I ordered a lot of food and he seemed pleasantly surprised even if he was a bit shocked at the quantities of sushi I ate. We didn't stop conversing and were amazed at how much we had in common, like jail. Among other things it was established we had both led our lives over the edge at times and were rebellious by nature. At 5:30 PM the restaurant manager asked us to please leave. They needed time to prepare for the dinner seating. We had been so engrossed and consumed with each other that we lost track of time.

Duane walked me to my car and right before we got there he hugged me.

I stepped back and he hugged me again and again. The fourth time he pulled me close and kissed me. It was in slow motion. I was used to my very A+ type personalities who always came on hot, hard and heavy (except for Alain). Not Duane. Our kiss was over the top gentle, sweet and mesmerizing. We kept kissing and hugging and it was magical. When we finally got to my car, I got in and rolled the window down. He put his head through the opening and we started kissing again until his body was halfway on top of me over my seat. It was rather passionate!

We had to tear our bodies apart, eventually. We said our goodbyes and I went home to reflect on the day. I was riveted and confused. Oh no. It was sweet, but risky. I knew it and was very conflicted. Since both of us had significant others I assumed we could have this mad passionate affair and when it burned out we'd be with our normal steady people again. We would say goodbye with a light, breezy kiss and best wishes. Not.

This was a fire that wouldn't be put out.

CHAPTER 125

D UANE WOULD MEET ME AT PEET'S, MY FAVOR-
ite coffee house in Santa Monica, as many days as he could during
the week. We'd take one look at each other and start making out on the street
in public. That definitely had never been me!

The fifth time we met I said to him "Listen, the next time you come
to see me we are checking into a hotel and doing it. We can't keep doing this
on the street."

He was a bit taken aback, but said, "YES!"

I had never been that forward and never had to pursue anyone.
Problem being I wasn't able to control my mind or body when I thought of
him. There was no stopping my feelings.

I was hoping when we finally did it, it would be OK and not great.
I knew if it were really good I'd have a problem being with Alain and that
would not be good.

We met on Sunset Boulevard at the Summit Hotel where many affairs
took place. The dining room was simple with very good food and the rooms
were done in gray, white and black. The maitre'd sat us at a secluded table
in the corner and we ordered. We were talking again non-stop while trying
to eat. Time was passing and I said we should head to the room now. He
didn't argue.

After he opened the door he turned around, grabbed me and we fell
on the bed in a mad passionate embrace. I quickly got up and went into the

bathroom. I looked at myself in the mirror and said, flow with it. It will be what it's supposed to be.

I came out naked. He went in after me and also came out naked. Our skin, our bodies were on fire, our attraction was chemical from another planet. I wanted to be near him physically, mentally, emotionally in every way. He just felt better. I loved to look at him. He was ruggedly handsome, 5'11," pitch black hair, brown eyes, naturally wide shoulders, with muscular legs and thighs that wouldn't quit. He was as close to my physical ideal as I had ever seen. I really liked his Zen, low-key quiet personality that I would never have appreciated, as I mentioned, if I hadn't been with Alain.

We stayed in the room for four hours making crazy mad raw sensual sex and laying in each other's arms before I told him I had to leave. I quickly rinsed off, kissed him goodbye and left. So many things flooded through my mind regarding Duane and Alain. I knew this fling or what I had thought would be a fling was becoming more serious.

I couldn't stop thinking about Duane. He intrigued me because he wasn't as expressive or verbal as most of the men I had been with. His actions were telling me he really liked me, but he wasn't verbally expressing it. For the first time in my life I was somewhat anxious about a new romance. I knew if I could ever love again after Jacques, it would have to be with somebody completely different who would take me by surprise.

I was getting this weird feeling about Duane and knew I really liked him. I reflected upon my relationship with Alain since I had recently told him that I was finished dating and it would be the last time I broke up with him. I certainly did NOT expect to meet Duane, but wasn't about to give him up. We continued sneaking around to be with each other and our feelings were catching up with this unbelievable chemistry. The intensity was increasing and the fire was steadily exploding.

We went sailing on a friend's boat. I was lying next to him and gazed up at the sky while listening to the gentle lapping of the waves. I suddenly realized I was falling big time for this man. It hit me like a ton of bricks.

Sparkling water, powder blue sky, the gentle wind, love. This was life…this was life moving on. Could I be falling in love?

When our sailing excursion was over we went back to my friend's condo and played a card game. My emotions were all about Duane and my sudden epiphany. I could hardly concentrate on the game, but for some odd reason I won.

We drove back to my house and Duane plopped himself onto my sitting room couch. I was standing in front of my bed looking at him when I had a moment of complete clarity. This would be the second time in my life I felt this kind of awareness. Jacques, of course, was the first. My words revealed my thoughts. I looked at Duane and said, "I don't want you to respond, but I really think I love you." I was so surprised I had blurted that out. He looked at me and smiled and of course, said nothing back.

I had never exposed myself like that and even though I told him not to answer I hoped he might say something. Nothing!

We were getting closer and closer and I knew I had fallen in love with Duane. Wherever we went people stopped us to say how beautiful we were together and how wonderful it was to see a couple so in love. He finally told me he was madly in love with me, which made me feel a whole lot better. I knew in my heart I would have to tell Alain soon. Even if it did not work out with Duane, having the feelings I had for him wouldn't be fair to continue with Al. I would rather be alone than to have something less than a full-on loving relationship. I dreaded that conversation with Al, but it was impossible to hide my feelings for Duane any longer.

I decided to do it on the phone rather than in person. It would be too emotional if I had to look him in the eye. My stomach was doing somersaults. I dialed his number and said Hi.

"I have something to tell you," As I was trembling, "And I feel devastated about it. I met a man a few months back and had no intention of falling in love again, but it happened."

I was gripping the phone hard enough to break it in half as I continued on.

"You can't predict or help who you fall in love with, but I swear when I said that I was finished dating, I truly believed it was the truth. I'm so sorry. I've hurt you in the past and I have to let you go. I don't want to hurt you anymore. You've been a wonderful understanding partner and I will always be grateful to you for your incredible kindness and support."

There was a brief moment of silence before Al responded, "I don't want to see you for at least a year. I'll see how I feel after that. Goodbye."

And that was that. I wasn't sure what kind of reaction he would have, but this one was interesting to me. We hung up and I waited for my emotions to kick in. I felt sad, but relieved, free and in love. I called Duane and told him about my conversation with Alain. He was still with his lady friend, so I told him that even if we didn't work out for some bizarre reason I would be fine and content knowing I had a second shot at being in love.

CHAPTER 126

I TRULY BELIEVED WE'D BE TOGETHER AND SO DID Duane, but with my life experiences I knew that if you make a plan the universe laughs.

I was now free to be with him when he was available. He had informed his friend and was making necessary arrangements to leave by the end of the month.

We were together as much as time allowed, but there was suddenly bad news regarding his friend. I'm going to call her Ann and not by her real name. She went to the doctor and was diagnosed with an abdominal aortic aneurysm. She had to be operated on soon and would need help recovering for several months. Duane said he would stay during her recovery to make sure she was alright. I felt sorry for Ann, but this put a crimp in our plans. This was difficult for all involved, especially because he had already informed her that they would be parting.

I was pleased to hear he was going to take care of her. This showed me his core character and that he was a good person. I knew if something ever happened to me he would be there as I would for him.

A friend of mine wanted to host a party to introduce him to a particular circle of my buddies and that would be just two days before Ann's operation. I figured we wouldn't be seeing one another too much for a while and at least I wanted him to attend the dinner. The morning of the party Duane called me and said he couldn't make it because Ann wanted him to stay with her. She was scared and nervous about the operation. I said the evening was planned around him and this would be the last outing we'd have for a while. I was prepared to do my own thing while he was occupied and only wanted him to go out that evening. I was not happy, so last minute I invited an old high school friend Cary Ross to accompany me. We had a great time even though he wasn't Duane. Everyone liked Cary.

When I was dropped off at home I was still angry and went to bed with questions in my mind. Was he weak? Was he still into her? If it had been the reverse situation I would have said to Alain, "I'll be taking care of you during your recovery and just want to go out with a few friends for dinner so, I'll see you later. I'm not asking permission because I don't need your permission."

But, that's me. Anyway, Duane was surprised when I told him how upset I was. I then hung up. He called me the next morning, but my greeting was not warm and welcoming. I needed a couple of days to process my feelings. I didn't trust anyone after my life in France. When you're in politics you learn very quickly you can't trust what people say. Sometimes, even their actions aren't honest. So when it came to men, if there were lies or any disrespectful signs of behavior I would leave quickly without hesitation, especially in the beginning of a relationship.

But for whatever reason I couldn't get Duane off my mind. I called him a day later and we talked it out. I explained to him my reasons for being hurt. I was acting differently with him than I had ever acted with any man from my past. Everyone had said Jacques had met his match with me, but for the first time I realized I might have met mine.

As we continued on our journey, this incredible magnetic pull kept us physically and emotionally inseparable. Our chemistry was undeniable and over the top.

Here I thought I wouldn't be seeing him during his friend's recovery, but he was driving almost daily on the 10 Freeway through all the terrible congested traffic just to be with me even if it was only for an hour. I thought, isn't that a sign of love?

He pretty much had the perfect physical form, but I didn't think he had the perfect name. He didn't look like a Duane to me. Since he was so sexy and hot I thought he needed a name that was more appropriate. I gave him the French nickname "Beau." He was handsome and beautiful. He reminded me of a Japanese Mark Wahlberg, rugged, buff, athletic and smart.

CHAPTER 127

I WAS INVITED TO THE WEDDING OF THE SON OF my oldest and dearest childhood friend, Laurel Warner. We became best friends at nine years old. Her wonderful husband Ken became my patient personal lawyer who gets me out of most of my predicaments. The wedding was also the same day Beau was to leave Ann since her recovery had gone so well. He gave me his word.

I was nervous because even though he told Ann he'd be leaving once she recovered, there still was drama when he headed towards the door. She didn't want to let him go. It wasn't easy and he was late getting to my house. I was almost ready to invite my friend Cary again as proxy.

He finally arrived, quickly put on his tux and off we went. I was so happy for us to finally be together and to introduce him to Laurel who I've known for 66 years and her husband Ken. Anyway, the wedding was beautiful and it was the beginning of our unbelievable partnership. It was an auspicious start for Beau and me.

We both had lived abroad and coming back home to live in L.A. was becoming more and more distasteful. Things had been changing for the worse with the influx of too many people and overcrowding. This in turn brought overcrowded freeways, wall-to-wall traffic in the city, too much crime and filth from people moving in and not respecting our laws, traditions and way of life.

Having lived in a socialist country, I was shocked that anyone looking for a better life and moving to the U.S. would bring that disrespect here and then demand all the freebies and benefits with an entitled attitude. They'd create chaos and violence if they didn't get everything they demanded. The world had gotten out of hand as I had discovered with my travels and now it was coming to the United States as I predicted.

I began warning people about this in 1976. Tragically, I was right.

CHAPTER 128

W E EVENTUALLY DECIDED TO MOVE TO Montana, which at the time seemed like a dream. Beau and I had just spent August in Bozeman and, oddly enough, found the perfect diamond for my engagement ring. Many of my friends to this day do not believe I lived there for 12 years. I have to admit Montana, and especially Bozeman, has changed with all the people who are coming in droves from California and other sanctuary states. However, it's still a safer place to live than most places in the country. We appreciated Montana because people are respected for being more independent and conservative as a whole. After all the glitz and glamor, I yearned for a less complicated life with friendly residents who respect the boundaries of their neighbors.

Beau and I were becoming symbiotic, wanting to be physically and emotionally together all the time. As stated previously, my dad had passed away and I had built a small wing onto his home. I sold my historical condo in West Hollywood and moved in with my step-monster who, according to my father's will, could live in the house until she died.

During this time, I wrote my cookbook, "The Exiled Countess's Cookbook." I had never taken cooking lessons, but I was experimenting with recipes I had made by changing ingredients and revamping my mother's and grandmother's specialties.

So that was the deal. I would live in my wing and be responsible for shopping and preparing meals as I previously said. My housekeeper and sous chef, Anna, was hired additionally to take care of my stepmother. She needed assistance because of her very bad COPD, back problems and horrible migraine headaches as I mentioned.

Beau and I got engaged and decided to get married in March of 2010. I was going to introduce him to India in late October of 2009. As we were discussing plans for this trip, I thought about our elaborate wedding the next year and asked, "Why don't we get married in India?"

Beau pondered the idea for a moment and said, "Yes! Great idea!" He thought it would be more comfortable and was quite agreeable.

My mother was hosting our wedding reception, so I told her about our decision and asked if we could just have a party in March. She thought that was an interesting and unique concept. I told Shirley (step-monster) our plan and we took off on our adventure. She would be fine in our absence with Anna taking care of her.

We landed in Delhi where I introduced Beau to my local travel guide Selvan who had become my good friend ever since my first trip to India. This would be my 12th visit. I was hoping Beau would find this other fascinating culture as wonderful as I had. Selvan and I showed him around the city and then we flew south to Mumbai.

I loved staying at the Taj Palace Hotel in Mumbai each time I went. We usually refer to it as "The Taj." However, on this particular trip there were haunting echoes of the horrible massacre by Muslim terrorists one year prior. There was definitely heightened awareness with armed security apparent in Mumbai and metal detectors at every access point to the hotel.

I was there just one week before the attack in November 2008, on a solo trip right after meeting Beau. Again, I can thank Ganesh for his timing and keeping me safe. I am an irreverent person and my beliefs are mine and mine alone. I do believe Ganesh had protected me.

There had been numerous horrific attacks lasting four days in Mumbai with the terrorists murdering 175 and injuring over 300 innocent people. The Taj had been one of the main sites targeted where they detonated explosives, took many hostages and killed at least 31 persons in the hotel. The damage to the hotel had been extensive and while much repair had been completed, the Heritage section was still being renovated during our stay one year later. Within walking distance of the hotel they attacked the Leopold Café where I frequently dined at my special table in the back corner of the restaurant. The Leopold took a heavy toll when the terrorists opened fire from the sidewalk outside. Using automatic weapons and grenades they killed 10 and injured numerous other innocent victims. I learned much of this in shock and horror from watching TV news just nine days after returning from India. I could see victims' dead bodies surround my favorite table at Leopold with blood scattered everywhere. It was ghastly.

I loved the cafe because it was a central gathering place with good food and a lively crowd. Having been depicted in the incredible book "*Shantaram*," the intrigue is what attracted me there the first time and every time after. However, my attraction for danger almost put me at the wrong place at the wrong time. The book is the true-life story of convicted Australian bank robber, Gregory David Roberts, who escapes from a maximum-security prison and ultimately flees to Mumbai, where he starts a new life. He and his friends always met at the Leopold Café and he became quite a legend. So I loved the book, the hotel, the cafe and the delicious food.

CHAPTER 129

I LEFT AN ANNOUNCEMENT ON MY PHONE'S VOICE-
mail before I departed giving the names of my hotels and their phone
numbers. I had just met Beau the month before and I wanted to keep in touch.
He was supposed to call my home phone, retrieve the info and then contact
me. I never heard from him, so when I got back I decided not to call as he
obviously didn't want to get in touch with me.

Three days went by and I was feeling sad. In the past I never would
have called a man who had neglected or forgotten me because as my wise
grandmother explained, " Always let the man chase you." I heeded her words
until then. I picked up the phone and dialed his number.

I said, "Hi, I'm back. I was wondering if there was a reason I didn't hear
from you because I thought we really liked each other." I'm sure there was a
little anger in my voice.

I continued by saying, "It's OK if you don't want to see me, I just wanted
to know why."

He responded by saying, "I was hurt because you were supposed to call
me from India, and I've been waiting and waiting to hear from you. I thought
you didn't want to see me again."

Phew! I suddenly felt a lot better and told him I had left my coordinates on my voicemail and was waiting for him to call me. That was our first
miscommunication and he just misunderstood. I told him to hang up, call
me back and I wouldn't pick up so he could listen to my message.

He called and said how sorry he was for not understanding he was supposed to call my home phone and wanted to see me as soon as possible. I couldn't wait. We got together the next day. I gave him a crystal Ganesh for luck and told him all about my trip. Seeing the terrible carnage nine days later on the news, he couldn't believe how lucky I was to not have been there at that time.

I knew this was something special we had going on and I was becoming more and more amazed at my uncontrollable attraction to him. This was the first time in my life I'd fallen for someone who was not at least 20 years older than me and thought this could really be serious. It was different because even though he was six years my junior, we basically were from the same generation. Although he was 100 % Japanese, he was raised in Los Angeles as I was. We had gone through the 60's with similar fun and wild experiences. I was comfortable with him and it was fun sharing tales of our youthful adventures. We had listened to the same music, went to many of the same restaurants and clubs and were both very family-oriented. I was like the Road Runner with my abundant energy, and he was the turtle being slow, calm, methodical and steady. Those traits made us a perfect combo with an edge even though we were opposites.

I gave him my high energy, fantasy and fun, and he gave me the feeling of an iron fist with a velvet glove. He was gentle with a solid steady foundation underneath. These were such different feelings than I had with Jacques, who was a dynamo, over the top charismatic, did all the talking and definitely was not a relaxing kind of man. He was a triple A+ personality who rarely sat still. He had been raised in a political family, which was in his blood. He had been the love of my life, but Beau…I somehow knew would be the second great love of my life.

After deciding to get married, I realized he must really be a good sport. I made plans to have the ceremony in Udaipur, India with Lakhsmir's help. He coordinated the traditional Indian wedding for us that was one of the most fascinating experiences of our union together. Of course, I needed to do something over the top and this was it. I'd been married a few times before so this had to be beyond memorable and knew our love had to be celebrated in my divine haven that had added so much meaning to my life. The Indian wedding had tremendous significance for me and hoped Beau would feel the same. I still hadn't realized what a great sport he really was.

CHAPTER 130

I CHOSE A SET OF INDIAN PARENTS TO GIVE ME away to my soon-to-be husband since my dad had passed away and my mother wasn't available. Lakhsmir took care of all the legal arrangements, our conversion to Hinduism, the wedding ceremony and special vows. It required a lot of coordination and planning to make all the arrangements.

He also notified the media who filmed us every step of the way. The first day we went to the lawyer-notary to sign 17 separate legal papers. When we entered his tiny office, the lawyer was sitting not behind (what appeared as) his desk, but on top of it with his legs folded. He was elevated one tier above us in a room that was the size of a small bathroom void of any other furnishings. He wasn't wearing a shirt, only off-white gauze pants and a turban.

It took around 45 minutes for everything to be signed and notarized by this smiling official who didn't speak a word of English. He beamed while continually nodding his head at us and seemed very gracious and kind. When we were presented with the bill I was completely stunned. It would have cost thousands of dollars to have all this done by a lawyer in the states. But our man only wanted 75 cents from each of us (75 cents for me, 75 cents for Beau), totaling $1.50 for all his expertise and time! To this day it's still hard to fathom the price for his service.

We then drove to one of my favorite tailor shops because Beau decided he wanted to wear something other than what he packed for the wedding ceremony. I picked out the most beautiful material, white satin with gold threaded designs for his wedding jacket. They took his measurements on the spot and said it would be finished later that night. It was ready as promised and hand delivered to our hotel room.

The second time I was in India, Alain and I explored the southern part of the subcontinent. That was how I discovered the Taj Hotel, in Mumbai. There was a top Indian designer who had a shop in the arcade. Passing by I noticed a beautiful white, very long tunic with pants and a shawl embroidered with beautiful multi-colored flowers decorating the sides of the outfit.

The top was made of shimmery satin and the pants and shawl were gauze with the colorful flower embroidery trim. The designer had recently dressed the mannequin with the outfit. It was around size 8. I asked if I could try it on and he asked, "When are you getting married?" I laughed and said, "I'm not getting married and didn't realize it was a wedding ensemble. I love the material and design so, if it fits me I'll purchase it."

Of course, it fit me like a glove. I never thought one day I would be getting married in it, but then I never thought I'd fall in love again. So I packed my outfit and eventually came to the conclusion that the purchase was preordained.

Beau and I were getting ready for the day of the conversion ceremony. Lakhsmir escorted us to the temple to meet a Hindu holy man. I was wearing a lightweight sky blue silk jacket with a Nehru collar. It was extremely hot and there was a fire pit we gathered around. The priest guided us through the steps as we converted to Hinduism. Afterwards, we practiced the seven traditional marriage vow steps, making seven circular rounds of the small room and performing the Saptapadi, the seven steps of a Hindu marriage ceremony. After the seventh round the couple legally becomes husband and wife. We were just practicing and getting ready for the real event the next day.

Upon completing our real ceremony at the temple the following day we went on to my special Ganesh Shrine. While normally orange, Ganesh had been painted gold especially for us to receive a final blessing. We offered the resident priest a basket of fruit including a pineapple with a monetary donation and in return he blessed our union. Ram, our driver, then took us back to the Lake Palace, my favorite hotel in the world. The floating palace was built between 1743 and 1746, under the direction of Maharana Jagat Singh the Eleventh (62nd successor to the Royal Throne of Mewer, in Udaipur, Rajasthan). It was for his wife's summer retreat, constructed in the middle of Lake Pichola on Jag Niwas Island and subsequently converted into a hotel by the Taj Group. The hotel provides a motor launch to transport guests to their dock, which takes around 10 minutes. When you disembark you are showered with rose petals by a small entourage of smiling faces who also refresh you with a non-alcoholic healthy juice on a silver tray.

We entered our lovely suite to see rose petals again strewn across the bed and in the bathroom a heated rose-petaled tub. There were baskets of fruit, champagne, a triple dark chocolate cake and cookies. On another table local handmade umbrellas, a mosaic tile of the hotel with a stand and a shawl were displayed. These were gifts from the staff as souvenirs of our marriage. It was one of the happiest days of my life. Everything seemed surreal, colorful, loving and I felt our future was bright. I knew we'd grow together in every way because we were so much in love and the physical attraction was beyond extreme. We became inseparable, like magnets. Little did I realize at the time how much I'd already grown in ways that I couldn't yet even fathom.

CHAPTER 131

U PON RETURNING HOME TO LOS ANGELES, MY
mother gave us an elaborate wedding reception at Lawry's, the famous
prime rib restaurant on La Cienega Boulevard.

Beau had invited his mother Rose for lunch to meet me five months
after we started seeing each other. We knew it was serious and Beau wanted
to introduce me to his mom. She reminded me of my dear grandmother
Nana Belle; tiny, sweet, welcoming and classically dressed with low heels and
a nicely coordinated outfit with matching accessories.

We bonded immediately and I thought if this fantastic woman raised
Beau, he had to be a very good, caring man. I was introduced to the rest of
the family later at an Easter party in Northern California. I met his middle
brother Jon, his eldest brother Michael and their wives. I sat next to Jon, who
is nostalgic like I am about the past. We both loved reminiscing about the
classic old style, romantic earlier days when there was respect and family
loyalty. He was so nice and welcoming. We enjoyed each other's conversation.
The rest of the family was skeptical of me except Mama Rose. With time,
they decided I was for real and not like some of Beau's previous women. I
had the impression when they first met me they thought I was like Beau's
second to last ex and that was not a good thing. This ex, I understood was a
terribly dishonest woman who had hurt him deeply. I didn't want anyone to
think I was like her. I hate being pre-judged because I may appear a certain
way. I have no pretenses. I treat everyone with the same degree of respect

with which I wish to be treated. What people visually see on the outside is not who I am on the inside.

Interestingly enough, Rose and Jacques had the same birthdate, May 5th (Cinco de Mayo). One of my closest high school friends Merry Elkins, a former "Golddigger" on the Dean Martin Show, also has the same birthday. Those two women are the sweetest ladies you could ever meet. Jacques, on the other hand, was completely different. They all had the same earthy Taurus traits, but he was unrecognizable as their birthday buddy.

The night of our wedding reception was a gathering of both our families and close friends.

Again, it was one of the happiest moments of my life and everyone who attended was supportive and extremely enthusiastic we had found each other at this stage in our lives. There were wonderful toasts, family introductions and good vibes that permeated the room.

I was dressed in a colorful red, Indian, long flared skirt with sequins, dangling crystals and gold threads. My top was an off-white, satin waist length blouse with a flowered embroidered scoop neck. I had lots of Indian bangles and my treasured ruby and diamond Indian necklace that I had acquired years before at Amrapali, one of the top jewelers in India.

Beau wore his beautiful gold brocade jacket that had been made for him in Udaipur. We had written words to express our love for one other after the family toasts. I read mine telling him how I adored and loved him. He of course, got so smashed he couldn't even read his. Oh well. I forgave him after he woke up the next day and read it to me as I was cradled in his arms. This was one of my most significant moments to remember as well as the grand celebration the night before.

We were married and ready to experience our lives as a couple. Beau was a rebel like I was. We knew our path would be different from the norm. He had taken big risks in his earlier life regarding health and business. I lived beyond the edge and there was many a time I lived in danger. While we both had tested and exceeded our boundaries during those years, we thankfully had settled into a less volatile existence. We sought a purer and simpler life with the dark clouds of our past dissipating into faded memories. Being with Beau and writing my memoir has been a cathartic experience. Both have helped me move beyond the thoughts of jail, escaping and losing almost everything of my personal possessions in France, living in fear in Uruguay, and being married to Lee who lied to me about everything.

I was too fragile after Jacques' and my ordeal. I somehow survived the golden staph infection that almost killed me. Then after coming back to L.A., living with PTSD, trying to re-acclimate and fighting desperately for my daughter, I was drained and exhausted.

When Lee and I married he swore he would protect and watch over me. Another betrayal and multiple lies I didn't sign up for, especially after all the challenges I had tried my best to overcome. Lee had hurt me mentally and emotionally, bringing back traumatic memories of France and Uruguay. My anxiety reappeared again because I realized I was not in control of my personal destiny. Why? Because, again, my partner wouldn't tell me the truth.

Now, I believed it would be different. In my heart I wanted to trust that Beau wouldn't put me in harm's way. He wasn't like anyone else I had ever been with. He was younger than my previous husbands and wasn't a megalomaniac. Those were the personalities I had always been attracted to: those high-powered men who were over the top and had death-defying egos. I experienced them first hand. This time I knew it would be safer. That was a 100% understatement. I never could have foreseen how different it was going to become.

It would not be easy or a bed of roses.

Beau tested my feelings to a point that if I hadn't loved him as much as I did I would have ended the relationship, but I didn't and worked for love to survive. That's when I knew I had evolved to a point that even I didn't recognize myself. This was a new and better me.

Our destiny has been an emotional rollercoaster, sometimes harrowing, never dull, but always passionately over the top. Neither one of us could ever have imagined how our future would evolve. We have been together 16 years and married 15. We're still in love and still working it all out. Who da thunk it?

CHAPTER 132

I N 2010, MY STEP-MONSTER PASSED AWAY AND MY father's estate was settled.

I asked Beau, "What do you think about moving to Bozeman?" Los Angeles was turning into a toxic cesspool, much like what I had witnessed in France. We were always proud to be from L.A., but unfortunately, we knew what was coming. We realized the downward spiral was quickly changing our beloved city and it was time to move. Beau had skied in Montana during the early 70's and spent summers on a friend's cattle ranch in Ennis, which was an hour's drive from Bozeman. More recently, we had just spent the month of August there.

Needless to say, he was not particularly enthused to remain in L.A. considering how it was unraveling. We were both very pleased about relocating and Beau managed to negotiate a remarkable price for our new home there. We were basically alone and happy to be that way. All my friends were shocked we left L.A. and had relocated to Montana. Some were so astonished they actually asked if we had indoor plumbing and electricity, but they were serious! Did I really have to answer that question?

It would be a tremendous move and would be the first time since I left my parent's home when I had all my belongings in one place. We had five garage sales, gave away half of my things and still had a moving van almost a block long packed to the gills.

We arrived in Bozeman two days ahead of the moving van. Since our master bedroom was undergoing a remodel, we slept in one of the upstairs guest bedrooms. The rest of the house was empty. So, it was Burger Bob's for great charbroiled hamburgers, our first meal downtown on Main Street. The food was delicious. Must have been the mountain air.

Two days later the movers arrived and even with all the furniture that was brought, the house seemed empty. It was a large house and took us three months to initially set everything in place. We worked sometimes through the night until five in the morning and wouldn't stop until we finished. I found new acquisitions to fill the empty spaces, paintings were all hung by Beau and for the most part it was finally almost furnished. Lol.

Now, it was time for social events and going out into the "community." We started attending local venues, met some fun people who introduced us to a couple who had moved around the same time as us and found a group of eclectic buddies. We were the talk of the town because "the group" met every weekend and partied at someone's home or out to a restaurant. Our favorite places were Blackbird, the best restaurant in town for real homemade Italian cuisine, Plonk for drinks, and the Second Street Bistro about 20 minutes away in Livingston for the French touch. We loved to party.

Brian Menges, the owner and chef at the Bistro became a good friend. When we were first introduced he said he had studied in Nice and had a close friend, like an adoptive uncle, who gave him Jacques Médecin's international cookbook *"La Cuisine du Comte de Nice,"* to study. Juilliard published it in 1972.

Did I say "Jacques' cookbook?" Yes. It happened like this. The group was out together, and we were all waiting happily for the entree and "Bri" was explaining the dish he had prepared for our table. He had studied the cuisine of Nice, France and was using various French words to explain his dishes.

I listened to him, smiling and later took him aside. "Brian," I said, "I know we just met, but I speak French. Please don't take offense, but you should pronounce the words correctly in case you're speaking in the future to Frenchies. They won't take you seriously if you pronounce their language incorrectly." The French can be condescending and snotty about everything, especially their food.

He appreciated that I had explained this to him privately and wanted to know why I was so fluent. I said I'd lived in France for 15 and a half years, mainly in Nice. When Jacques was Minister of Tourism we lived in Paris for the first year and then moved back to Nice. Brian then asked if I had ever heard of the Mayor of Nice, Jacques Médecin, who wrote this famous cookbook and was such a dynamic figure.

I chuckled and replied, "Why yes, I knew him well."

His eyes opened wide and said "Really! How did you meet him? What was he like?"

I said he was one of the most charismatic men I'd ever met in my life and oh, by the way I was his wife.

Brian almost fell over. He got on his knees, started kissing my hands and hugging my legs in front of the entire restaurant. Our friends and his clients in the room were so shocked their mouths hung open.

He turned to everyone and said, "Do you know who this woman is?"

He went on and on and everyone looked at me quite surprised. From that moment Bri and I established our bond. He's been featured on Anthony Bourdain's food and travel show, "*Parts Unknown*." He's one of the best chefs in Montana, and a great guy who married a beautiful woman Rheanna, who studied in France. They have two young children, a boy and a girl.

Our Montana friends knew very little about my past because I didn't speak about it unless questioned. I'd told them I lived in Nice, France and had been married to a French politician. They weren't quite sure what to say when Bri poured out all this wild information about me. They just stared.

The thing I really like about the Montana is that no one knows or cares who you were or who you think you are. It's jeans and cowboy boots from the locals to the billionaires, and I won't mention their names. People's individual rights and property are generally well respected here.

Our wild and crazy group lasted many years. Unfortunately, there were a couple of misunderstandings among the men. We all started going our separate ways, but the girls would still get together for lunches. Beau and I became less social and were enjoying our alone time. I didn't even have lunch with the ladies as much after a while. I became a bit of a recluse. Before moving to Bozeman, my whole life had been involved with the public in some capacity. As a result of all my experiences I was relishing the fact that my life had become somewhat less complicated. I wasn't immobile or frozen in place of course, but being at home became more and more appealing. Like the Road Runner I was still running, but mostly by myself. Beau and I only went out to dinner a couple of times a week. We became good friends with another couple, Jimmy T and Lucia. JT, as we called him, was of Italian descent hailing from New Jersey. Lucia was Italian from Bologna, which was a plus for me having lived on the Italian border and appreciating someone of European descent to chat with. JT and Beau became great buddies. The four of us were tight and had so much fun together. The friendship filled a gap in our newly toned down, comfy cozy lifestyle. Things started evolving in a more honest, real direction and I was loving being a homebody, which I hadn't been in my previous life.

Whether it was my age or the climate my temperament certainly improved for the better in Montana. It really is wonderful to sit by the fireplace with a beautiful swirling snowstorm outside. However, I hoped the snowstorms kept more people from moving there.

I'm fascinated by the weather in this state because of the wonderful seasonal changes. During our typical cold dry winters, we call the snow "cold smoke" because it is so light and dry. I get bored easily, but it's never boring watching the Montana weather. It's fun for moi.

Main Street downtown is 10 minutes from our home. The hospital is seven minutes away. That sadly became one of the most important factors in both my daughter's and my life.

There was practically no traffic. The locals were so friendly I thought I was reliving my youth in California, where everyone used to nod and smile at you and say, "Hello, have a nice day." Tragically, in L.A., now they scowl at you and tell you off or worse.

I really liked my new home even though I didn't have much experience living in a rural area. It was certainly different from Beverly Hills and the Côte d'Azur. Living in Uruguay was another kind of rural experience and something I never want to repeat. I wasn't there under the best of circumstances and was still under Jacques' control. He didn't want or expect me to do anything around the house or anywhere else for that matter. He always handled everything. I was a semi-prisoner who had nothing to do.

Bozeman wasn't like Punta. We have year round heat, electricity and running water. Not like in Punta. We even have snowplows clearing the roads after one of our furious snowstorms.

CHAPTER 133

S O, HERE I WAS FINALLY HANDLING THINGS ALL BY
myself without parental guidance or instructions from a husband. I
believe I was beginning to make better decisions and hoped I had learned
from all the lies and previous experiences. The lying mostly applied to both
Jacques and Lee. Jacques had lied to me about the charges against him when
we escaped France and about all the things that led up to us having to flee the
country. Lee lied to me about everything regarding his financial condition,
relationships with past wives and his marriage to the Las Vegas scammer.

I decided no more BS and no more lies. That's how I live my life now. I
learned a long time ago that people do not want to hear the truth because they
would have to look at themselves, admit they were wrong, confront facts, and
try to rectify the situation. That does not happen very often, especially today.

Look around and tell me if I'm wrong. It's not just family members. It's
everyone you have to deal with on a daily basis. My best advice as I age is to
be true to yourself. Believe in your ability to make your own decisions. If the
outcome is not what you had hoped for, at least learn from the experience
and don't repeat it. New mistakes are more palatable because we learn new
lessons from them. Old repeated mistakes are like hitting your head against
a wall, waiting for the pain to stop. Of course, it won't stop if you insist on
repeating the same behavior. It's when you realize you've had enough and
quit bashing your head in, is when progress is made.

My relationship with Beau was so different and I believed what he told me.

Unfortunately, he avoided some important items that I should have been privy to in the beginning, but he never lied about them. He didn't tell me until the last minute there was an issue. I would only find out in increments over the years.

But this time was different and I had changed. My reaction, after letting Beau's news simmer for a few days, surprised me. I loved Beau and stayed. Money and family are usually the challenges couples deal with. Our physical attraction and chemistry seemed to be the glue that held us together. Thank Ganesh, we had that going for us. Plus, Beau's an extremely bright and sensitive man with a good heart.

We communicated more easily and honestly than I ever had before. I really was experiencing a partnership instead of being my husband's little girl. Also, the fact that Beau was younger than me made a huge difference. He had been raised in L.A. We understood the 60's. We knew what the other was talking about. Need I say more?

Life in Montana was going well. I was invited to join the Board of Directors for the Bozeman Symphony. Our conductor, Matthew Savery, was the reason we decided to become donors. This man had so much energy and charisma on stage I couldn't keep my eyes off him. Since Jacques had been Minister of Tourism and Nice had 22 sister cities around the world we had the opportunity to attend many fine concerts performed by outstanding orchestras over the years. Matthew was among the best. In addition to the regular season, he worked exceedingly hard to put on a 4th of July concert and a Christmas concert each year that were spectacular and always memorable.

I have always appreciated the arts in its many forms. I met an artist, Linda Williams, from whom I purchased a still life painting. I asked her to make a slight change to it if she could. She agreed and told me she would drop it off at our home when finished. When she walked through the door she smiled. Our home contains a lot of eclectic art with pieces from all over the world.

She looked at me and said, "I would like to start an art museum in Bozeman. Would you like to decorate it?" I will decorate anything from homes to jewelry, clothing, food, humans and even Belle, our wiener dog. So, my answer was a huge "YES."

Linda laughed and said there would be a lot to do before we'd be ready to decorate. We had to get donors, find land, and then of course, build the museum.

That was the beginning. We've made incredible progress over the years and have established our first temporary location for BAM (Bozeman Art Museum). Land is being donated where the permanent museum will be erected, and I have sketched my vision for the design of the structure.

During my time in Nice, Jacques asked me how I would decorate the Acropolis, his new concept for an exhibition center. I explained, "Large public institutions are decorated mostly in drab gray, white and black." I love color and suggested, "Why not do all the rooms in different color schemes?"

He was amused and asked, "For instance?"

I told him to envision a combination of shades of purple, turquoise and pink that would stand out with coordinating fabrics on the chairs. He mulled it over and agreed with my idea. The Acropolis was voted the most beautiful exhibition center of its kind in France, and one of the top four most beautiful and easy-functioning venues in Europe. Accordingly, that was my inspiration for BAM.

Linda Williams is a doer and go-getter. She reestablished art for middle school children in Bozeman after the school district had discontinued it as a subject. She and an assistant teach the students about art on a fundamental level twice a week, gratis.

We decided the permanent museum collection would showcase Western art. Additionally, there would be traveling exhibits from around the world with a variety of subjects, artists and styles. On the Côte d'Azur there are over 1000 art museums. In Bozeman, this will be the first one. We have the Museum of the Rockies, which is world-famous with their primary focus on paleontology. It's a great tourist attraction. Plus, they put unique dinosaur exhibits on tour for other museums in the States and Europe. But, we're one of the only "larger" cities in Montana that doesn't have an art museum. That's why my mentor, Linda, and I are passionately pursuing this worthwhile goal.

I was very busy with my Bozeman projects while still traveling to L.A. to see my daughter, brother, friends and my mother in Rancho Mirage, near Palm Springs.

Being a traveling addict, Beau and I were extremely happy flying every year to our favorite countries. India, Italy, Thailand, and Mexico, just to mention a few. And, of course, Hawaii.

CHAPTER 134

Here's a word I don't like to hear... "UNTIL." Everything was going along great, "UNTIL." The honeymoon was wonderful, "UNTIL." She was a beauty, "UNTIL." The treatment was going perfectly, "UNTIL."

Beau and I were cruising along UNTIL his daughter, Tara, started having custody issues with the man who had fathered her second child, Keidin. They were not married. Tara had a drug problem that she was hopefully solving and was staying sober. Nevertheless, the father was pushing for total custody of the child and was creating a huge mess. He was wasting his family's money, which he hadn't earned, and my husband's money as well by forcing us to hire lawyers and go to court. It was a typically stupid, dirty, very expensive legal battle. It went on for three years of back and forth non-stop fighting. In the end, the judge came to the same conclusion he'd previously come to in the beginning before the lawyers got involved.

Beau spent so much time and money. The child should have been with Tara, but due to the former drug issues she only got part-time custody. Unfortunately, it took too much time, money, effort and anger to get there. It put a damper on our marriage.

Those three years put Beau under tremendous pressure and strained our relationship. He wasn't in a good mood most of the time and I was getting tired of it. He would spend a good portion of every meal on the phone with lawyers. It seemed they always wanted to talk during dinnertime. If we were at a restaurant he'd take the call outside as I finished the meal with friends or by myself. I wanted to get away from this and wasn't pleased.

I decided to go to Thailand and India with my friend and traveling buddy, Trish Rust. We love doing all the same things such as shopping, eating, sightseeing, shopping, eating, and shopping and eating. All we do is laugh and giggle. We're a fun pair.

The first time "Twish" (as I call her) and I went to India together we were in Jaipur, the capital of the state of Rajasthan. Near Jaipur is the Amer Fort where tourists can ride elephants. We had to arrive by 9:30 AM for the last ride of the morning. I shouted at her in the bathroom to hurry up. The door finally opened and here came Twish in a beautiful long, pastel pink, yellow, light blue, cream-colored fluffy layered dress with snazzy rhinestone gilded sandals. She was covered in jewelry and sported extravagant rings on fingers and toes. Her hair was perfectly coiffed.

I actually gawked at her and threw my head back laughing. "Twishette, you cannot dress like that to ride the elephants! It's dusty and dirty. You don't want to call attention to yourself."

"But i (for Ilene), I want to look pretty for them," she declared.

"Do you honestly think the elephants care about what you're wearing? No, they do not! Now change into jeans, tennis shoes, take off all the jewelry which is an eyesore and let's go."

That's my quirky Twish. We had a great time riding the elephants up to the fort.

On the way back we walked down the hill followed by a herd of Indians selling their wares. Of course, Twish needed my help to rescue her from all the merchants surrounding her. Even in her jeans she still looked like the perfect target. They knew they had found their mark. I wormed my way through the crowd to grab her hand and drag her away telling the men to leave us alone. I am fiercely protective of my family and friends and have no problem confronting any situation that has put them in harm's way.

If no man is present, I'm the designated protector. I have a volcanic temper and am not afraid to pounce when being threatened or attacked, especially when it's someone I love. That is why Trish liked traveling with me. I always did my best to keep her safe from harm.

CHAPTER 135

AFTER THE COURT WAS FINALLY FINISHED, TARA was granted part-time custody of her son. Beau was still worried about his daughter because Los Angeles was not the best option for her following rehab and recovery. He asked me if Tara and Marshall, her elder son, could stay with us for two or three months until she was settled and found work. It would only be Marshall staying with us, who was ten at the time. I told Beau to give me a little time to think about it because my personal life was not what I had envisioned it would be heading into the latter part of my years. Those last three years had not been a picnic.

I knew I still loved him because I was hanging in, but he was presenting new challenges that were unlike my past challenges. These were new difficulties that I hadn't wrestled with before. I mulled it over and decided to make him happy and said OK, let them stay for a few months.

Well, a few months turned into years and not only were Tara and Marshall still there, but my own daughter, TK, relocated to join us. She didn't want to live in Los Angeles anymore either, because it had become dangerous, filthy, toxic and too expensive. Beau and I moved her to Bozeman in July of 2019.

She was planning to start esthetician school in September. I knew it had been a while since TK had undergone a full health check-up. Before her arrival I scheduled an appointment with my primary care doctor three months in advance because he was always booked up. I wanted to make sure she started her new life and career with a clean bill of health. This was just routine…" UNTIL."

Two days before her doctor's appointment TK came to me and asked if I could feel a tiny lump in her right breast. There was something there alright. I could feel it, but didn't think it was serious. She had dense tissue, which I knew something about and told her the doctor would probably recommend a mammogram. We both thought it was hormonal and believed it would disappear with her next cycle. Still, we were on pins and needles waiting to hear what the doctor had to say.

The nurse led us to an exam room and waited until Dr. Spinelli came in. He listened to TK and her concerns. I left the room for him to do the exam and then was called back to hear the diagnosis. He said he was not too concerned about the lump but still wanted her to have a mammogram.

It was scheduled for a few days later.

I drove her and sat in the waiting room working on my laptop.

Finally, a nurse came out stating they found a lump that was confirmed by the ultrasound. It was deemed questionable and needed a biopsy. I was shocked. The first tremors of fear and alarm ran through me and I wanted to see my daughter. They let me in the operating room while they were prepping for the biopsy. TK and I looked at each other in disbelief. I told her whatever the results were we would handle it, not imagining or not yet allowing myself to imagine it could be what it turned out to be. The worst, most awful word no one ever wants to hear, cancer. That horrible feeling in the pit of your stomach because that frightening word is so devastating it feels like an out of body experience.

That's what we were told after the test result. It was cancer. They wanted her to come in for one more biopsy and further clarify if there was anything else that might show up.

She was scheduled the next day. This time they dug deeper into her tissues and it was quite painful. My baby, my darling daughter who hadn't had an easy life was now going to have to fight for her life. I can say that if you or someone close to you is diagnosed with this insidious repulsive disease it does change your awareness and lifestyle. It is so much more complicated than one can imagine. All I can say is thank goodness our home is a convenient 7-minute drive from the hospital and cancer center.

During the next week she had labs, counseling, shots to prevent a drop in her white blood cells, shots to save her eggs and on and on.

I had heard about one of the oncologists at the hospital, Dr. Hensold, who came highly recommended by my personal doctor in Beverly Hills. His reputation was one of the top in his profession. Lucky for us he was assigned to TK and luckier for us the cancer center was an outstanding facility. We were in the best hands to face this terrible disease.

The day came for the lumpectomy. We were braced. Once the surgeon had cut her open, he had to remove more than originally planned. The lump was larger than expected and even though her lymph nodes were not infected they removed six of them as well. The news was not getting better. More unexpected challenges and more procedures. They decided to implant an infusion port in her chest, which was a good idea, certainly better than having to find a vein for the chemo each time.

Of course, the nurse hit a tiny vein in her wrist and popped it causing more pain. A male nurse finally entered with an ultrasound device that would search for hidden veins. He spent close to 20 minutes poking her until he was able to get one to perform and register on the machine. I was cringing watching my girl go through this. When she was moved out of the room on a gurney I broke down. That was not a pleasant experience. So much was required to combat this horror. It hurt and as I would learn, the hurt wouldn't stop.

The catheter for the infusion port was routed through her neck. It was intrusive and she couldn't turn her head because of it.

The following day was TK's first chemotherapy session. We were both so scared. We knew nothing about any of this and chemo is a scary word. It seems the less you know the more frightened you are.

We arrived early in the morning and were assigned to a private area with just us, the nurse and her assistant.

There were so many pre-chemo medicines to inject into her body before the actual blast of chemo. That made us more nervous. It seemed like the needles were endless.

We were blessed to have one of the best nurses I have ever dealt with. Thank goodness she was compassionate, knowledgeable and empathetic.

Her name is Jenny Welsh. She explained everything in detail to us telling TK what she would feel with each medication being injected, all the reasons why they were necessary, what they would do to her and how she would feel during and after.

It was like attending a cancer seminar. Her chest was very sore with the implanted port and the catheter was terribly uncomfortable. I couldn't believe how courageous my daughter was. When she finally finished the treatment they removed the catheter, which was a huge relief. The port would then be ready for all following sessions.

We were there ten hours that first day. This had been an extremely long session and hoped the other infusions would not be as lengthy as we were definitely not looking forward to them. I have to mention Jenny's credentials. They're impressive. She's an RN, BSN, OCN and an FNP. I'm giving her accolades which she richly deserves. She made a difference in my daughter's life and mine, a tremendous difference. Thank you! We finally got home and TK went straight to bed.

We were waiting for the side effects to emerge and they did. Nausea, body aches, mouth sores, enormous fatigue, loss of taste and the beginning of hair loss. She bought cancer caps and rocked them. I shopped only for organic foods and had to force feed her. She started feeling a bit better after five days and was able to function a bit more. Then her hair started coming out in clumps.

She said, "Mom, I can't watch myself go bald so I've decided to shave it." I told her whatever you feel you need to do, do it. So she shaved it and I have to say TK has a beautifully shaped head and looked like an angel. Those were disturbing weeks watching her go through all the changes. It has been a process for me as well, her caregiver.

Cancer shows who really cares about you. We heard from people sending prayers, love, and support who I never thought would keep in touch, and then there were friends who didn't contact me at all. I called them about TK and never heard a word after.

One of my best childhood friends who had breast cancer never contacted me to find out how my girl or I was doing. I thought being a survivor she would be able to give me some kind words of encouragement and support. But nothing from her, and I was very shocked because she really liked TK who was the inspiration for her having a son. So, there went 60 years of friendship. It was such an eye opener and terribly painful. This experience showed their true colors and as TK said, "No more BULLSHIT!"

She finished with chemo and radiation on the first of March 2020 and has been in remission since. If it weren't for the pandemic, I was planning a trip to India to go visit my Ganesh Temples and put loads of pineapples at his feet in thanks. This trip will still take place once it is safe to travel there.

When you watch your loved one go through a fight like this, it's heartbreaking. I would have gladly taken her place and if necessary, substitute my life for hers. That wasn't possible, so I needed to remain strong to be able to take care of my only child.

CHAPTER 136

O NE MUST ALWAYS BE SPECIFIC WHEN YOU PUT something out in the cosmos or it can be misinterpreted.

I delve inside myself from time to time to do inventory. As I grow older it seems to occur more often. There has been much reflection as I watch myself age and evolve, especially now with all the pain and sorrow that came with TK's illness.

My Sagittarius traits are apparent in the way I've lived my life. I truly embrace fairness and fighting for the underdog. I'm truthful to a fault and always curious to understand and find out why. I have an addiction to travel around the world and discover new cultures. Then, I incorporate those experiences into a logical vision of how I want to live my life. That's very Sagittarius. The benefit of embracing my traits has been tremendous for all that I have learned.

My life completely changed when I met and married Jacques. It was phenomenal at the beginning, but tragic and frightening at the end. I have deeply reflected about our relationship as well as the trauma of my near-death experience and PTSD. I reflect daily about my relationship with Beau, his family and my daughter moving here just in time to discover cancer. If TK hadn't moved to Montana, would we have discovered the cancer in time? I think very possibly not.

I believe I am alive today because I had to be here for my daughter. For my first 60 years I was the one who was taken care of. Now, I'm the one taking care of others. How do I feel about that? Blessed.

There were five people and three animals in our household: Beau, TK, Tara with her young son Marshall, and myself. Our wiener dog, Ms. Belle, TK's cat, Zoey, and Milo, the chinchilla enjoy all the benefits as part of a one big integrated family.

So, after all my experiences living and traveling around the world, I found myself in Montana. Since that move I've started tackling household chores like doing lots of dishes which I hadn't done before. I grocery shop three or four times per week. I cook, bake, clean, and try to make healthy organic meals for TK and my crew with lots of decadent desserts.

Thankfully, she's in remission now. This cancer debacle takes at least a year out of the life of the caretaker, the family and close friends, and of course the cancer patient. Then, there's the aftercare for the rest of the patient's life. We've been on quite a journey together. I love my daughter more each day for being the incredible fighter she is, for her courage and attitude that enabled her to beat this cancer and win. I reflect every day on this life-changing event and how grateful I am for the incredible support and prayers coming from people around the world who care for my TK.

Being such an independent wild child, my personal journey has been a challenging evolution. The trauma and fear of escaping my adopted country of France to live in exile in Uruguay was a terrifying experience. I lost most of my precious personal belongings that were stolen by the socialist French government, only to be further humiliated by my unjust arrest and imprisonment. If it wasn't enough, that episode ended with my near death and being separated from my daughter for six long years.

I chose to marry a man like Lee Rich, who lied to me about his true situation and almost put me in financial jeopardy. I witnessed the first love of my life Jacques, completely fragment because of the mistakes he'd made. He was responsible for the demise of a 150-year family dynasty in Nice and the Côte d'Azur. I had chosen to marry a man who brainwashed our daughter against me because I refused to expose myself any more to his toxicity. I had no idea Jacques could turn on his family as he did.

These life events slapped me back and forth to the point of no return. A few times I was sure I wouldn't make it physically or emotionally. My body has been through hell. The golden staph destroyed my mucus lining from my esophagus down through my stomach into my bladder. The pain was so excruciating I almost jumped off the balcony of the Préfecture.

Emotionally, I felt destroyed for years. Being separated from my daughter almost did me in. Fighting for her return was intense and the journey to help her heal was so difficult that I would double over and weep in pain. All I cared about was wanting her to overcome her fears and the abuse she had suffered in Uruguay when I wasn't there to protect her. I only learned about her horrid experiences after the fact when she came back to me. If I had a clue how it really was when I wasn't there I would have taken action, but her father had such a hold over her that she played up to him in front of me and hid the truth of her abuse. She had become a compliant victim. He threatened her and she feared him.

TK later revealed she was so unhappy that she tried to put herself in harm's way and end it several times. Jacques was a monster in the house. TK told me one night she was in the shower washing her hair and ran out of conditioner. Jacques came into her room and TK asked him to buy her some more because she'd run out. For some warped reason that enraged him. He was unbalanced and crazy during those years. Jacques grabbed her by the hair and threw her across the room! If only I had known!

She blurted this out in a therapy session. I was so angry I could hardly be contained. I was blind with rage, but it was all too late. Sadly, I learned about these incidents only after they occurred.

I'm fiercely protective of the people I love and will go to any length to ensure their safety, even putting myself in danger, which I've done instinctively without thought many times. When it comes to my daughter, there would have been a physical fight with Jacques if I had been in the house. Believe me when I tell you, I would have come out punching and won.

There were so many secrets of his brutal abuse. The respect or trust I had for Jacques was gone.

His unfathomable lies altered our lives and put us in bad situations with dangerous people. He became very unstable not knowing his next irrational move. His actions affected not just our family, but French politics as well. What Jacques did in Nice, didn't stay in Nice. It rippled around the world. I doubt if he ever thought of that in his self-obsession and concern for only his needs.

CHAPTER 137

THE FRENCH RIVIERA WAS THE GO-TO JET SET vacation spot in Europe and the world. Anyone who wanted to be somebody, anyone who wanted to be seen by the world or wanted to be famous would show up in their finery to make a movie deal to get their name in the papers. The richest of the rich came there for sport and to play and make deals. They all came to the French Riviera.

Jacques and I were part of that, but tragically the real glamor of the Côte d'Azur is now over. He ruled Nice and the Riviera with an iron fist, keeping it safe from terrorists, nasty muggers in the streets and bad people doing bad things. He kept the city immaculately clean, but no longer. You could have a great time in Nice, a wild time and not worry about it. But, the carefree days are gone. Monaco is the only little country in the world where one can still wear jewelry and furs without being sprayed or attacked.

What once was is no longer, and I don't have any faith that those days will ever return.

When I was a young girl in Beverly Hills, we grew up riveted to Walt Disney movies. It didn't take me long before I realized I wanted that fairytale life. I was of the generation when many young girls shared the same dream. Whether it was real or not, I was never deterred from wanting it.

In general, young girls today don't dream like that. All they know is to be connected on their phones. Many are lazy and self-indulgent from being given too much at an early age. They feel entitled because they've been so pampered and privileged and believe the world owes them a living. NOT. One thing you learn as you get older is to not have expectations or think you're owed anything because you aren't.

I knew it would take a lot of work fulfilling lofty goals and striving towards something positive. I just didn't realize it would be that hard hooking up with Jacques. It was the best of times and the worst of times. As I said, the only thing that didn't happen to me was I didn't die. I felt like I was the Phoenix rising from the ashes of despair after the escape from France. I was physically ill on the edge of death and separated from my daughter.

All these events led me to finally write my memoirs revealing what happened over a 75-year span of time. Four ghostwriters attempted it, three producers wanted to make a movie, many articles have been written, and there was almost a television series. I reached the point where I didn't even consider doing the project anymore.

Anyone who's asked me about my life always said it should be a book. Who better to write it at this juncture than me after all the previous failed attempts. I finally succumbed. This is the honest, down to earth, real me. I think you must have realized by now I write how I speak. I don't lie and if unable to answer or discuss a subject I will say I cannot. I've just scratched the surface with revelations in this book and could easily write 1000 pages, but it wouldn't be wise at this time. There are hidden skeletons not to be dealt with until maybe a future book. Hopefully, what I've written so far will still burn up the pages. I've told as much as I can for now. The older I get the more I don't care about what is exposed. We'll see.

I was so young when Jacques and I were together. I was 26 years old. There were no rules or protocol prepping me when I became First Lady.

I am pretty logical and always try to use that quality in dealing with anybody or any circumstance. I was used to making quick wardrobe changes during my modeling days, so whatever event I was scheduled for I quickly changed outfits suiting the occasion. I became pretty adept at shaking hands, hugging and kissing. I became familiar with French politics and could gab about various aspects of it in French. In other words, "I winged it."

CHAPTER 138

T HE POLITICIANS I MET WERE ONLY INTERESTED first and foremost in their own power, control and status. They only cared about being re-elected and not so much for their constituents. Jacques was uniquely unlike that. For all his faults, he loved his roots and the Niçois. He protected them and in return they loved and adored him dearly which he craved. There were very few major crimes committed when he was mayor. If there was one, Max would handle it and no one would be the wiser.

I entered into this new political world very naive, but with compassion and empathy towards my fellow man. Boy, did I learn a lot about human nature. No matter what you want to believe, it's not all good. In fact it was startling and frightening the things people asked of me. Could I buy them a new home? Could I make someone disappear? Would I adopt their child? Could they use my American passport for the 25% tax discount? Could I donate land to build their family home? Could I give them my old clothes and jewelry, etc.?

I even had one couple literally demand they move into the Préfecture and live with us. Now, that takes nerve.

We traveled around the world connecting with our 22 sister cities. There were people who would ask for my help and beg me to give them money. There was no difference in cultures around the world. Many of these people thought it was my duty to subsidize them.

I never quite understood why it was my responsibility and not their government leaders who they elected. This is how I formed my opinions about politics. The more I saw first hand, the more I realized men and women were not as innocent or good as they claimed to be.

I also didn't understand the kind of anger that festered inside of them. Many of these people were from Western cultures where they had the opportunity to be educated, work and raise a family. Yet, they were the ones who acted the most entitled. I did as much as I could to help those who were really in need. I was touched by a few, appalled by others and saddened that I couldn't do more to help those I hadn't met.

With the experiences I've had in my life, I sometimes feel like an alien. When I speak with people I feel like I'm watching myself through a camera lens. How can a regular person understand the highest of highs I reached and the depths of hell I experienced?

Politics is a nasty profession where power and greed are the priorities and those envious enough will stoop to any means including, sex, cheating, lying, and even murder. It's hard for one to understand that way of life unless you've lived it.

I'm jaded, skeptical and on the defensive regarding how I deal with life now. I am more compassionate and empathetic to real, honest human beings, but intolerant of people who don't contribute to society. My motto is, "Take care of your own family and responsibilities, period." That's what I was taught and that's how I conduct my life.

I escaped to Montana from all that was crazy in the world and was ecstatic to be there for 12 years. Small town, no traffic, really friendly helpful citizens, no sales tax, an easy comfortable and safe life.

NOW, our once small town has exploded with a mass influx of people and an overburdened infrastructure. As a result of the pandemic with the new paradigm shift of remote working many people have now realized they can easily afford to live and work from any location they choose. I was hoping the weather would be a deterrent for potential newcomers, ha ha. There's so much new construction that it's turning into, as they call it, "Bozangeles." I think it's good for business, but I resent out-of-staters coming here and voting to turn Montana into the states they left. Bozeman has changed and not for the better. The quality of life that was once so comforting is now in decline. It may be time to move on and we're thinking about Wyoming. It's one state that embraces freedom and respect for our country.

I think about India and her people who are fundamentally happy, kind and generally non violent. And, of course, there's Ganesh. I must share the Ganesh story. It's a trip! He's the son of Shiva and Parvati, two gods who were lovers in the Hindu pantheon.

Shiva, the Supreme Lord who creates, protects, and transforms the Universe was always away when there were wars. Before he left for another war, Parvati, his wife, told Shiva she wanted a child to comfort her while he was away. He would be gone for such a long time and she would be alone. He said No, you must wait for my return to have a child.

So, Shiva departed to war. Parvati waited over a year, and then decided she must create her own son. She shed her skin into the shape of a boy and he came alive. She named him Ganesh.

One day while she was taking her bath she posted Ganesh at the door to prevent any intruder from coming in. Shiva unexpectedly returned from the war after three and a half years and wanted to see his wife. Ganesh stopped him at the door to his mother's bath and said to Shiva, "You cannot enter." Not knowing Parvati had created Ganesh, he was outraged that this unknown creature would dare deny him entrance to his own wife's bath!

Because he was a warrior, he cut off Ganesh's head.

Hearing the commotion Parvati rushed out of her bath, but it was too late. The boy was dead…decapitated. She was devastated by this horrible slaughter. She told Shiva to immediately go out into the world and find a mother who had turned her back on her child. She ordered him to cut off the head of the baby and bring it back to put on Ganesh's body. He immediately went on his search. He looked high and low, but couldn't find a mother who had abandoned her child. So, legend has it he went to the sacred elephant grounds and saw a mother elephant who had left her calf behind. Shiva chopped off the baby elephant's head and brought it back to Parvati, explaining this was the only child he could find that its mother turned her back on. The head was placed on Ganesh's body, but one of the tusks shattered. Ganesh is depicted holding the broken piece in his hand.

Ganesh survived as the elephant-headed Hindu God of Beginnings. He is traditionally worshiped before the start of any major enterprise and is the patron of intellectuals, bankers, scribes and authors. He is the remover of obstacles and is wise. If you ask Ganesh for something he doesn't think is good for you he will deny your wish, but will find a better outcome in the future.

I find it a fascinating philosophy with all the drama of life in addition to a colorful and amusing way to think about things. To me, the peaceful Indian demeanor and way of existence is amazing. It has appealed to my transcendental awareness and introspection. I'm as enchanted with India now as I was then.

The poverty in India is not like any other poverty I've experienced. People accept it and even though the government builds public housing for them they return to the streets in three to four months. They smile, yes they beg, but it's normal for them. They seem to be happier on the whole as a culture than any other country I've visited. I keep going back to experience their natural serenity which I crave for myself. I've written a lot about India and its effect on my life. It's astonishing to me how this culture captured my heart and soul.

CHAPTER 139

AGING IS A FASCINATING PROCESS. I SEEM TO reflect on my past more and more. There have been highs and lows that were more exaggerated than most people have ever experienced. My life has had such extremes that it's been very difficult at times to understand who the real me is.

I understood my unique personality has led me to fascinating destinations with incredible outcomes. Being fulfilled with a diverse range of experiences has enabled me to take a different perspective on my life now. I have learned well enough not to repeat past mistakes. I am certainly thankful to be alive and continue to live my life to the fullest.

Onward and upward, as my journalist friend Joel Stratte-McClure always says. Joel is an American journalist who lived in the south of France for a long time. We became friends at a Reagan rally that Jacques and I sponsored in Nice, just before he became President. Joel, who is nothing if not flamboyant, strutted into the room wearing a Jimmy Carter mask. We were introduced, and I said to him, "I think you better leave. Your mask is out of place here!" He was stunned and started to laugh. He apologized and asked if he could stay. I said maybe, but take that horrible mask off. From then on we became buddies.

Many years later we were at a gala event. Joel came to our table and asked Jacques if he could have a dance with me. As we were whirling on the floor he said, "Can I ask you a personal question?"

I replied, "When haven't you asked me a personal question?"

With this little grin he said, "Out of all the women in the world, Jacques chose you. Why do you think you were the one?"

I gave it a moment of reflection and said, "If I answer truthfully, it better be off the record."

"Of course," he replied

I looked him straight in the eye. "Well," I declared, "it's because I gave him the best blowjob he ever had."

I thought Joel was going to choke on his spit! I said again, obviously, this is off the record. He looked at me with a frightened expression on his face. "Jacques will have me shot if anyone heard you say that."

I laughed and assured him, "Not to worry, he'd just do away with both of us."

For once, Joel looked serious and blurted out, "Really?"

I heartily laughed and said, "Of course, you know if I can't tell the truth I won't answer."

We still remain in contact to this day even though he published our private conversation in his first travel book. LIAR! It wasn't off the record.

CHAPTER 140

IN MY TEMPESTUOUS JOURNEY THROUGH LIFE there are a few people whose karma and behaviors I wish I could have avoided...especially those who tried to destroy Jacques and me. I would like to see them just one last time to bestow upon them what they did to us.

Life changed radically after jail. It was a challenge coming to grips with the danger I had been subjected to so unexpectedly. The court case in Grenoble never died, and I was convicted "in absentia" as I try not to think about it. I lived there in the best of times, but now being socialist, France will never be the same. The glamor and allure are gone. It has been replaced by socialist policies allowing rioting, taxing citizens beyond reason and entitlements for foreign immigrants who have bled government funds dry while extending the retirement age for hard-working citizens. There's an ongoing anger permeating in the air which is another failure of socialism.

I must admit to missing the perks from my other life sometimes. Men kneeling on the sidewalk and kissing my hands with respect wasn't so bad. A little more of that would be nice. There was my peace of mind with my bodyguard Jean-Claude and the Niçois Mafia who always protected me. I miss the incredible freedom of being able to do good things for deserving people who appreciated my help and genuinely smiled when they crossed my path. I miss traveling to our 22 sister cities around the world and learning about their fascinating cultures and of course, the respect I was accorded in those cities as First Lady of Nice.

It's amazing to me how disrespectful it is today to even mention the word respect. The world has changed too much, and I don't see respect coming from most of the younger generations or for that matter from many of the baby boomers who have forgotten the basic rules of boundaries and decency. Would someone, anyone, please explain to me how all this disruption is acceptable to normal human beings just wanting to live their lives, raise a family, be decent citizens, and appreciate with loyalty the United States that afforded them those freedoms? I don't recognize the cities where I lived much less the country because of this chaotic violence and crime in America. Socialism has never worked nor will it ever work. Yet, there are those who continue down the path of blind idealistic destruction out of jealousy, laziness and greed.

Having been in politics, I experienced many types of regimes around the globe. I have seen the horrors and dregs of the earth. I've witnessed leaders who promised to lift their people out of poverty only to betray them.

Instead, one leader took foreign aid sent by other countries only to spend it on personal luxury items for himself and family. They let the rest of their population wallow in filth and starve. I remember Jacques telling me he sent aid to an African president years ago. People were starving in the country. The grain had to be shipped to Africa and the last leg of the journey was by train. The train cars were full of grain and other staples to feed the people. The cars had to stop before they reached the villages because the railroad tracks had never been completed. The food rotted. All that time, money and effort were wasted because this tyrant didn't care about his people. Yet, he owned a fleet of the most expensive automobiles in the world. So, no one will ever convince me I'm wrong. Unless you experience this type of corruption, you cannot understand. That's why I've started my own political party. The "Logicist" Party.

My followers vote logically and only logically. Should I run for office? My platform would be that no personal issue would be on the ballot. Government does not have the right to insert itself into personal private matters. Government has the obligation to follow the constitution and the will of the majority of the people by protecting our borders against threats, stabilize the economy, and have a strong military ready to protect and defend the country and citizens.

Government has gotten way out of hand. As I said, it's the people's will and not the will of elected leaders. Jacques truly loved his citizens. He kept Nice and the Côte d'Azur prosperous, clean and safe. He was one of the very few elected officials who created positive outcomes for his city and the region, fulfilling most campaign promises. Even Mitterrand, the socialist president of France, praised Jacques as the finest and best mayor in the country.

CHAPTER 142

B EAU WILL BE MY LAST HUSBAND AND TRUE LOVE. We started our personal journey testing our bond and here we are today, still in love. He's a very unusual man. Being raised in a Japanese American family his parents wanted their three sons to be totally American. They both had been in internment camps during the war and worked very hard to raise a tight knit group with respect and manners. I'm sure that was a challenge with three boys. The one who gave them the most worry of course, was my husband. Beau's a very kind and sweet man but with an edge. I need that edge or I would walk all over him. Did I mention he's the only man in my life that has ever stood up to me? It makes me laugh because he has such incredible nerve. Actually, I'm still mystified why I'm so relaxed about it. It must be my age or frankly, I'm just burnt out.

Now, I don't mean to say I'm scary, but when my tether is stretched to the limit my guts erupt and I can be very frightening. I've dealt with the strongest personalities in the world and will never back down or run from a confrontation when I know I didn't do anything to deserve such behavior. It may take me a long time to get to that point, but when I'm disrespected, taken advantage of or mistreated, it's GAME OVER!

Jacque would be intimidated by me even though he had a violent, dangerous temper. I've dealt with prison authorities and stood up to them. My encounters have encompassed murderers, heads of state, and assorted political figures, with some insane personalities among them. I've stood up to them all.

These experiences were not always by choice because I was obligated to function in certain roles. Now, being free from those roles enables me to direct my strengths along more positive avenues. At this point in my life I choose not to waste my energy with toxic people.

There are so many things I wish I could reveal at this time, but it wouldn't be wise. Too many people have allegedly disappeared because of the things I was privy to as Jacques' wife. Even though most of the dangerous people have died, I won't take chances by consciously putting myself in harm's way again.

Well, that's politics for you. What I have written is the truth, the whole truth and nothing but the truth which is racy enough for this memoir.

Regarding my untold stories, there may be a more appropriate time (post mortem) for them to be published.

I am very grateful to share these chapters of my life story with hope the readers can fathom my first-hand experiences. It would make me happy if my story serves as an inspiration for others to seek and fulfill their own true dreams. I have always pushed my life to the fullest to accomplish my goals and, as harrowing as it's been, I now believe I have succeeded in finding the correct path.

When India becomes safe for travel again, I will plan my next trip to Udaipur. I shall pay homage and thank Ganesh for his loving guidance and support. I'm just waiting for the word "GO," to get on that plane.

Until then, I wish you all, "NAMASTE!"

THE END